Collector's Guide to Classic Video Games

Billy Galaxy

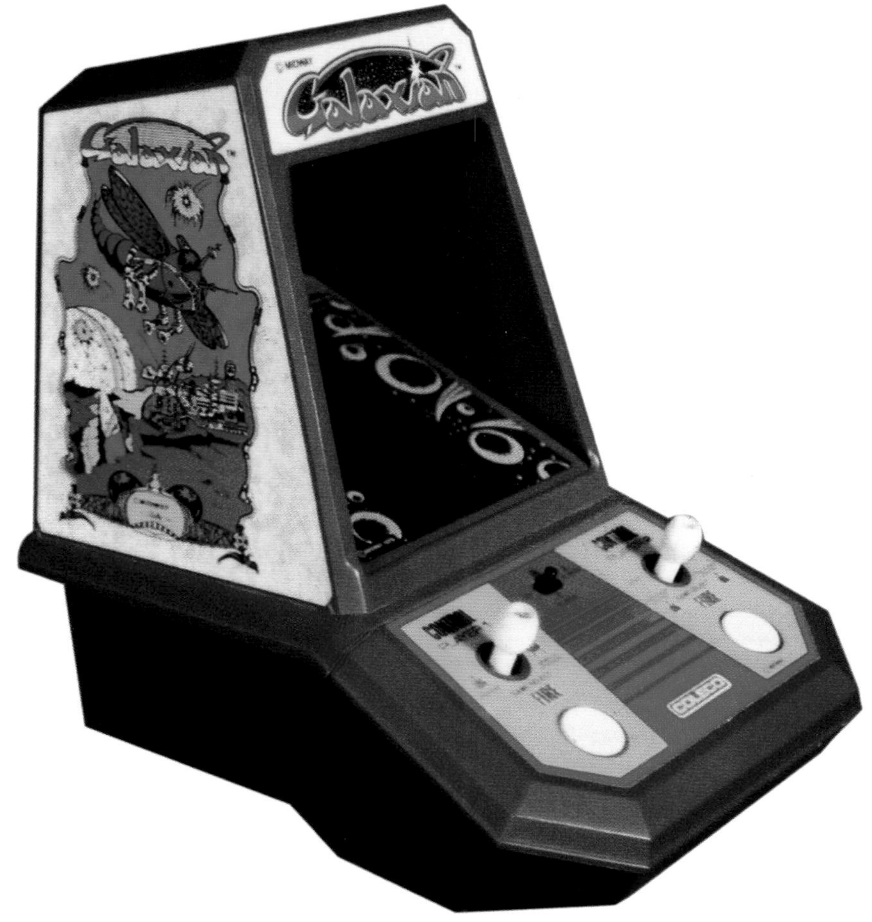

Library of Congress Control Number: 2001094156

Designed by John P. Cheek
Cover design by Bruce M. Waters
Type set in Futura Hv BT/Zapf Humanist BT

ISBN: 0-7643-1456-4
Printed in China
1 2 3 4

Published by Schiffer Publishing Ltd.
4880 Lower Valley Road
Atglen, PA 19310
Phone: (610) 593-1777; Fax: (610) 593-2002
E-mail: Schifferbk@aol.com
Please visit our web site catalog at
www.schifferbooks.com
We are always looking for people to write books on new and related subjects. If you have an idea for a book please contact us at the above address.

This book may be purchased from the publisher.
Include $3.95 for shipping.
Please try your bookstore first.
You may write for a free catalog.

In Europe, Schiffer books are distributed by
Bushwood Books
6 Marksbury Ave.
Kew Gardens
Surrey TW9 4JF England
Phone: 44 (0)20-8392-8585
Fax: 44 (0)20-8392-9876
E-mail: Bushwd@aol.com
Free postage in the UK. Europe: air mail at cost

Acknowledgments

Extra big portions of thanks and gratitude to Kim Gilbert, Toby Wickwire, and Miriam Elman for lots and lots of help and patience.

Thanks again to Toby Wickwire, and also Rick Weiss, for sharing great stuff from their collections.

Thank you also to: Mitsuwa Sakamoto, Grandma & Grandpa, Mom, Gerry, the Spoons, Tina Skinner, Jeff Snyder, Thundarr the Barbarian, Marion Almond, Tim + Mya, Paul, the Coolest Jet, and last but certainly not least — Peter Schiffer and Schiffer Publishing.

Contents

Introduction

This book is for collectors, dealers, and video gaming enthusiasts of all types. It is by no means a complete record of this fascinating era of electronic history; but, inside you will find excellent pricing information, extensive photographic reference, and an extremely varied content. This book not only covers all of the classic home video game systems from the very beginning, but goes on to include all sorts of electronic games and related memorabilia from the 1970s and 1980s. It would be virtually impossible to include everything pertinent to this field in one volume, or even several volumes for that matter (a book this size could be written simply on label variation of Atari 2600 games). I consider this to be simply a brief overview of the hobby as a whole. As collectibles, home video games, and "electronica" in general are a fairly recent entry. That is one of the factors that makes this hobby so exciting — the chance to uncover something previously undocumented, possibly even to own a one of a kind item! Not only that, but it is one of the most interactive of all fields of collecting. You can actually play with most of the items in your collection, causing little or no wear. Yay!

Many may not realize that the primitive computer memorabilia contained herein is in fact what programmed the majority of the fast forward culture that we live in today. Home video games have had a massive impact on the way that we use, accept, and interact with computer technology that previously had been beyond both the means and the comprehension of most people. What began as a simple black & white electronic table tennis game (i.e., Pong) in the early 1970s quickly exploded into a virtual wonderland of sight, sound, and color, going on to change the world into to the computer friendly place we all recognize today. Early home video games helped along many technologies that have become so familiar to us today. For example, Intellivision playcable and the Atari Gameline Master modem had a hand in the development of the internet and cable television delivery systems. An early attempt at virtual reality was made with the 3D Imager for the Vectrex system. On the human side of things, two then Atari employees that created the arcade game Breakout went on to found the Apple Computer company. Or take Nolan Bushnell for instance, founder of Atari and considered by many to be the father of the video game industry; he went on to found Chuck E. Cheese Pizzatime Theaters. This updated version of the classic pizza parlor came complete with animatronic characters, cheap eats, and of course video games!

About the Prices in This Book

All prices listed in this book are for items in Near Mint to Mint condition, which means games boxes, manual, etc. should be free of residue, scratches, tears, folds, and should be in working condition. Prices in this book have been determined from a number of factors, including but not limited to: dealer price lists; internet auctions; prices at toy, antique, and collectibles shows; current market trends; correspondence with collectors and dealers worldwide; and the author's own experience. This book should be treated as a guide, not a bible. It is for appraisal only and does not set market value. Prices frequently fluctuate. For instance, increased demand may drive prices of some items to several times that of those listed in this book whereas a warehouse find may drastically reduce the value of other items. Remember, collectibles such as these are only worth what one is willing to pay for them.

Atari 2600

While the Atari 2600 was not the first home console, it is the most famous and, thus, has the largest library of software and peripherals. Actually christened the Atari VCS (short for Video Computer System), the console's model number seemed more catchy and became the moniker that is remembered by most today. Released in 1977, this system remained popular in many parts of the world into the 1990s. While other systems coexisted with the 2600 during this era, it was the system with the largest impact. It was not only the first system to have third party software produced for it, but it was also the first system for which video games based movies, television, comics, etc., were licensed. The Atari 2600 more than any other system gained a foothold in the hearts, minds, and pocketbooks of people everywhere.

The Atari 2600 is the most challenging and exciting system to collect for. It would be virtually impossible to "complete" a 2600 collection, as numerous prototypes and one of a kind items, previously unheard of foreign only releases, and other new items are still being unearthed today. In addition to there rarities, there are literally thousands of items that could be counted as part of the 2600 collection. Below you will find a brief overview of some of what is available. Cartridges in this section are listed alphabetically by manufacturer, then title.

Atari 2600 Systems

Here are a few systems released by Atari and others.

Early 6 switch model of the Atari 2600. Boxed specimens can bring $100 - $500.

The common 4 switch wood grain version. Model 2600A. $75 - $250 for boxed examples.

Atari 2600 promotional box. Also included a 2600 unit branded for promotional use only on the bottom. One in the condition shown is valued at around $100, while an unused one may bring over $400.

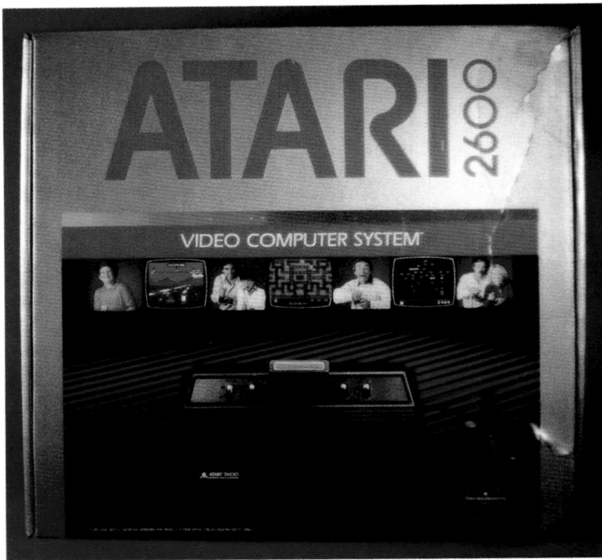

Later release of the 2600. Only included 1 joystick. $75 - $195.

Second version of the Atari 2600 6 switch. Note: Straighter front than the first version pictured. This version also weighs much less than its earlier counterpart. $75 for a complete, functioning system.

Standard 4 switch version of the 2600 is nearly identical to the later model pictured, with the exception of the color, of course. $65 complete and working.

First version of the Atari 2600 is significantly heavier than subsequent releases. Note more rounded front and thick plastic bottom. $100 for a complete, functioning system.

This all black version of the 2600 is sometimes referred to by collectors as the "Darth Vader". $60 complete and working.

Several different owner's manuals for the aforementioned systems. $5 - $9 each.

Small rainbow version of the Atari 2600 junior. $25 console only.

Slightly harder to find large rainbow version of the 2600 junior. $30 console only.

Boxed European issue of the Atari 2600 junior. Includes different style controller and European power supply. $150 complete in box.

6 switch Sears version of the Atari 2600 — the Telegames Video Arcade. $45 console only.

Sears Video Arcade. This 4 switch model is much more difficult to find than the 6 switch video arcade. $175 complete in box.

Sears Video Arcade II. An unused example may bring up to $350.

Nearly identical to the Japanese Atari 2800, this Sears Video Arcade II is valued at $95 for a complete, working system with all original parts.

Coleco's version of the Atari 2600 — the Gemini. $75 complete.

The extremely rare Columbia Home Arcade is nearly identical to the Coleco Gemini and was available via mail order only from Columbia House. $250 complete.

Activision Games

Pinkish box is the later blue label release of Activision's Boxing. $12 complete in box.

Barnstorming. $16 complete in box.

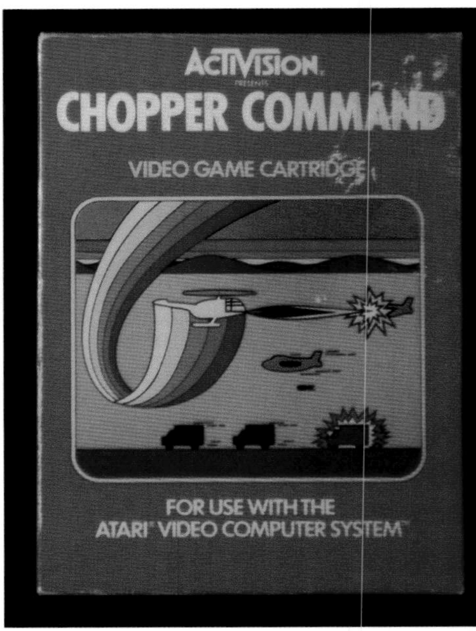

Chopper Command. $13 complete in box.

Bridge. $21 complete in box.

Red box is the first issue of this Boxing game by Activision. $10 complete in box.

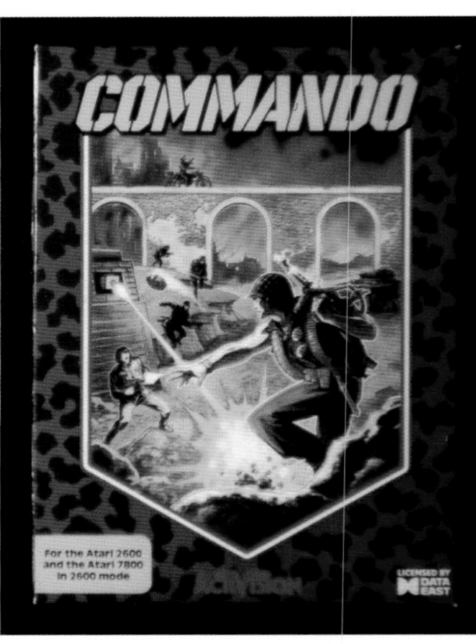

Commando. $20 complete in box.

Crackpots. $25 complete in box.

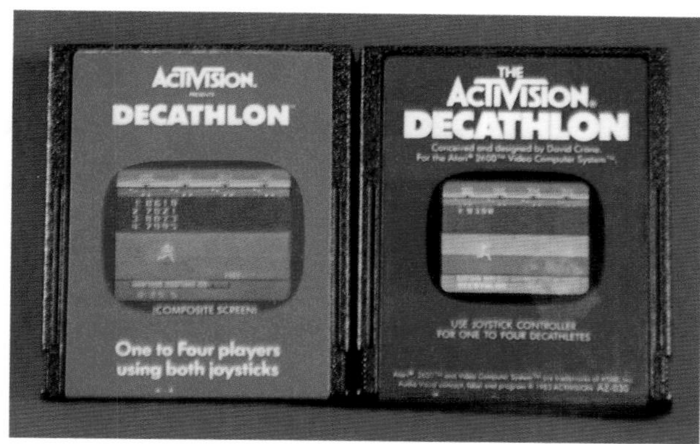

Two label variations of Decathlon. Right is the standard version valued at $7, left is an odd variation valued at about $15.

Decathlon. $12 complete in box.

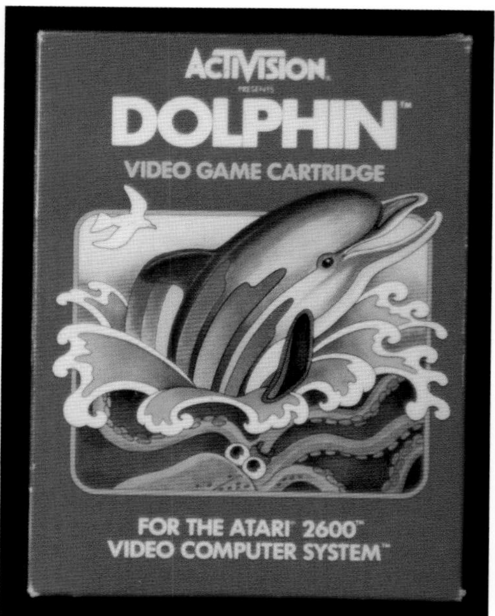

Dolphin. $20 complete in box.

Dragster. $12 complete in box.

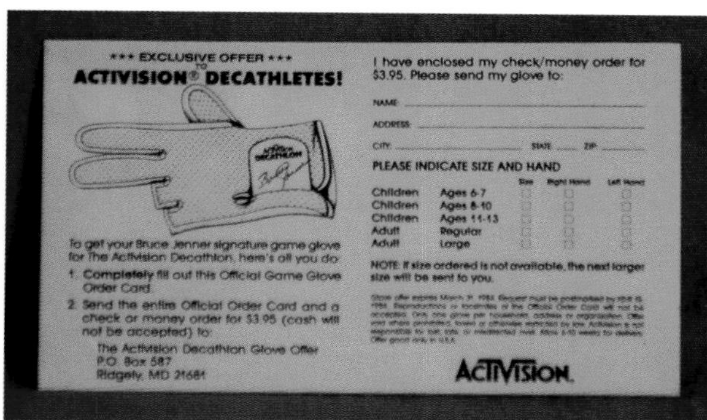

*** EXCLUSIVE OFFER ***
TO
ACTIVISION® DECATHLETES!

To get your Bruce Jenner signature game glove for The Activision Decathlon, here's all you do:

1. Completely fill out this Official Game Glove Order Card.
2. Send the entire Official Order Card and a check or money order for $3.95 (cash will not be accepted) to:

The Activision Decathlon Glove Offer
P.O. Box 587
Ridgely, MD 21681

I have enclosed my check/money order for $3.95. Please send my glove to:

NAME ______
ADDRESS ______
CITY ______ STATE ____ ZIP ____

PLEASE INDICATE SIZE AND HAND

		Size	Right Hand	Left Hand
Children	Ages 6-7	☐	☐	☐
Children	Ages 8-10	☐	☐	☐
Children	Ages 11-13	☐	☐	☐
Adult	Regular	☐	☐	☐
Adult	Large	☐	☐	☐

NOTE: If size ordered is not available, the next larger size will be sent to you.

ACTIVISION

Order form for the Bruce Jenner signature game glove for Activision's Decathlon. $5

2600 version of the arcade classic Double Dragon. $20 complete in box.

Enduro. $15 complete in box.

Frostbite — standard early version. $28 complete in box.

Frostbite — later European white label release. $25 complete in box.

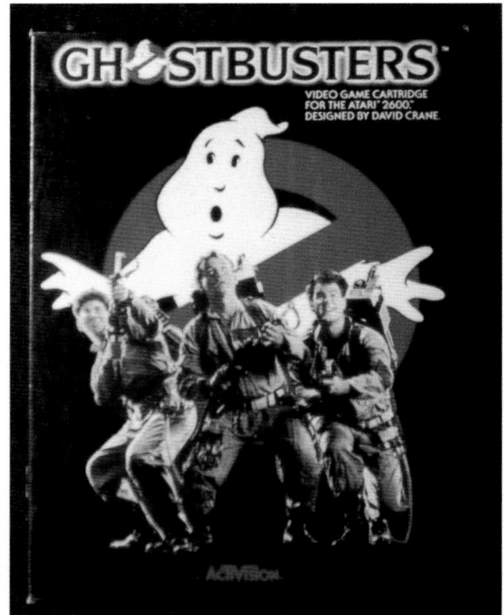

Ghostbusters. $38 complete in box.

Ghostbusters II was only released in Europe. $35 complete in box.

Standard early version of Grand Prix in purplish box. $13 complete in box.

Later blue label release of Grand Prix in reddish box. $15 complete in box.

Keystone Kapers. $12 complete in box.

Laser Blast. $10 complete in box.

Kung Fu Master. $21 complete in box.

Ice Hockey. $12 complete in box.

Megamania. $12 complete in box.

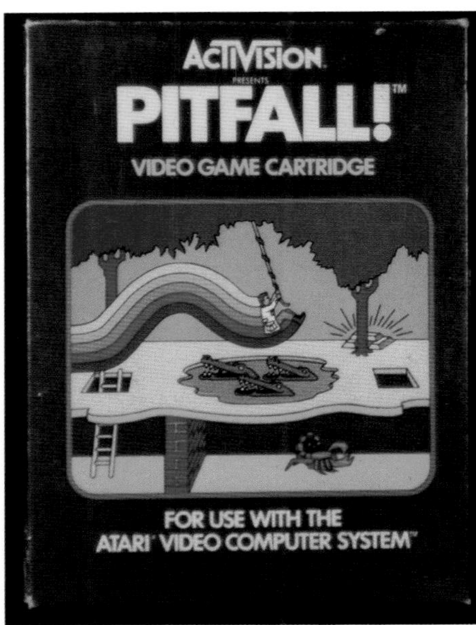

Clockwise from Top left:

Oink. $25 complete in box.

Perhaps the most famous of all Activision games — Pitfall. $18 complete in box.

Pitfall II. $25 complete in box.

Plaque Attack. $28 complete in box.

Pressure Cooker. $35 complete in box.

Private Eye. $25 complete in box.

2600 home version of the arcade classic — Rampage. $25 complete in box.

River Raid. $14 complete in box.

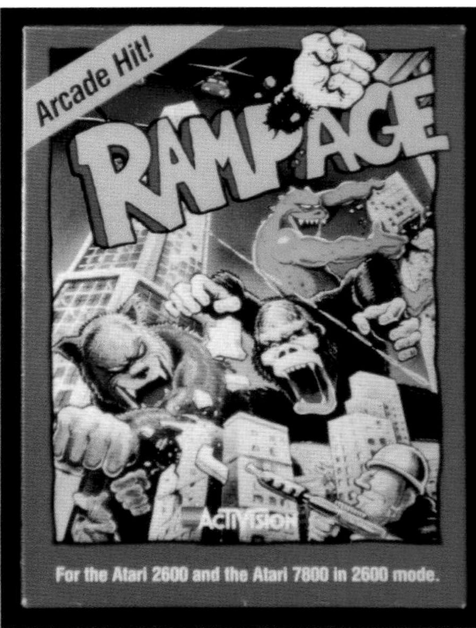

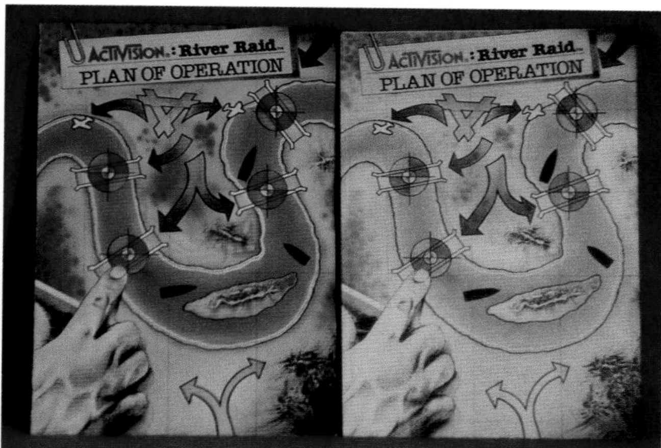

Two variations of the instruction manual for River Raid. The one on the right came with the later blue label release. $3 - $4 each.

Space Shuttle. $20 complete in box.

River Raid II. $29 complete in box.

Seaquest. $19 complete in box.

Spider Fighter. $18 complete in box.

Robot Tank. $15 complete in box.

Skiing. $12 complete in box.

Stampede. $15 complete in box.

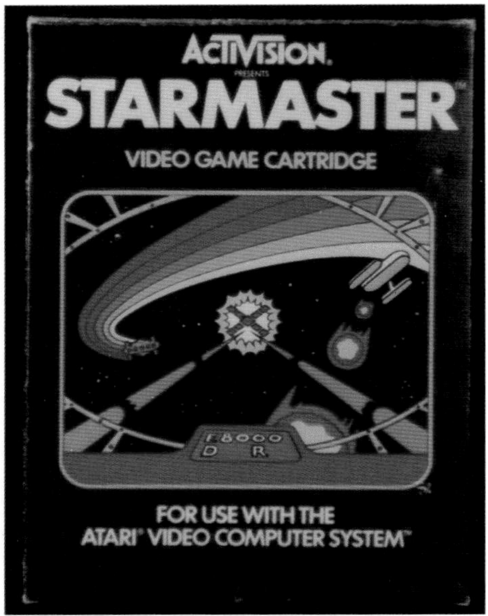

Starmaster. $15 complete in box.

Super Hit Pak, primarily an Australian release that included multiple games on one cartridge and was packaged in an oversized plastic casing. $50 complete in box.

Tennis. $15 complete in box.

Rad Action Pak, primarily an Australian release that included multiple games on two cartridges and was packaged in an oversized plastic casing. $50 complete in box.

Sports Action Pak, primarily an Australian release that included multiple games on one cartridge and was packaged in an oversized plastic casing. $50 complete in box.

An inside view of the aforementioned Rad Action Pak. $50 complete in box.

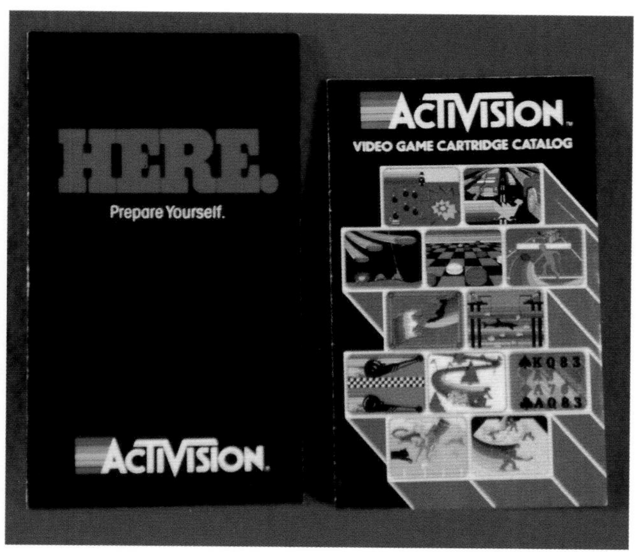

Two of the earliest Activision catalogs, released in 1981. $3 - $7 each.

Two late release Activision catalogs. $3 - $6 each.

Complete series of seasonal Activision catalogs from 1982. $3 - $5 each.

Two Activision catalogs released in 1983. $3 - $5 each.

Late release Activision catalog, also featuring games by Absolute & Imagic. Imagic games were later released by Activision with blue labels. $4.

Atari Games

Activision labels of three different styles. The white labels were distributed in Europe by HES, the picture labels were the standard issue, and the blue labels were later releases of the games. Keystone Kapers' values, from left to right: $10, $6, $9.

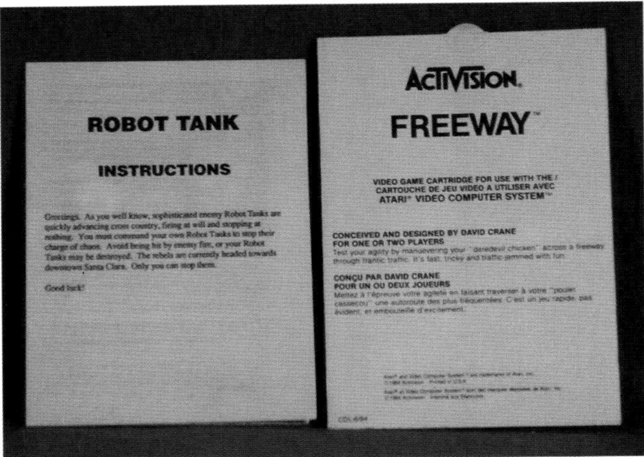

Two of the Activision catalogs that were included with the later release blue label games. $2 - $6 each.

Patches could be earned by photographing your high scores and sending them to Activision. $30 - $75 each

Different patches were available for the same game, depending on your score. A rare patch may bring as much as $75.

3D Tic-Tac-Toe. $18 - $20 complete in box.

A game of Concentration in full color early release box. $25 complete in box.

A game of Concentration in full late release gray box. $23 complete in box.

Asteroids. $9 complete in box.

Adventure — the first video game to contain a hidden "Easter egg" (this one was the programmers initials in a secret room). $40 complete in box.

Four different Asteroids label varieties. $3 - $12 each.

Air Sea Battle. $10 complete in box.

Backgammon. $15 complete in box.

Clockwise from Top left:

Early release of Basic Programming. $20 complete in box.

Late release gray box version of Basic Programming. $19 complete in box.

Standard early release of Basketball. $10 complete in box.

Late release gray box version of Basketball. $10 complete in box.

Battlezone. $9 complete in box.

Red box and label version of Battlezone. $35 complete in box.

Berzerk. $11 complete in box.

Big Bird's Egg Catch. $20 complete in box.

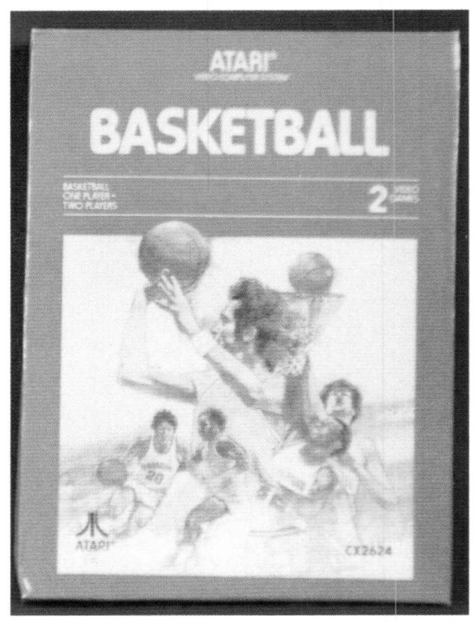

Clockwise from Top left:

First release book style box for Blackjack. $19 complete in box.

Bowling. $11 complete in box.

Bowling in late release gray box. $12 complete in box.

Brain Games. $20 complete in box.

Breakout. $10 complete in box.

Casino. $15 complete in box.

Centipede. $10 complete in box.

Championship Soccer. $12 complete in box.

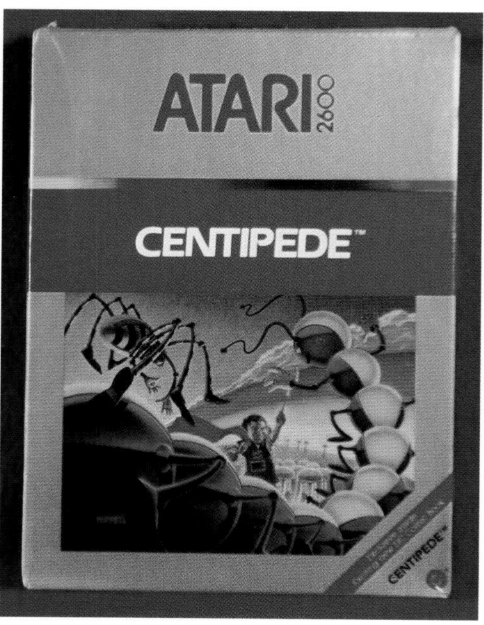

Clockwise from Top left:

Circus Atari. $12 complete in box.

Codebreaker in late release gray box. $20 complete in box.

01 Combat book-style box. Box opens from the front, like a book, and is labeled 01 on the side panel. Cartridge should also be labeled 01. $15 complete in box.

Combat. $5 complete in box.

Cookie Monster Munch. $20 complete in box.

Crystal Castles. $15 complete in box.

Red box and label variant of Crystal Castles. $35 complete in box.

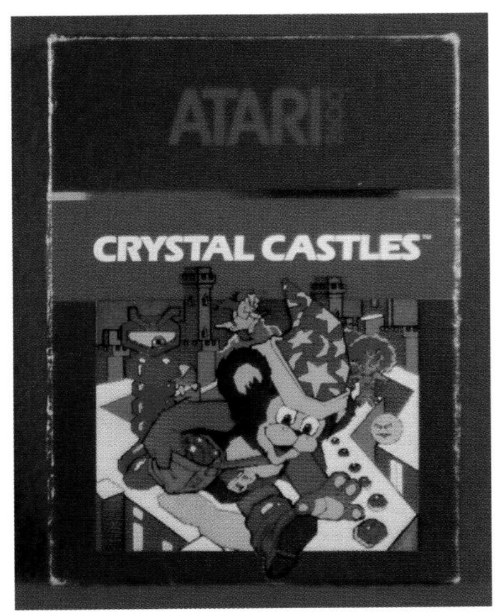

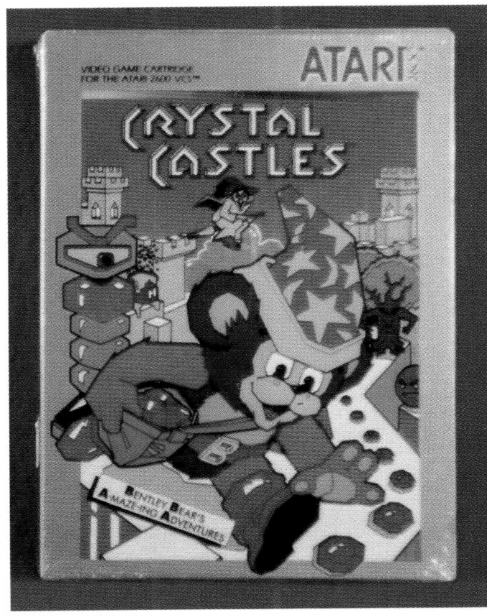

Crystal Castles cartridges with and without the Bentley bear logo. Valued at $7 and $15 each respectively.

Desert Falcon. $15 complete in box.

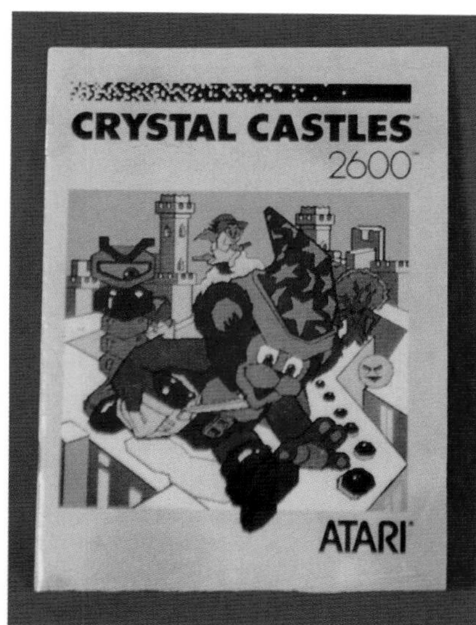

Crystal Castles instruction booklet sans Bentley bear logo. $5.

Demons to Diamonds. $12 complete in box.

Dig Dug. $9 complete in box.

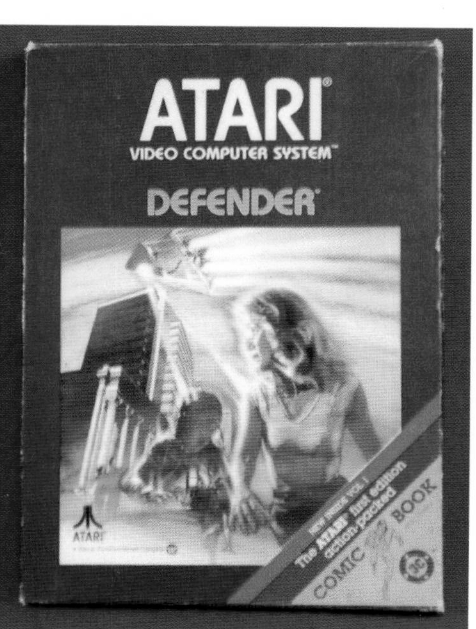

Defender. $9 complete in box.

Demons to Diamonds in late release gray box. $13 complete in box.

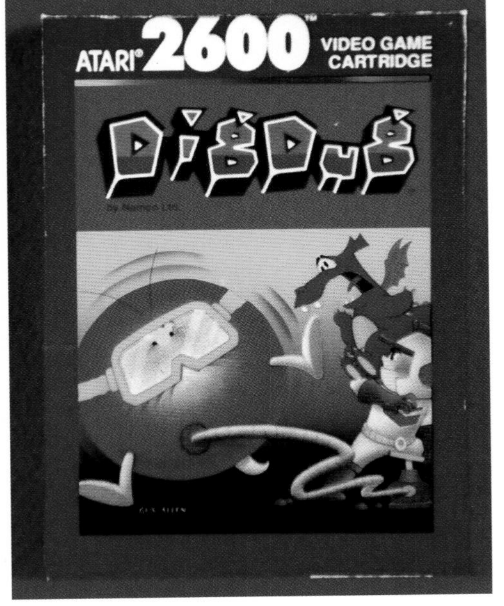

Clockwise from Top left:

Dig Dug in rare European release red box. $29 complete in box.

Double Dunk. $19 complete in box.

E.T. $10 complete in box.

Tip sheet for E.T. $3.

Fatal Run. $40 complete in box.

Flag Capture. $20 complete in box.

Football. $9 complete in box.

Fun With Numbers in late release gray box. $25 complete in box.

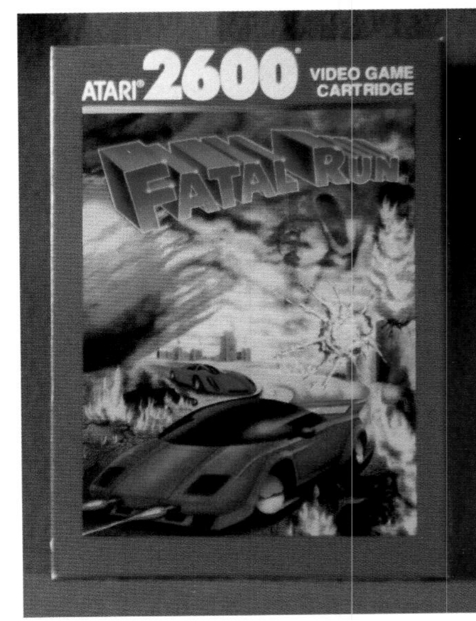

Clockwise from Top left:

Galaxian. $9 complete in box.

Gravitar. $9 complete in box.

Golf. $15 complete in box.

Hangman. $25 complete in box.

Haunted House. $12 complete in box.

Home Run. $10 complete in box.

Human Cannonball. $15 complete in box.

Hunt & Score. $21 complete in box.

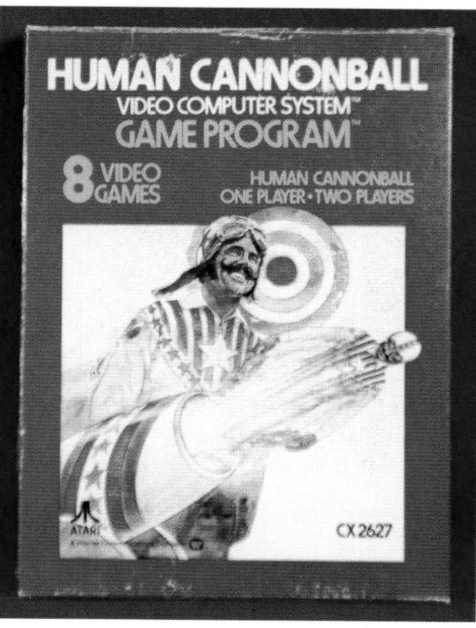

Indy 500. $12 complete in box.

Jr. Pac-Man. $9 complete in box.

Klax. $65 complete in box.

Indy 500 package with driving controller. $50 complete in box.

Jungle Hunt. $9 complete in box.

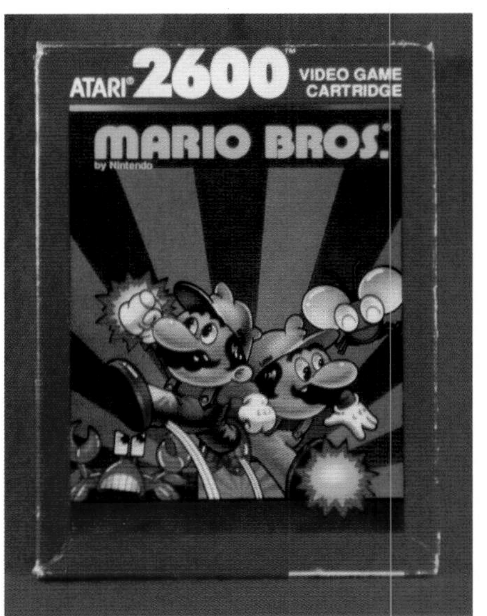

Mario Bros. in foreign release red box. $26 complete in box.

Joust. $9 complete in box.

Kangaroo. $9 complete in box.

Maze Craze. $15 complete in box.

Clockwise from Top left:

Midnight Magic. $12 complete in box.

Millipede. $15 complete in box.

Missile Command. $8 complete in box.

Missile Command in multilingual box. $10 complete in box.

Moon Patrol. $10 complete in box.

Atari re-release of Coleco's Mouse Trap. $14 complete in box.

Ms. Pac-Man in early style box. $10 complete in box.

Ms. Pac-Man in later release box. $9 complete in box.

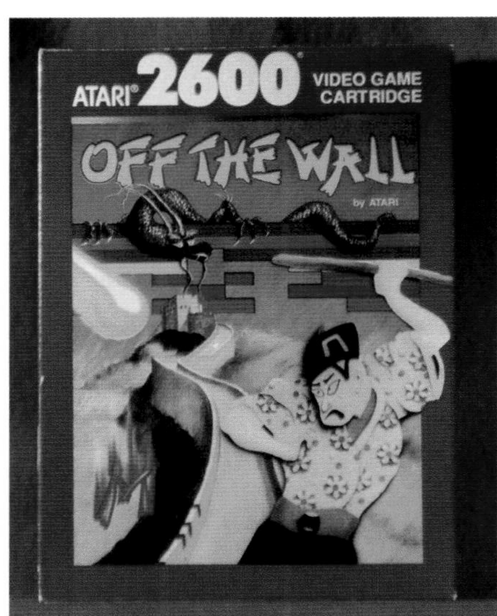

Clockwise from Top left:

Night Driver. $14 complete in box.

Off the Wall. $29 complete in box.

Outlaw. $12 complete in box.

Pac-Man. $9 complete in box.

Pelé's Soccer. $20 complete in box.

Pelé's Soccer in multilingual box. $22 complete in box.

Phoenix. $9 complete in box.

Pole Position. $9 complete in box.

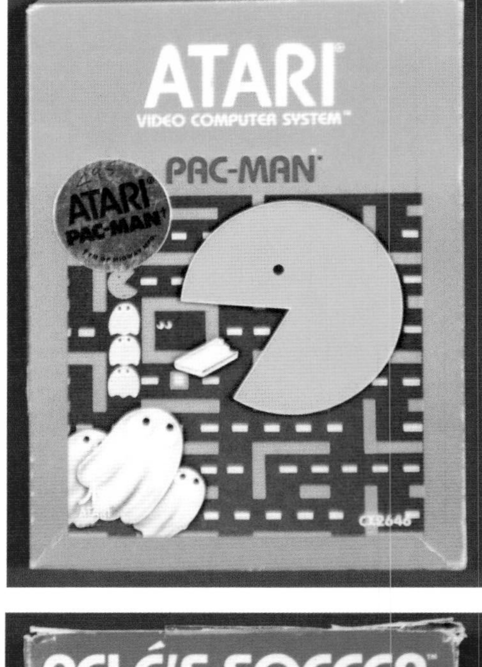

Pole Position in foreign release red box. $26 complete in box.

Atari re-release of Parker Brothers' Q*bert. $12 complete in box.

Radar Lock. $20 complete in box.

Raiders of the Lost Ark. $22 complete in box.

Scarce Japanese release of Raiders of the Lost Ark. $100 complete in box.

Raiders of the Lost Ark and its counterpart with a title error. Non-error cartridge $6. Error cartridge $15.

Raiders of the Lost Ark tip sheet. $5

RealSports Baseball. $10 complete in box.

RealSports Boxing. $15 complete in box.

RealSports Football. $10 complete in box.

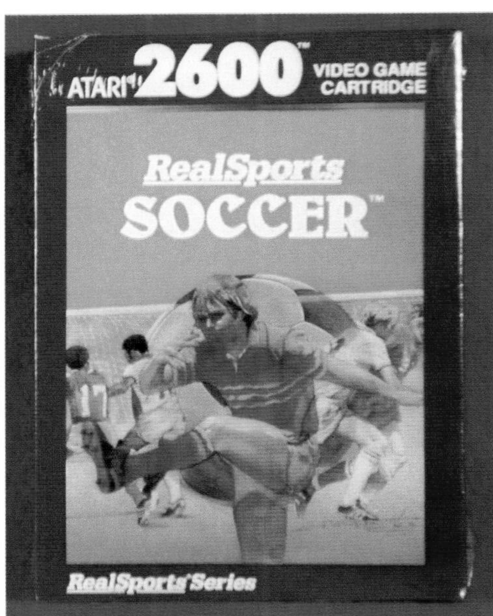

Red box foreign edition of RealSports Soccer. $25 complete in box.

RealSports Volleyball. $13 complete in box.

Some games, such as RealSports Football, came with multiple instruction manuals. $4 set.

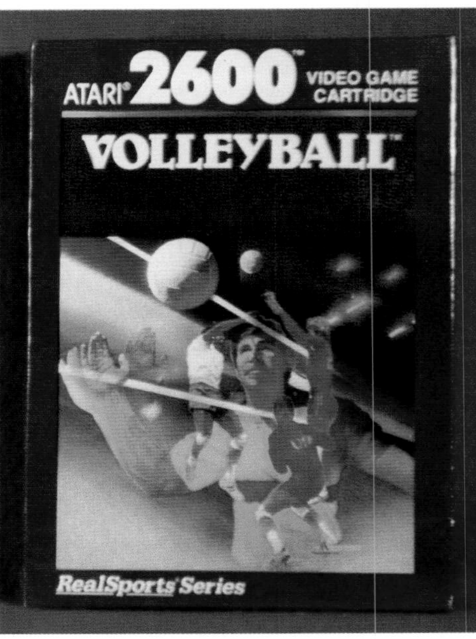

Red box foreign edition of RealSports Volleyball. $27 complete in box.

RealSports Soccer. $15 complete in box.

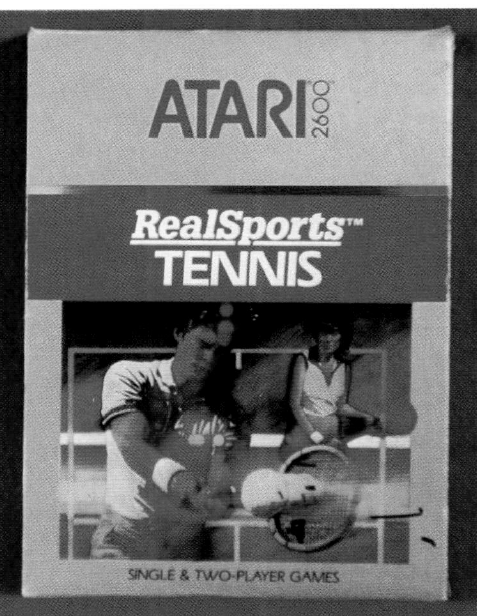

RealSports Tennis. $12 complete in box.

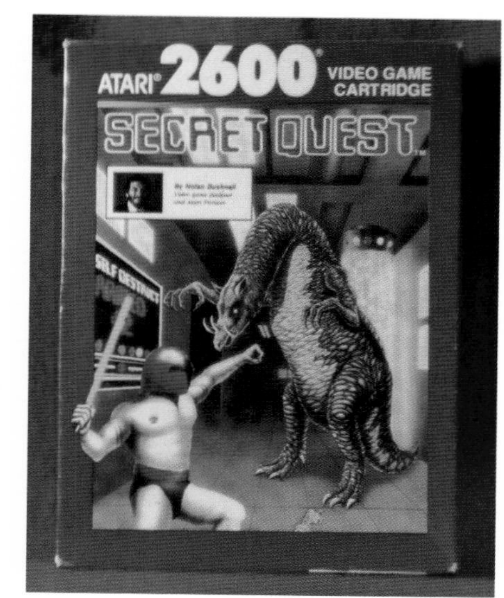

Clockwise from Top left:

Road Runner. $35 complete in box.

Early release of Secret Quest. $25 complete in box.

Secret Quest. Secret Quest was programmed by Atari founder Nolan Bushnell. $25 complete in box.

Sentinel. $22 complete in box.

Sky Diver. $20 complete in box.

Slot Machine. $35 complete in box.

Solaris. $9 complete in box.

Sorcerer's Apprentice is also of interest to Disney collectors. $49 complete in box.

Space Invaders. $8 complete in box.

Space Invaders multilingual box. $10 complete in box.

Sprint Master. $29 complete in box.

Slightly less common Space Invaders with yellow text box. $9 complete in box.

Space War. $15 complete in box.

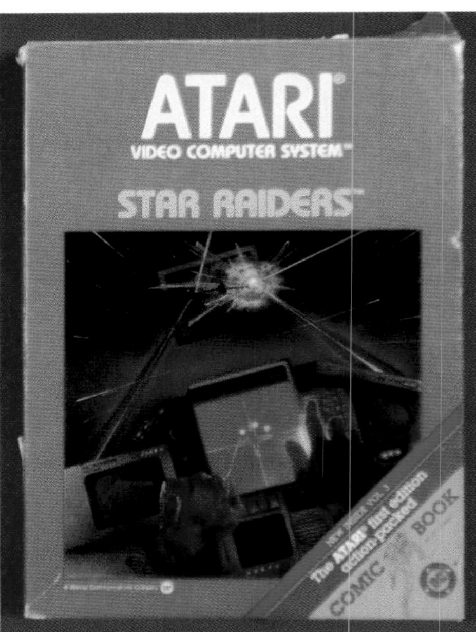

Star Raiders. $10 complete in box.

Star Raiders touch pad controller was necessary to play the game. Displayed here are the outer boxes these controllers were packaged in. $35 complete in boxes.

Stargate (a.k.a. Defender II). $14 complete in box.

Super Breakout in multilingual box. $16 complete in box.

Superman in first release box. $27 complete in box.

Super Breakout. $15 complete in box.

Super Football. $9 complete in box.

Superman in subsequently released box. $25 complete in box.

Surround. $15 complete in box.

Swordquest — Earthworld, first game in the Swordquest trilogy. $15 complete in box.

Instruction manual and guide book for the extremely rare Swordquest — Waterworld. $50 for the pair.

Swordquest — Earthworld certificate of merit. $50 - $60.

Taz. $37 complete in box.

Atari's re-release of Coleco's Venture. $9 complete in box.

Video Checkers. $18 complete in box.

Vanguard. $12 complete in box.

Video Chess. $18 complete in box.

Video Pinball. $11 complete in box.

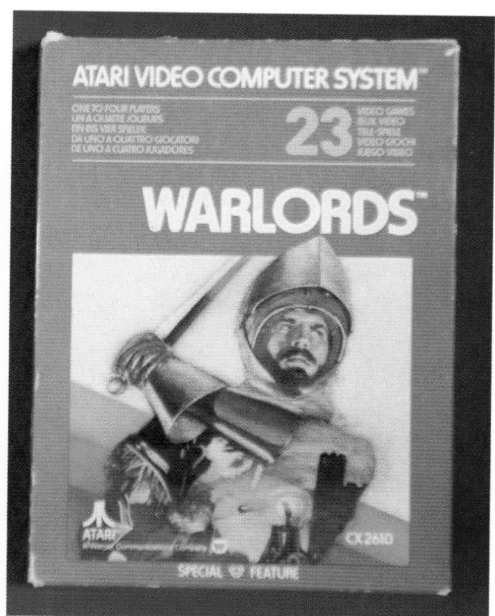

Warlords in multilingual box. $12 complete in box.

Video Olympics. $10 complete in box.

Warlords. $10 complete in box.

Yar's Revenge. $10 complete in box.

Four different versions of the earliest Atari catalogs. $2 - $6 each.

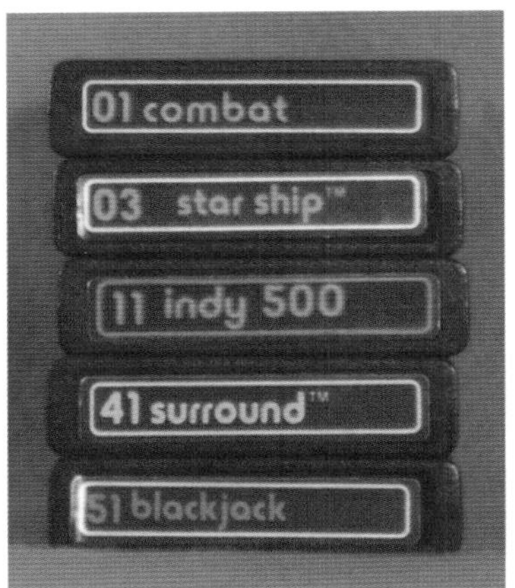

The earliest released Atari cartridges have numbered prefixes, they are worth a little less than twice that of their unnumbered counterparts. (See price guide section in this book for further details.)

Five different Atari catalogs that go from 42 games to 49 games. $1 - $4 each.

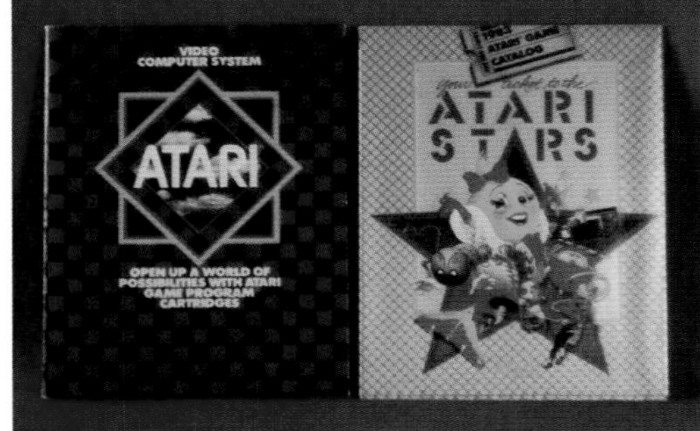

Two different versions Atari catalogs that fold out into posters. $4 - $6 each.

The early released numbered Atari games came in book-style boxes like this one. Combat, the most common of the lot, is valued at $15 complete in box.

Late release Atari stars catalog. $5.

Atari Video Cube was initially released as Rubik's Cube, but was soon changed to Video Cube, making the original release somewhat difficult to find. The Atari Video Cube cartridge is valued at $40, while the Rubik's Cube version comes in at about $85.

The Atari club made many items that were available to club members, making for numerous interesting and rare items. This special offer form was your chance to join the club. $5.

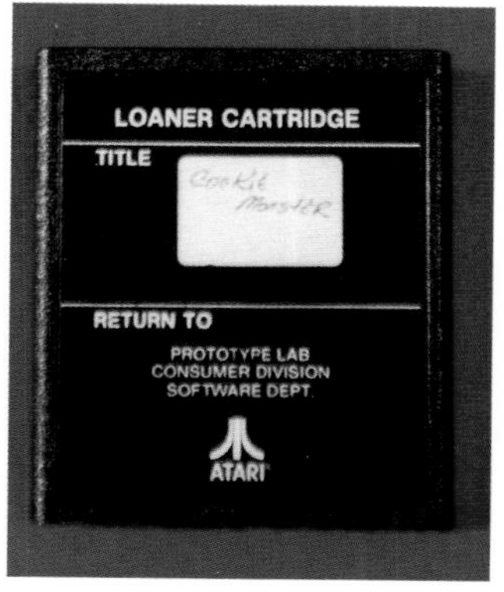

Atari lab loaner cartridges from the Atari prototype lab are very desirable items. Common released titles are $50 - $150 each, while an unreleased title can bring over $1000.

Atari Log Book alongside the offer that allowed you to mail away for it. Book in unused condition: $8, unused offer: $2.

Different sized catalogs were released for some Atari games; however, there is no significant difference in value.

DC Comics produced mini comics that were packed in with some Atari releases. Common ones will only fetch a dollar or two, while a rarity like the Swordquest #3 may bring as much as $50.

Coleco Games

Berenstain Bears was one of only two cartridges produced for use with the kid vid controller. $250 complete in box.

Inside view of the large Berenstain Bears box.

Mouse Trap. $12 complete in box.

Carnival. $16 complete in box.

Standard pack in catalog from Coleco. $2.

Venture. $17 complete in box.

Froggo Games

Donkey Kong. $9 complete in box.

Zaxxon. $27 complete in box.

Cruise Missile. $15 complete in box.

Karate. $15 complete in box.

Sea Hawk. $15 complete in box.

Sea Hunt. $15 complete in box.

Spider-droid. $15 complete in box.

Task Force. $15 complete in box.

Imagic Games

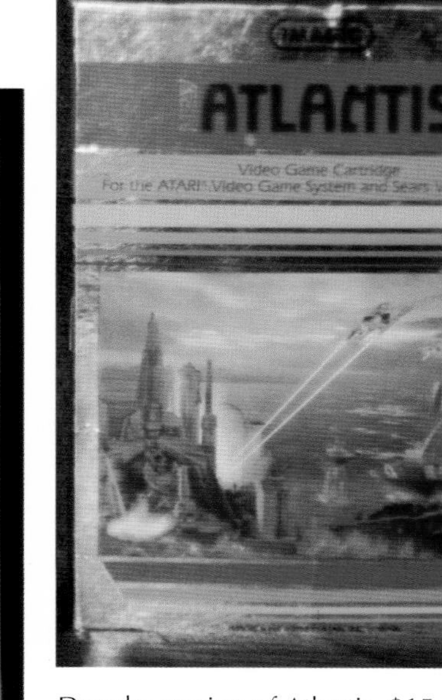

Day sky version of Atlantis. $15 complete in box.

Night sky version of Atlantis. $14 complete in box.

Cosmic Ark. $13 complete in box.

Clockwise from Top left:

Demon Attack. $11 complete in box.

Blue label version of Demon Attack in black box. $15 complete in box.

Dragonfire. $16 complete in box.

Fire Fighter. $16 complete in box.

Laser Gates. $65 complete in box.

Moonsweeper. $21 complete in box.

No Escape. $36 complete in box.

Riddle of the Sphynx. $15 complete in box.

Top left: Star Voyager. $15 complete in box.

Center left: Subterranea in foreign issue box (This is a white label version, which is how the game was released in Europe [where it was more common than it is in the U.S.]). The silver label U.S. release may bring over $95 complete in box. This European version is valued at $65 complete in box.

Bottom left: Trick Shot. $29 complete in box.

Left: Wing War in foreign issue box (this is a white label version). $65 complete in box.

Center right: Various Imagic catalogs. $2 - $6 each.

Bottom right: Part of an Imagic store display. $400 - $500 if complete, but about $150 as pictured.

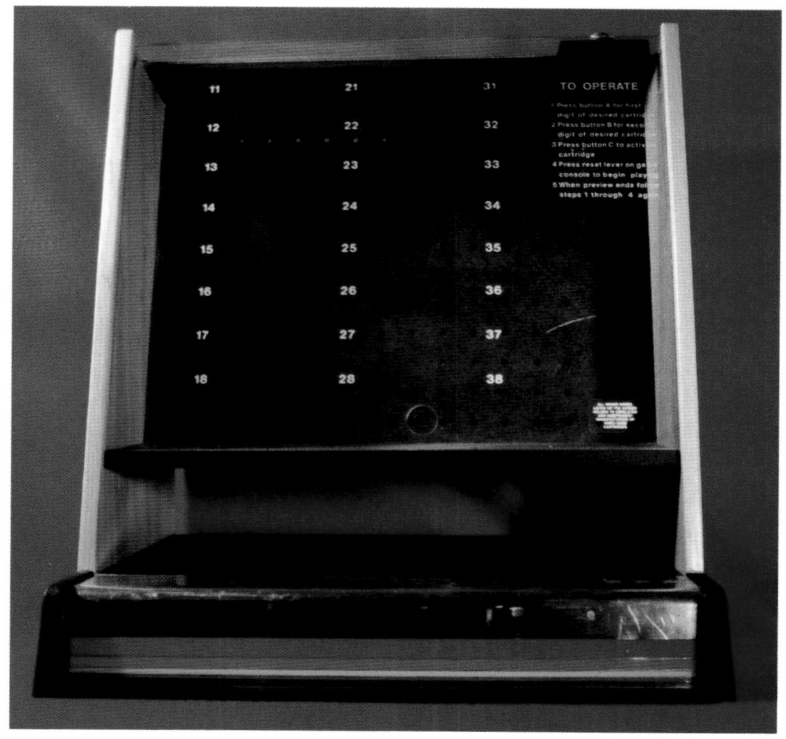

Mattel Games

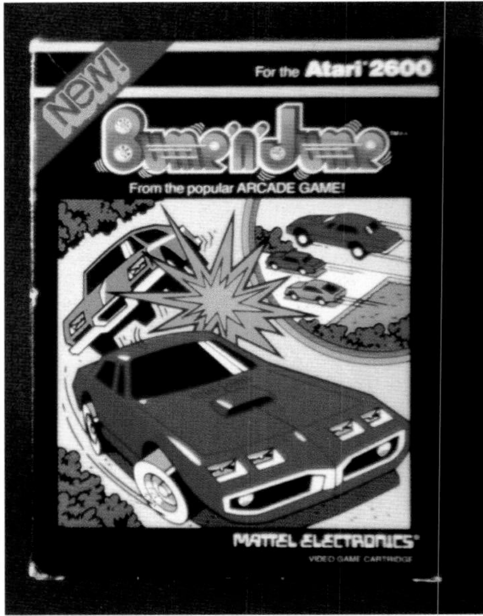

Clockwise from Top left:

Armor Ambush. $12 complete in box.

Astroblast. $9 complete in box.

Bump 'n' Jump. $25 complete in box.

Dark Cavern. $12 complete in box.

Frogs and Flies. $15 complete in box.

International Soccer. $19 complete in box.

Kool-Aid Man. $35 complete in box.

Lock 'N' Chase. $12 complete in box.

Clockwise from Top left:

Masters of the Universe. $35 complete in box.

Space Attack. $10 complete in box.

Super Challenge Baseball. $10 complete in box.

Super Challenge Football. $10 complete in box.

Tron Deadly Discs. $35 complete in box.

Assorted Mattel M Network catalogs, which were originally included in the cartridge boxes. $2 - $5 each.

Parker Brothers Games

Action Force. Action Man is the British equivalent of G.I. Joe. $51 complete in box.

Amidar. $14 complete in box.

Clockwise from Top left:

Frogger. $15 complete in box.

G.I. Joe. $19 complete in box.

Gyruss. $35 complete in box.

James Bond 007. $75 complete in box.

Popeye. $35 complete in box.

Q*bert. $15 complete in box.

Reactor. $16 complete in box.

Spiderman. $25 complete in box.

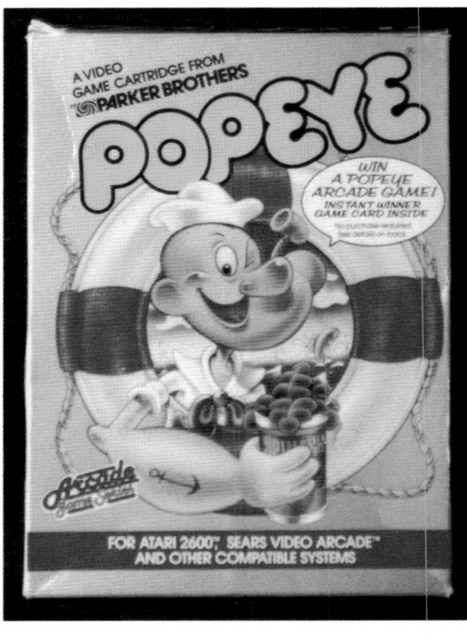

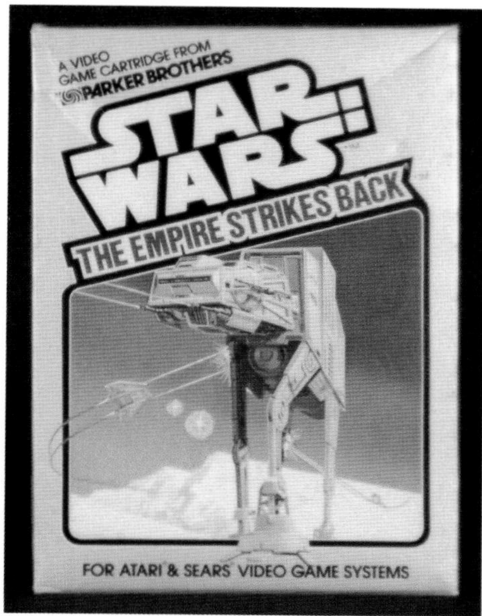

Star Wars: the Empire Strikes Back. $19 complete in box.

Instruction manuals for all four Star Wars games released for the 2600. $4 - $20 each.

Star Wars: Return of the Jedi Death Star Battle. $41 complete in box.

Super Cobra. $25 complete in box.

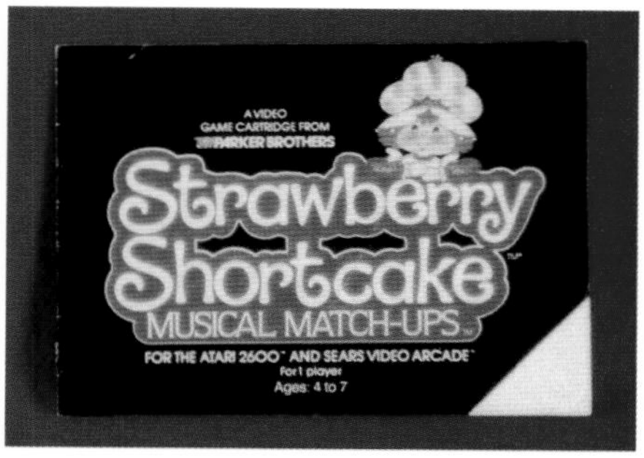

Parker Brothers instruction manuals often have the proof of purchase cut off. This reduces the value of the manual by approximately 20%.

Sweepstakes offer for Star Wars: Return of the Jedi Death Star Battle. $5.

Tutankham. $19 complete in box.

Parker Brother catalogs. The later issue catalog on the left features screen shots of many unreleased titles, including the Incredible Hulk, Lord of the Rings, Star Wars, McDonald's, etc. $5 - $10 each.

Sears Games

Note: these should not be confused with games from Telegames. All Sears games are marked "Tele-Games," but were manufactured by Sears, Roebuck and Co.

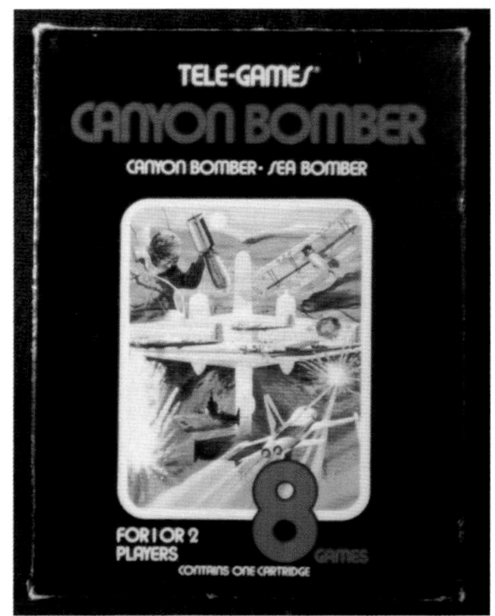

Canyon Bomber. $35 complete in box.

Outer Space. $26 complete in box.

Golf. $21 complete in box.

Missile Command. $15 complete in box.

Pong Sports. $21 complete in box.

Clockwise from Top left:

Race. $25 complete in box.

Space Combat. $35 complete in box.

Space Invaders. $18 complete in box.

Speedway II. $20 - $25 complete in box.

Star Raiders. $25 complete in box.

Tank Plus. $19 - $23 complete in box.

Target Fun. $15 complete in box.

Sears catalog of cartridges for the 2600 system. $4 - $8.

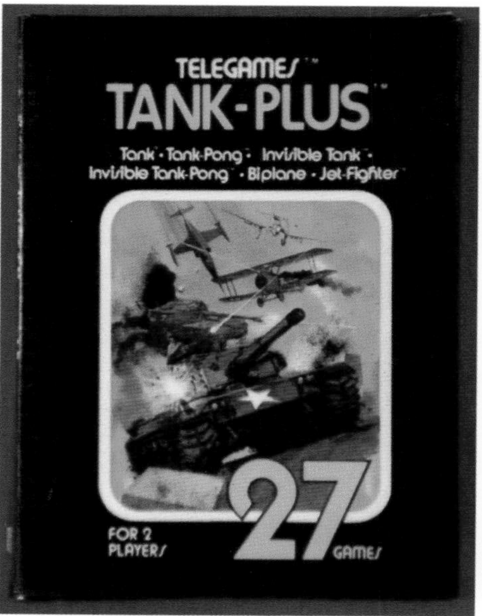

Three different Sears cartridge label variations. Note the slanted S's on the cartridge to the right; these slanted S variations, along with the picture labels, are generally harder to come by than the standard style in the middle. $8 - $13 each.

A few instruction manuals for Sears games. $4 - $10 each.

Telegames Games

This company has obtained both the rights and leftover stock for many older systems. Many titles are still available new from this company.

Adventures on GX-12, which is Tron sans the licensing. $20 complete in box.

Bogey Blaster. $20 complete in box.

Bump 'n' Jump. $20 complete in box.

Clockwise from Top left:

Frogs and Flies. $20 complete in box.

Glacier Patrol. $25 complete in box.

Kung Fu Superkicks. $25 complete in box.

Lock 'N' Chase. $20 complete in box.

Universal Chaos. $25 complete in box.

Telegames catalog. $1 - $4.

Twentieth Century Fox Games

Alien. $45 complete in box.

Bank Heist. $45 complete in box.

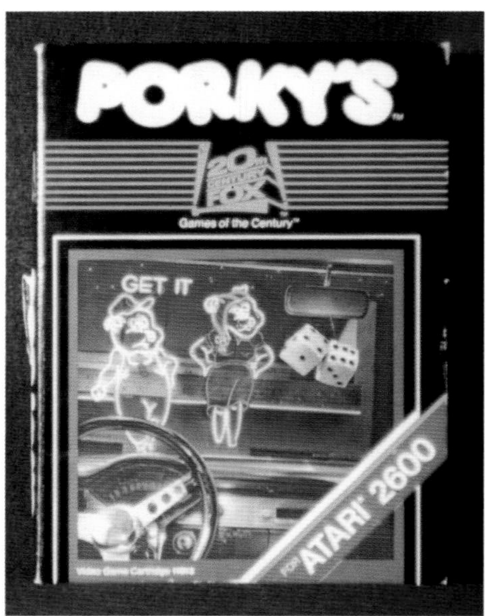

Clockwise from Top left:

Beany Bopper. $25 complete in box.

Crash Dive. $34 complete in box.

Crypts of Chaos. $45 complete in box.

Fantastic Voyage. $35 complete in box.

Flash Gordon. $39 complete in box.

MASH. $25 complete in box.

Mega Force. $45 complete in box.

Porky's. $29 complete in box.

Clockwise from Top left:

Revenge of the Beefsteak Tomatoes. $34 complete in box.

SpaceMaster X-7 is based on a little known 1950s science fiction film. $95 complete in box.

Turmoil. $28 complete in box.

Worm War I. $25 complete in box.

Pete Rose Baseball by Absolute. $25 complete in box.

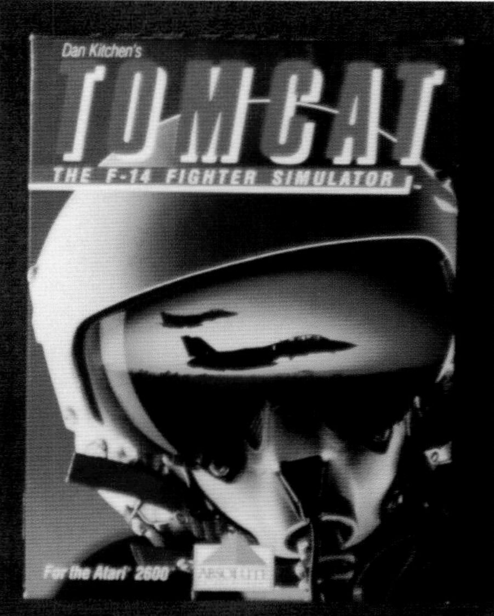

Games From Various Manufacturers

Skate Boardin' by Absolute. $20 complete in box.

Titlematch Pro Wrestling by Absolute. $20 complete in box.

Tomcat The F-14 Fighter Simulator by Absolute. $20 complete in box.

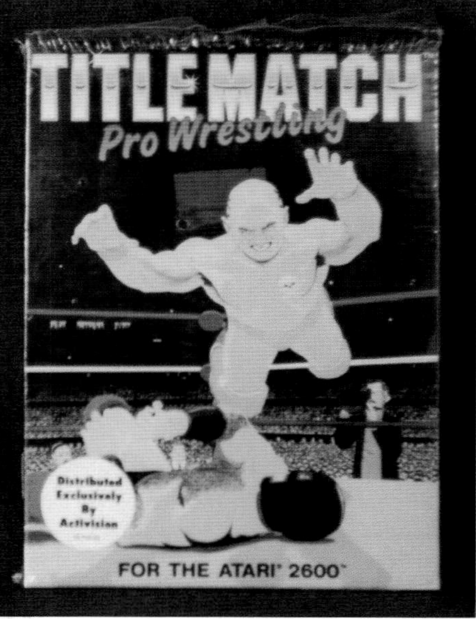

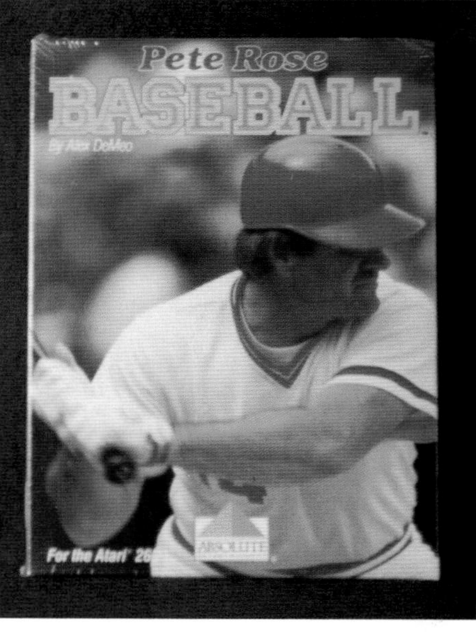

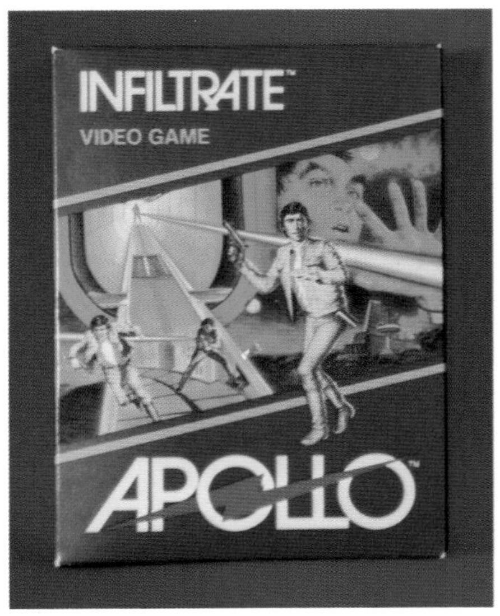

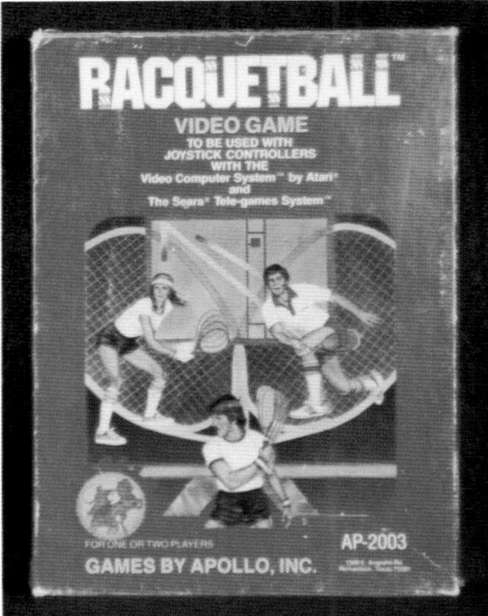

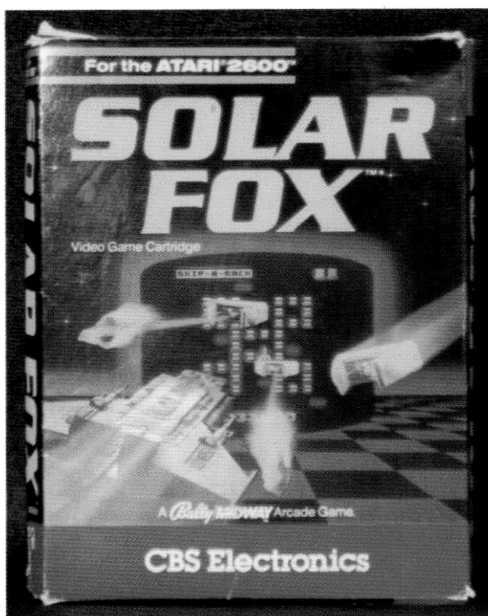

Clockwise from Top left:

Infiltrate by Apollo. $19 - $25 complete in box.

Racquetball by Apollo. $25 complete in box.

Shark Attack by Apollo was originally titled Lochjaw, but this was apparently too close to *Jaws*, so Apollo was forced to change the title, making the original release very scarce today. $29 complete in box.

Skeet Shoot by Apollo. $35 complete in box.

Space Cavern by Apollo. $15 complete in box.

Space Chase by Apollo. $20 complete in box.

Gorf by CBS. $22 complete in box.

Solar Fox by CBS. $29 complete in box.

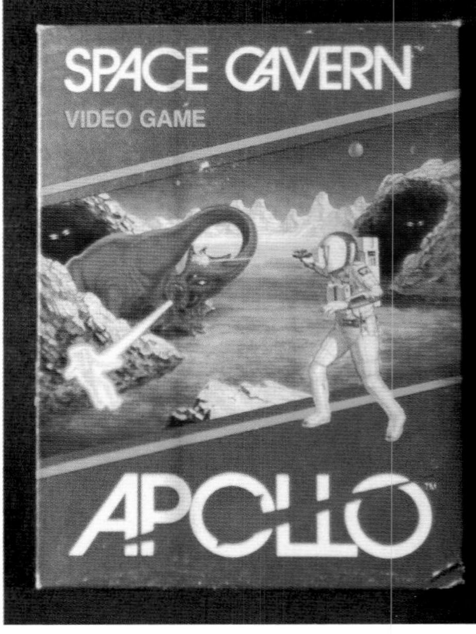

CBS video games fun voucher. $3 - $5.

Room of Doom by CommaVid. $110 complete in box.

Airlock by Data Age. $15 complete in box.

Bermuda Triangle by Data Age. $21 complete in box.

Bugs by Data Age. $15 complete in box.

Encounter at L-5 by Data Age. $18 complete in box.

Journey Escape by Data Age. $18 complete in box.

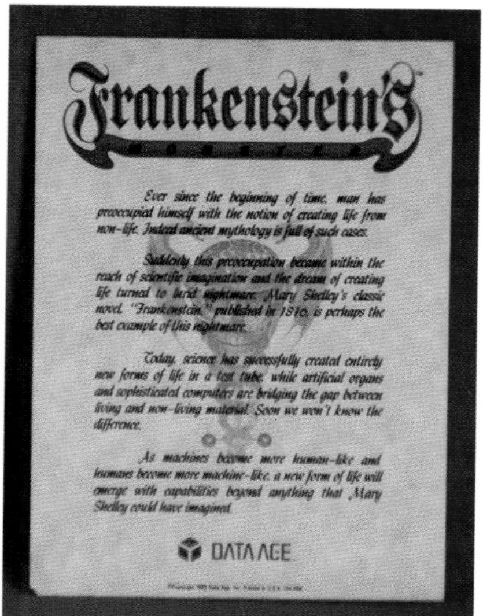
Frankenstein's

Ever since the beginning of time, man has preoccupied himself with the notion of creating life from non-life. Indeed ancient mythology is full of such cases.

Suddenly this preoccupation became within the reach of scientific imagination and the dream of creating life turned to lurid nightmare. Mary Shelley's classic novel, "Frankenstein," published in 1818, is perhaps the best example of this nightmare.

Today, science has successfully created entirely new forms of life in a test tube, while artificial organs and sophisticated computers are bridging the gap between living and non-living material. Soon we won't know the difference.

As machines become more human-like and humans become more machine-like, a new form of life will emerge with capabilities beyond anything that Mary Shelley could have imagined.

DATA AGE

Insert from the Frankenstein game by Data Age. $3 -$7.

Data Age catalog. $2 - $5.

California Games by Epyx. $15 complete in box.

Epyx games came in two different sized boxes. The larger box on the left is the standard American release, while the smaller box on the right is a European release.

Summer Games by Epyx. $15 complete in box.

Video Jogger and Video Reflex were the only two cartridges produced by Exus. They were both included with the "Foot Craz" controller and are valued at about $120 each.

Winter Games by Epyx. $15 complete in box.

Most of the Adult games produced by Mystique, such as Beat 'Em & Eat 'Em, were later released as double ended cartridges by Playaround. $50 complete in box.

The release Custer's Revenge by Mystique was met with outcry and protests by both Feminist and Native American organizations. $65 complete in box.

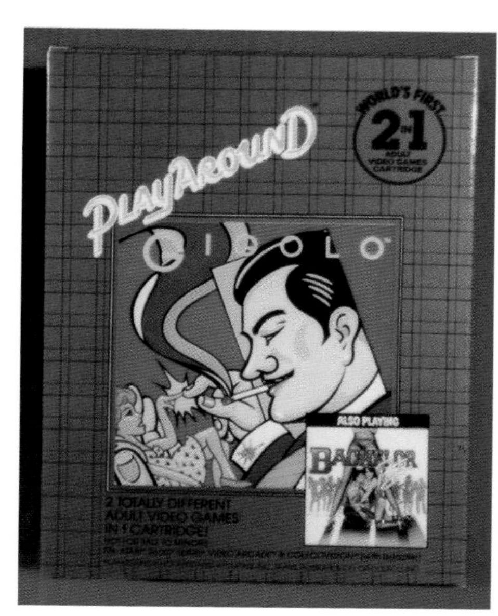

Clockwise from Top left:

Fire Fly by Mythicon. $39 complete in box.

One side of the double sided Bachelor Party / Gigolo by Playaround. $75 complete in box.

Other side of the double sided Bachelor Party / Gigolo by Playaround. $75 complete in box.

One side of the double sided Beat 'Em & Eat 'Em / Lady in Wading by Playaround. $75 complete in box.

Other side of the double sided Beat 'Em & Eat 'Em / Lady in Wading by Playaround. $75 complete in box.

One side of the double sided Bachelorette Party / Burning Desire by Playaround. $75 complete in box.

Other side of the double sided Bachelorette Party / Burning Desire by Playaround. $75 complete in box.

One side of the double sided Philly Flasher / Cathouse Blues by Playaround. $75 complete in box.

Other side of the double sided Philly Flasher / Cathouse Blues by Playaround. $75 complete in box.

Star Trek — Strategic Operations Simulator. $31 complete in box.

Inside view of a Playaround double ended cartridge, complete with two instruction manuals and a lock to keep the kids away from the game.

Tac - Scan by Sega. $28 complete in box.

Buck Rogers — Planet of Zoom by Sega. $25 complete in box.

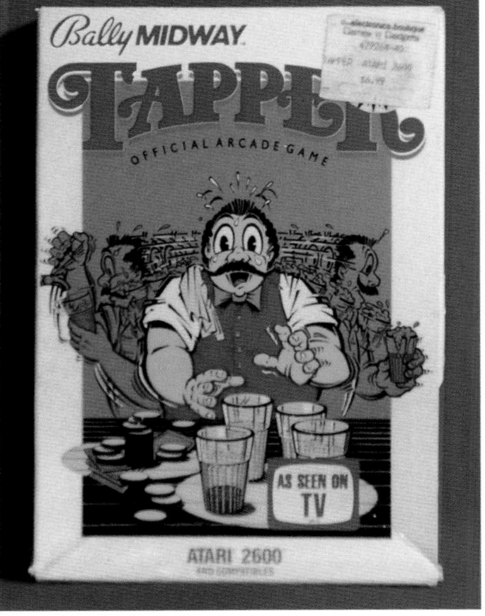

Tapper by Sega. $75 complete in box.

This instruction manual by Sega also folds out into a full color poster. $3 - $6.

Tape Worm by Spectravideo, which is an early name for the Spectravision company. $29 complete in box.

Fast Food by Telesys. $16 complete in box.

The extremely rare Music Machine cartridge by Sparrow was only obtainable via Christian outlets. $500 for a loose cartridge.

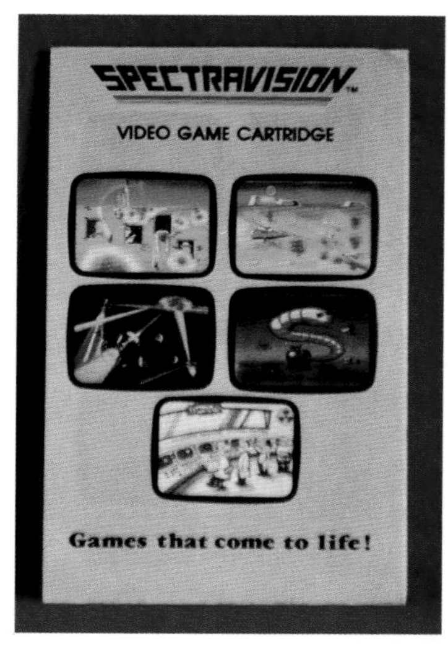

Catalog from Spectravision. $2 - $5.

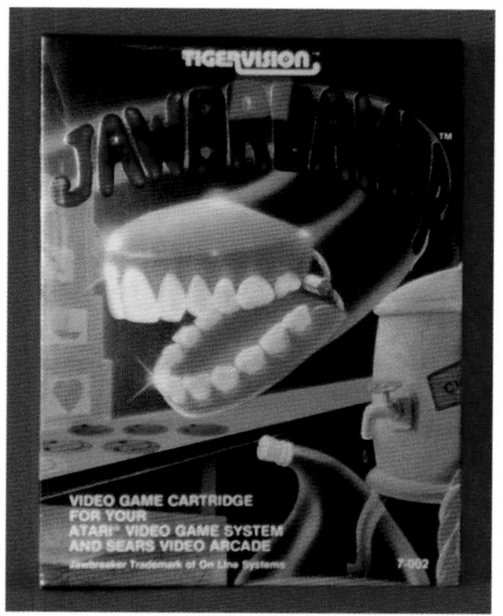

Jawbreaker by Tigervision. $75 complete in box.

Gangster Alley by Spectravision. $22 complete in box.

Coconuts by Telesys. $19 complete in box.

Miner 2049er Volume II by Tigervision. $155 complete in box.

Tigervision cartridges were released in very colorful casings. $29 - $40 each.

Various Tigervision instruction manuals. $7 - $10 each.

M.A.D. by US Games. $29 complete in box.

Name This Game by US Games featured a contest to actually name this cartridge. The eventual name was Octopus. $25 complete in box.

BMX Air Master by TNT. $25 complete in box.

Gopher by US Games. $25 complete in box.

Squeeze Box by US Games. $29 complete in box.

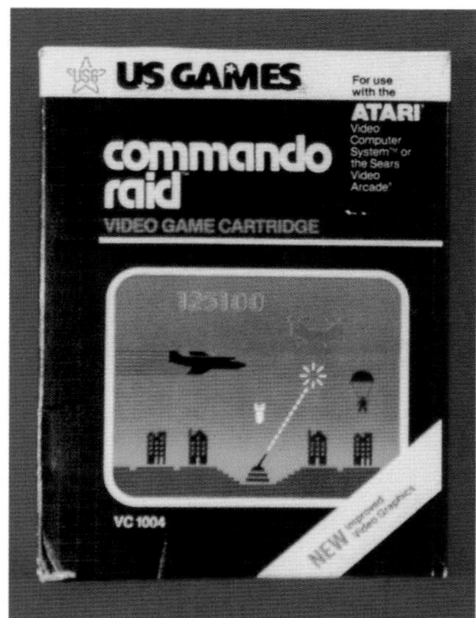

Commando Raid by US Games / Vidtec. $15 complete in box.

Word Zapper by US Games / Vidtec. $16 complete in box.

Surfer's Paradise, But Danger Below. $190 complete in box.

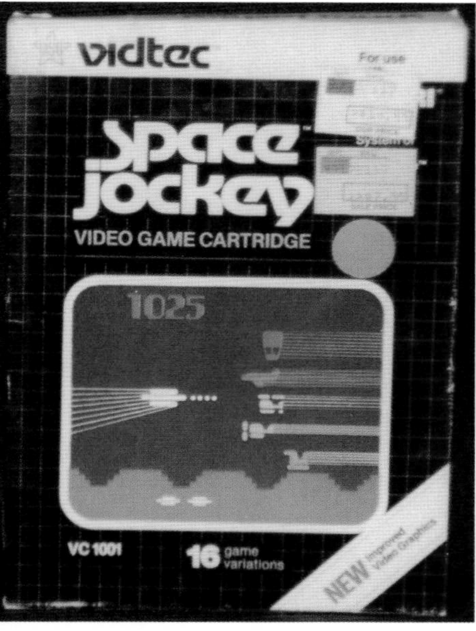

Space Jockey by US Games / Vidtec. $14 complete in box.

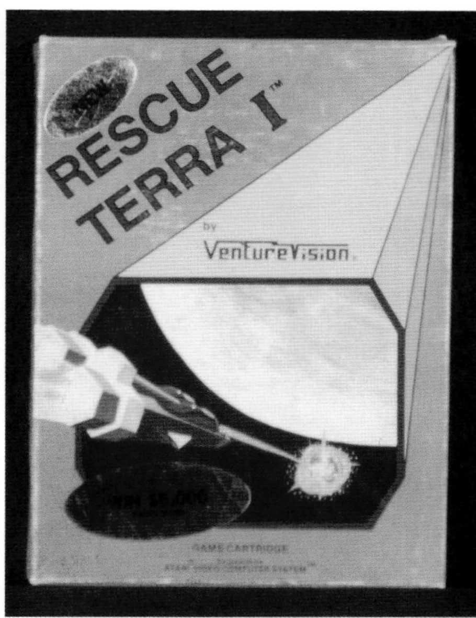
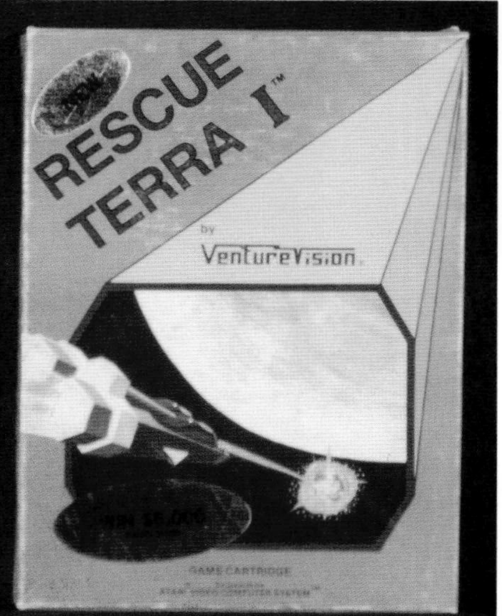

Rescue Terra I was the only game produced by Venturevision. $240 complete in box.

Halloween and Texas Chainsaw Massacre cartridges by Wizard Video. $125 each.

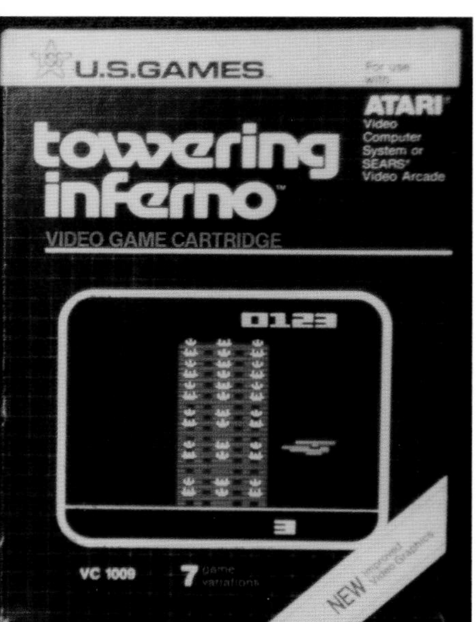

Towering Inferno by US Games / Vidtec. And, yes, it is based on the movie. $25 complete in box.

Instruction manual for The Texas Chainsaw Massacre. $25.

Foreign Games

Single ended cartridges by Xonox. Artillery Duel (left) is valued at around $35, while Tomarc the Barbarian (right), which was originally to be released as Thundarr the Barbarian, is valued at $60.

Assorted games from Brazilian manufacturer CCE. $30 - $50 each.

Some Xonox double ended cartridges. Note the different artwork on the European released cartridge in the center. $25 - $85 each.

CCE titles came on a blistercard rather than in a box. $65 - $85 mint on card.

Instruction manuals for various Xonox releases. $5 - $10 each.

Digivsion games from Brazil were packaged in small plastic cases. $50 - $75 with case.

The Brazilian company Polyvox released titles legitimately licensed from American companies. Loose cartridges are valued at $25 - $55 each.

Acid Drop, released by Salu in Europe. $27 complete in box.

This German release, which translates as "Snail Against Squirrel" is worth $30 complete in box.

This German release of "Open Sesame" is one of very few talking games released for the Atari 2600. $30 complete in box.

This Dynacom release of the adult title X-Man is slightly less desireable than the Gamex version, but still commands a hefty price. *Courtesy of Rick Weiss.* $150 complete with case.

My Golf, released by HES in Europe. $45 complete in box.

Pick' N Pile, released by Ubi Soft in Europe. $30 complete in box.

Wall Break, by Australian manufacturer Home Vision. Games by this company came in a VHS style plastic case. *Courtesy of Rick Weiss.* $120 complete in box.

European company Sancho released several titles, some of which were released by Froggo in America. $50 - $70 complete in box.

Pac-Kong was released in Europe by a large retail chain named Quelle. $25 - $35 complete in box.

HES of Australia released many different 2 Pak Specials. $40 - $65 for each complete boxed one.

Some Quelle cartridges outside of their boxes. $15 - $35 each.

Nightmare by Sancho. $35 - $45 cartridge only.

Similar in appearance to Taiwan released games, Zellers games were distributed in Canada and Europe. $20 - $35 each, complete in box.

ITT was another European company that released several interesting titles. $35 - $75 each for loose cartridges.

A typical Taiwan 2600 game. $20 - $30 each, complete in box.

Foreign issue 8 in 1 cartridge. See accompanying photo for list of games. $30 - $35 complete in box.

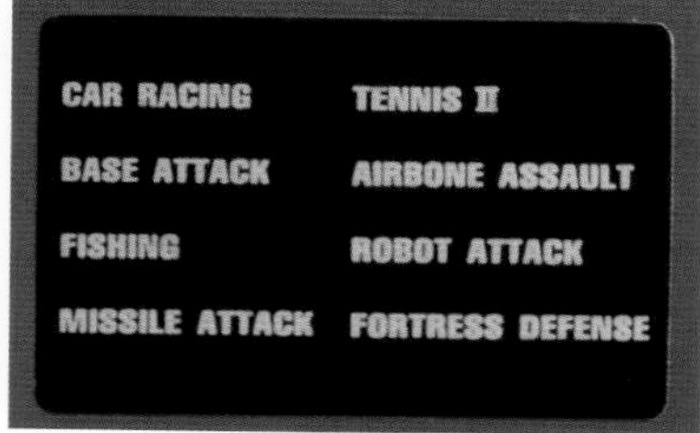

Sticker from the back of the 8 in 1 cartridge box.

Another foreign released 8 in 1 cartridge. See accompanying photo for list of games. $35 - $40 complete in box.

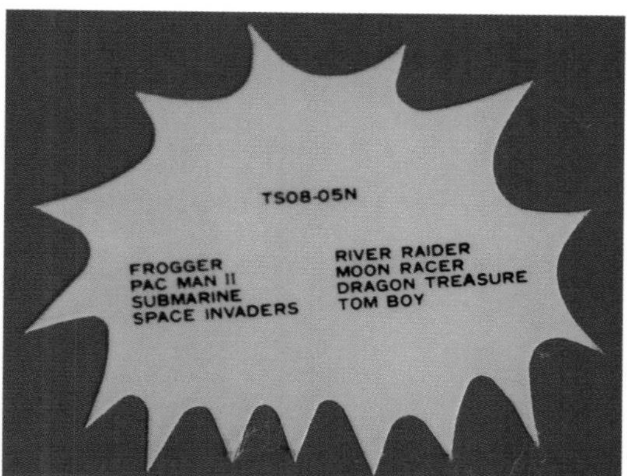

Enlargement of game list from 8 in 1 cartridge box.

A very cute Taiwan game, which was released in the United States as Dishaster by Zimag. $25 complete in box.

Fans of the Atari 2600 are still making games for the system. This particular game was made by a French programmer as an exclusive for an Atari convention in Las Vegas.

Assorted Peripherals and Memorabilia

In store display for Atari's release of E.T. $50 - $150.

Atari game library storage unit. $25 - $40 for a nice boxed example.

Atari Kid's controller for use with the Sesame Street series of games. $10 - $15.

Atari book-style cartridge storage case holds up to eight cartridges. $10 - $20.

Overlays for use with the Atari Kid's controller. $3 - $7 each.

Atari keyboard controllers, for use with several math and programming games. $35 - $40 for a boxed pair.

Atari joystick repair kit. $15 - $30 unused.

Full color and generic boxes for Atari brand paddle controllers. $25 - $30 boxed.

Atari remote control joysticks. $35 - $50 for complete working set.

A few of the several variations of Atari brand power supplies. $15 - $25 each.

'tari joystick in retail box. $20 - $30.

Boxed Atari Trak-Ball. $25 - $40.

The Supercharger, manufactured by both Starpath and Arcadia, allows you to attach you 2600 to a cassette deck to play games. $35 loose.

This game copier was released in the Netherlands. $60 - $110 with packaging.

Cassette games for use with the supercharger were also manufactured by both Starpath and Arcadia. $10 - $15 each.

Blank cartridge for the copier allowed storage of two separate games. $25 - $35 unused.

This Universum version of the Compumate keyboard for the Atari 2600, valued at $85, is much more common than the Spectravision version.

Milton Bradley's Flight Commander controller. $125 - $175 boxed.

Extremely rare Copy Cart set allows temporary transfer of most 2600 games to its blank cartridge. Estimated $200 - $300 for a boxed example such as the one pictured. *Courtey of Rick Weiss.*

Spitfire Attack was the game included with the Flight Commander controller. $15 for the cartridge.

Amiga's Joyboard was designed to stand on for skiing and surfing type games. $60 - $80.

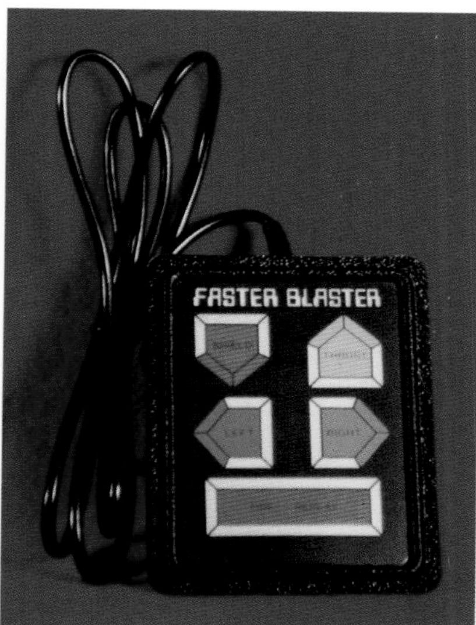

This Faster Blaster controller was built in an unusual pressure sensitive format. $15 - $25.

This high quality Wico brand joystick included three interchangeable handles. $25 - $45 boxed.

This Dynacom joystick was released only in South America, making it a rare find in the States. $30 - $40.

Beautiful translucent blue Tron joystick with retractable cord. $75.

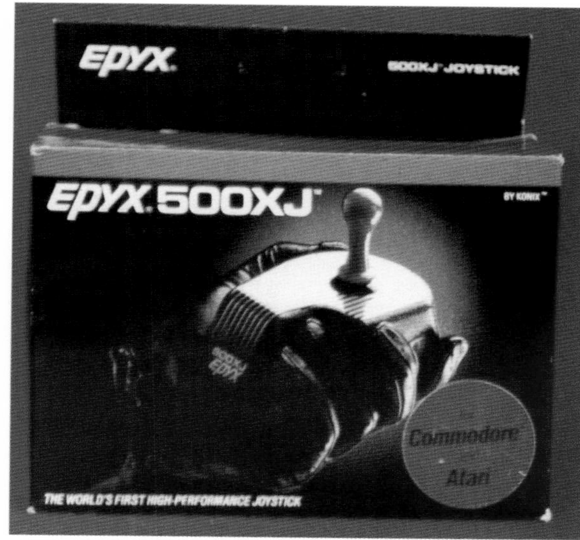

Epyx 500 XJ. $15 - $25 boxed.

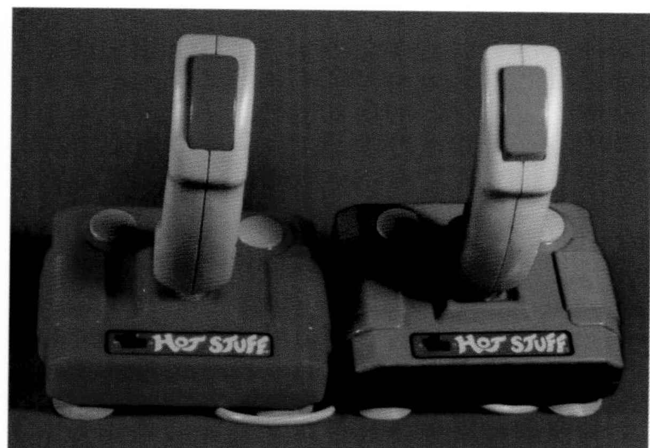

Hot Stuff controllers were produced in several different colors. $15 - $25 each.

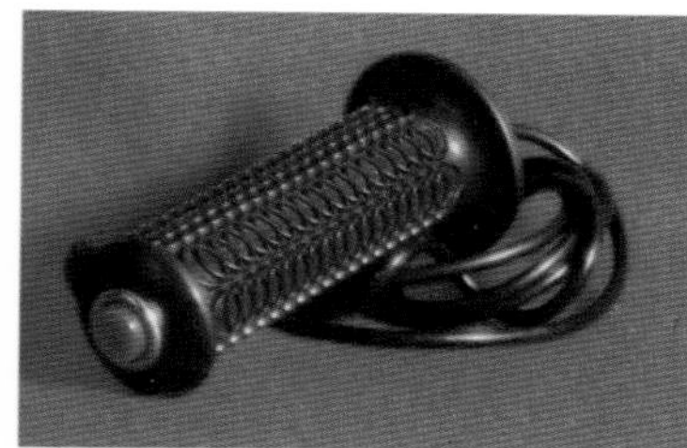

Le Stick is a mercury based controller which reacts to the movement of you hand. $25 - $40.

Slik Stik. $10 - $25 boxed.

Triggerstik adaptors allowed you to fire from the top of the joystick. $15 - $25 mint on card.

Unroller controllers from Roklan. $35 - $50 for a boxed pair.

Pointmaster Fire Control went between your joystick and the console to produce a rapid fire effect. $8 - $15.

Paddle controllers by Gemini. $15 - $25 boxed.

The Video Command controller is nearly identical to the controllers of the Fairchild Channel F. It was manufactured by Zircon, the company that bought the Channel F from Fairchild. $10 - $20.

The Video Game Brain allowed you to switch between six different games with the push of a button. $65 - $80 boxed.

Atari 5200

The Atari 5200, or the Atari Super System as it was originally known, was a stripped down version of the Atari home computers of the time. Graphics on some 5200 games were often identical to those of Atari 8-bit computer games, far superior to those of the already nearly antiquated 2600. The Atari 5200 also played a key role in the 1980s blockbuster movie *Cloak & Dagger*. When buying a 5200 system with the intent to play it, be sure to test out the controllers first as they were poorly manufactured and are often broken. Third party controllers are the recommended way to enjoy this system, if you can find them.

The Atari 5200 System

An Atari 5200 system complete in its original box will bring $100 - $200, while a unused example will be about twice that.

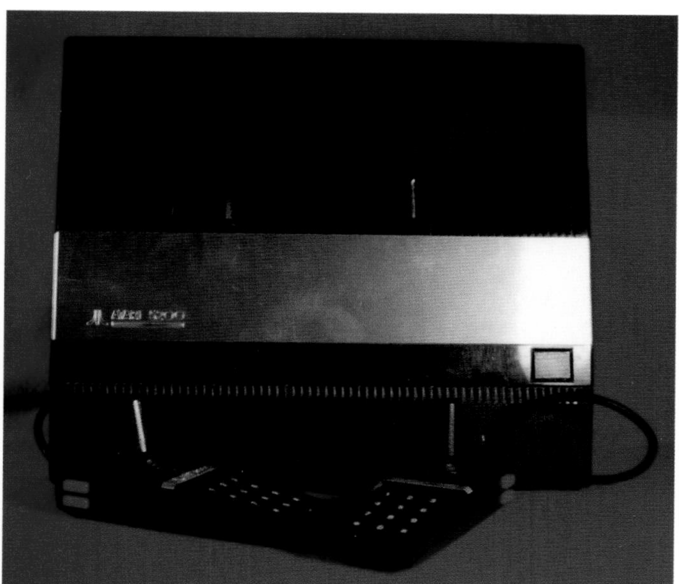

An Atari 5200 system complete and working (which is quite uncommon as the controllers are very delicate and prone to breaking) will bring $50 - $100.

Atari Games

Ballblazer. $30 complete in box.

Berzerk. $12 complete in box.

Dig Dug. $12 complete in box.

Jungle Hunt. $12 complete in box.

Centipede. $11 complete in box.

Galaxian. $11 complete in box.

Kangaroo. $11 complete in box.

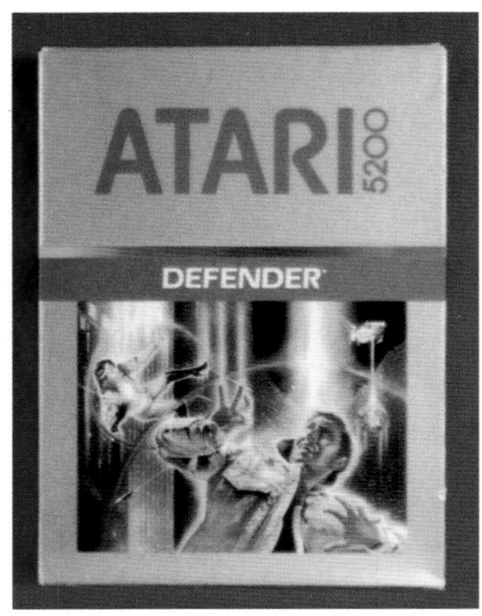

Defender. $9 complete in box.

Joust. $12 complete in box.

Moon Patrol. $12 complete in box.

Ms. Pac-Man. $11 complete in box.

Pengo. $37 complete in box.

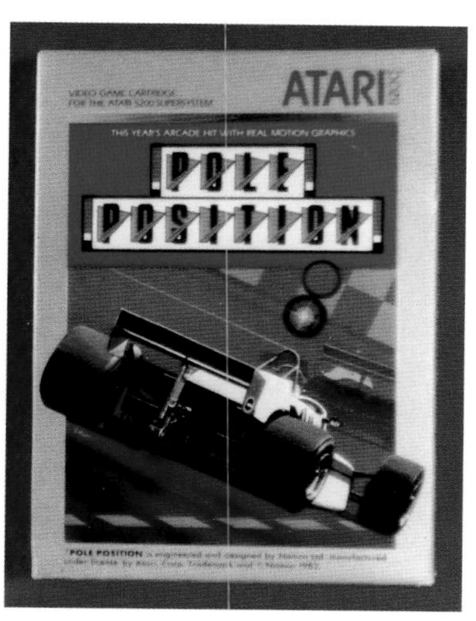

Pole Position. $11 complete in box.

RealSports Tennis. $12 complete in box.

Rescue on Fractalus. $65 complete in box.

Star Raiders. $11 complete in box.

Third Party Games

Astrochase by Parker Brothers. $35 complete in box.

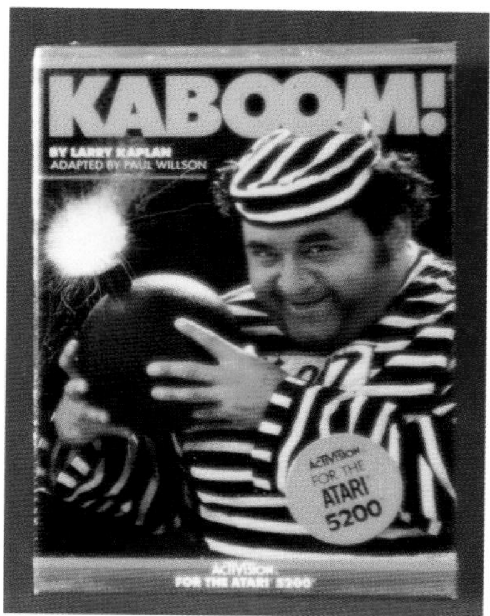

Kaboom by Activision. $25 complete in box.

Electra Concepts' Meteroites is one of the most difficult to find games for the 5200. $175 cartridge only.

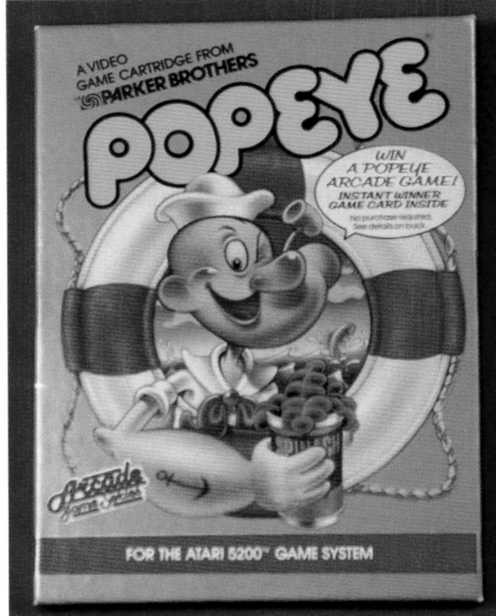

Popeye by Parker Brothers. $25 complete in box.

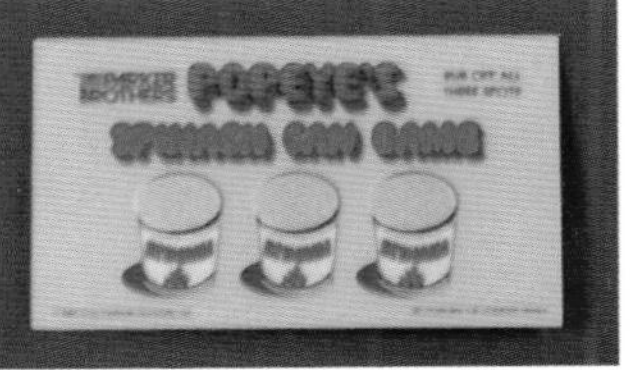

This spinach can game card was included, for a time, with the Parker Brothers release of Popeye for the 5200. $5 - $15.

Licensed titles for the 5200. Buck Rogers is valued at $15 for the cart only, while Star Wars the Arcade Game is valued at around $35.

Q*bert by Parker Brothers. $16 complete in box.

Super Cobra by Parker Brothers. $35 complete in box.

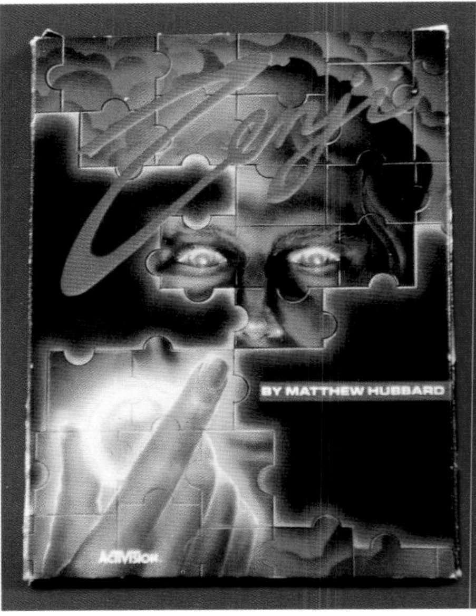

Zenji by Activision. $50 complete in box.

Star Trek by Sega. $40 complete in box.

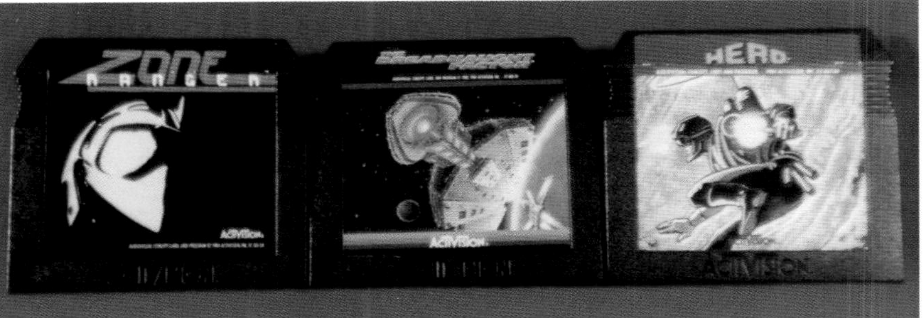

A few other releases from Activision, for the Atari 5200. $15 - $25 each.

Third party companies produced several different styles of cartridge for the 5200.

Assorted Atari 5200 Items

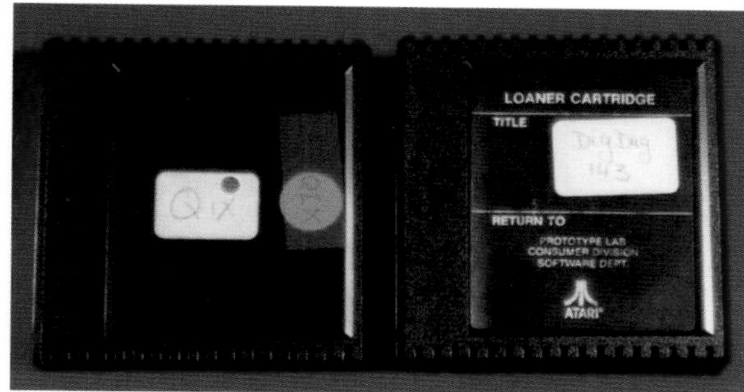

Two different styles of prototype cartridges. Beware of fakes. Since it is sometimes difficult to identify the real thing from a forgery, it is best to buy items such as these from reputable sources. A prototype of a common released title will fetch $40 - $100, while an unreleased game can bring several hundred dollars.

5200 Trak - Ball controller. $50 - $75 boxed.

Activision produced patches for the 5200 as well as the 2600. Although patches for the 5200 are more difficult to find, they are valued at approximately the same as their 2600 counterparts.

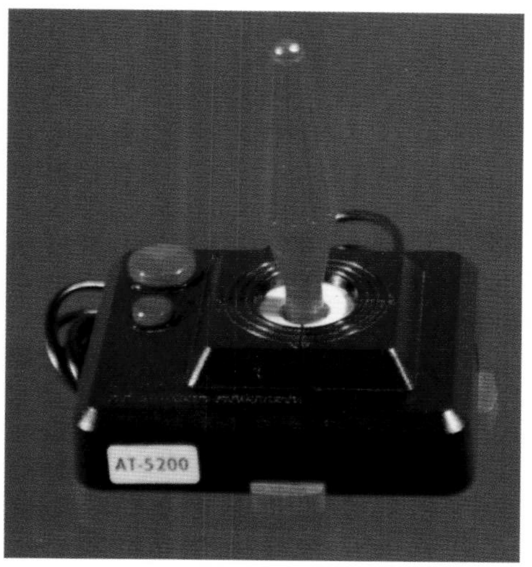

Wico brand joystick for the Atari 5200. $25 - $35.

This adaptor allowed 2600 cartridges to be played on the 5200 system. $25 - $40.

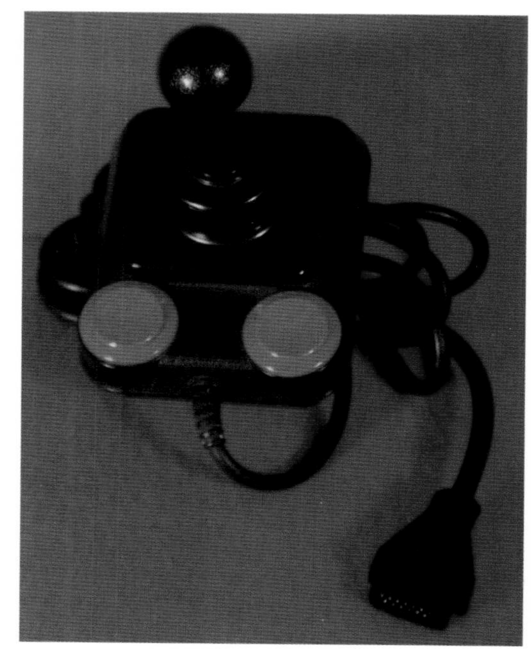

Third party joysticks for the Atari 5200 are very desireable, as the original Atari brand controllers are very prone to breakage. This joystick is valued in the $25 - $35 range.

Atari 7800

The Atari 7800 Pro System is an unfortunate case. It was ready a full two years ahead of its actual release, but the Atari home games division was sold to Commodore, who shelved the product until it was convinced by the success of the NES that there was a market for home video games after all. Nearly all 2600 games are compatible with the 7800 without the aid of any adapters or add ons. Like most systems of this era, a computer upgrade was announced but never materialized.

The Atari 7800 System

The Atari 7800 system is valued at $100 - $150 complete and working in the original box.

A complete 7800 system without the box, but in nice, working order will bring $50 - $75.

Atari 7800 Games

Ace of Aces. $15 complete in box.

Asteroids. $9 complete in box.

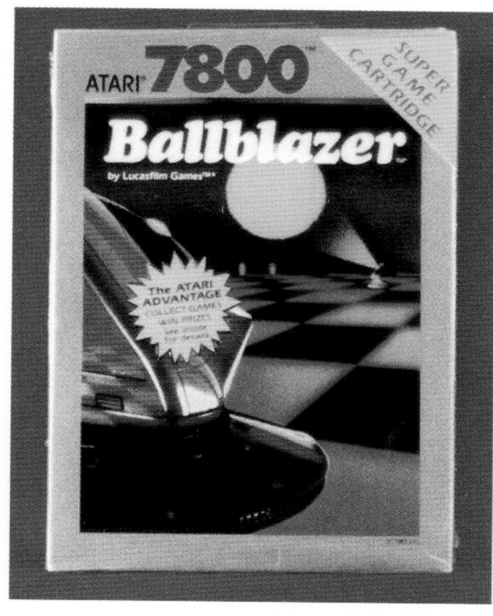

Ballblazer. $13 complete in box.

Crack'ed. $15 complete in box.

Dig Dug. $9 complete in box.

Fight Night. $15 complete in box.

Barnyard Blaster. $9 complete in box.

Dark Chambers. $9 complete in box.

Donkey Kong. $9 complete in box.

Food Fight. $9 complete in box.

Centipede. $9 complete in box.

Desert Falcon. $9 complete in box.

Donkey Kong Jr. $9 complete in box.

Galaga. $9 complete in box.

Hat Trick. $9 complete in box.

Mario Bros. $15 complete in box.

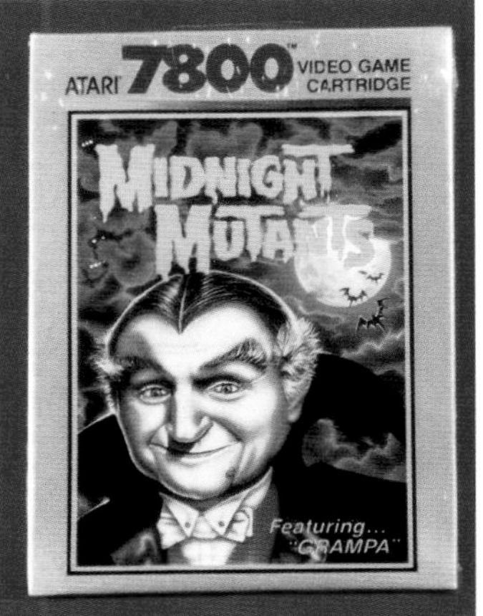

Midnight Mutants — featuring Grampa Munster. $25 complete in box.

One on One Basketball — featuring Larry Bird and Dr. J. $9 complete in box.

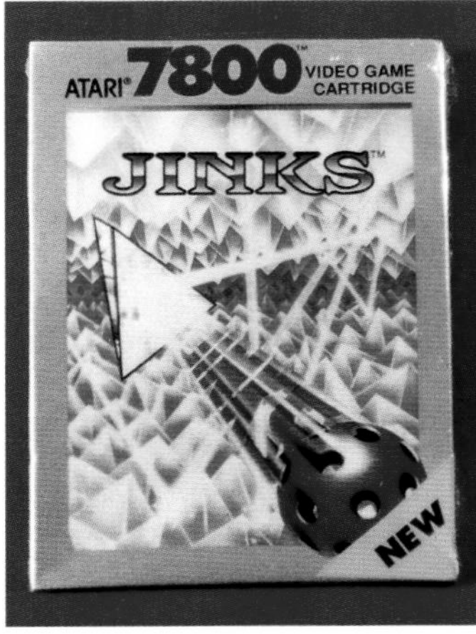

Jinks. $9 complete in box.

Mat Mania Challenge. $25 complete in box.

Ms. Pac-Man. $9 complete in box.

Pole Position II was the pack in game for the Atari 7800 system. $7 complete in box.

Joust. $9 complete in box.

Meltdown. $25 complete in box.

Ninja Golf. $25 complete in box.

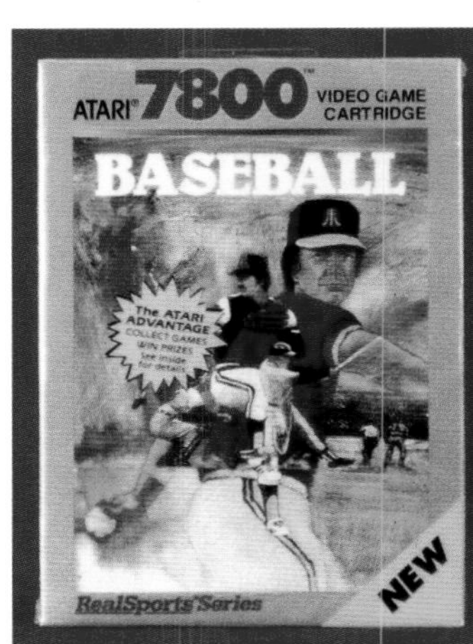

RealSports Baseball. $9 complete in box.

Robotron: 2084. $9 complete in box.

Super Huey UH-IX. $15 complete in box.

Tower Toppler. $9 complete in box.

Winter Games. $9 complete in box.

Scrapyard Dog. $9 complete in box.

Absolute's Title Match Pro Wrestling in foreign issue plastic box. $35 - $40 complete in box.

Water Ski by Froggo. $90 complete in box.

Xevious. $9 complete in box.

Sentinel was never released in the United States. $50 complete in box.

Touchdown Football. $15 complete in box.

Very few third party titles were released for the 7800. These three, all by Absolute, are valued at about $20 each.

Colecovision

A graphically superior system, the Colecovision was Coleco's (once known as the Connecticut Leather Company) perfectly timed and well executed entry into the video game marketplace. They nailed down licenses to home translations of many of the most popular arcade games of the day. In fact, designs of the boxes of Coleco games often emphasized this by featuring images of the actual arcade machines. For some unknown reason, boxes for Colecovision cartridges seem more difficult to locate than those of most systems. Coleco was one of the few companies to release a computer upgrade for their system, the Coleco Adam, which was big, bulky, and never worked very well.

The Colecovision System

Colecovision system. $100 - $150 complete in box.

Colecovision system. $50 - $75 complete and fully functional.

Front view of the Colecovision system.

Coleco Games

Antarctic Adventure. $35 complete in box.

B.C.'s Quest for Tires II - Grog's Revenge. $40 complete in box.

Burgertime. $25 complete in box.

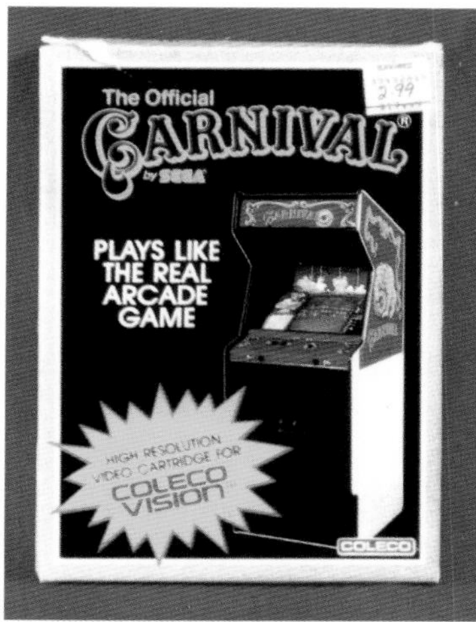

Carnival. $15 complete in box.

Cosmic Avenger. $21 complete in box.

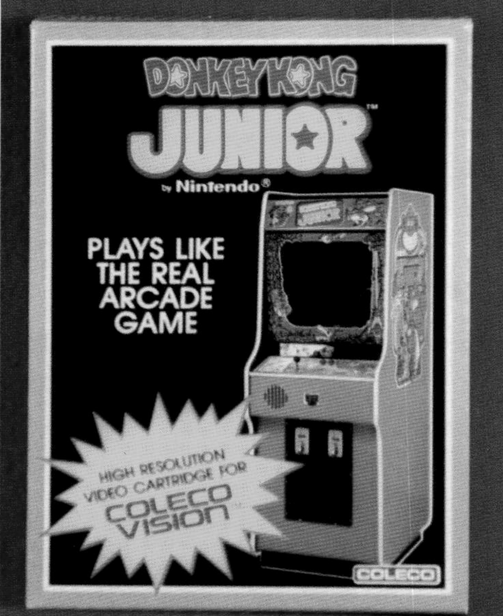

Donkey Kong Junior. $19 complete in box.

Cabbage Patch Kids — Adventures in the Park. $25 complete in box.

Front Line. $23 complete in box.

Illusions. $55 complete in box.

Lady Bug. $19 complete in box.

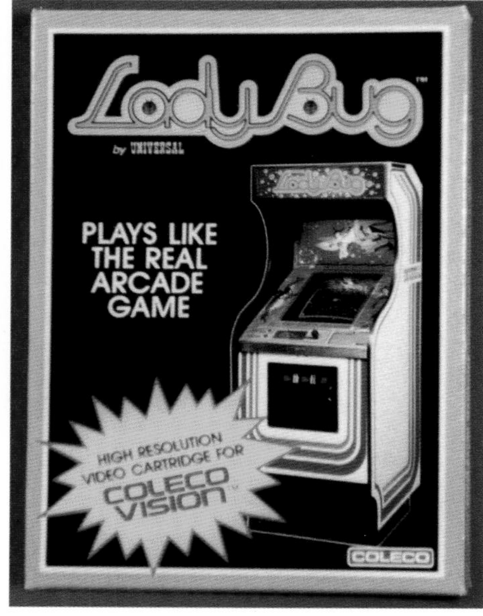

Looping. $19 complete in box.

Omega Race. $25 complete in box.

Space Fury. $18 complete in box.

Unlike most Coleco releases, Monkey Academy came in a larger plastic box. $55 complete in box.

Roc 'N Rope. $25 complete in box.

Space Panic. $19 complete in box.

Mr. Do. $35 complete in box.

Smurf — Rescue in Gargamel's Castle. $25 complete in box.

Two different label variations of the preceding Smurfs game. The label at left is valued at $15, while the more common version to the right is valued at $9.

Tapper. $58 complete in box.

Zaxxon. $15 complete in box.

Centipede by Atarisoft. $23 complete in box.

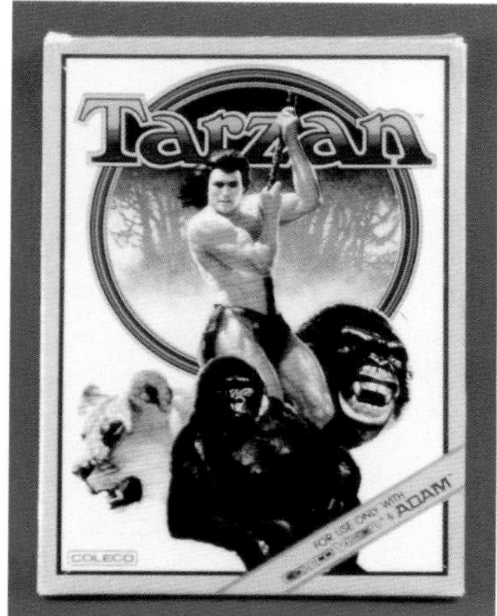

Tarzan. $50 complete in box.

War Games. $35 complete in box.

Third Party Games

B.C.'s Quest for Tires by Sierra On-Line. $39 complete in box.

Beamrider by Activision. $25 complete in box.

Defender by Atarisoft. $23 complete in box.

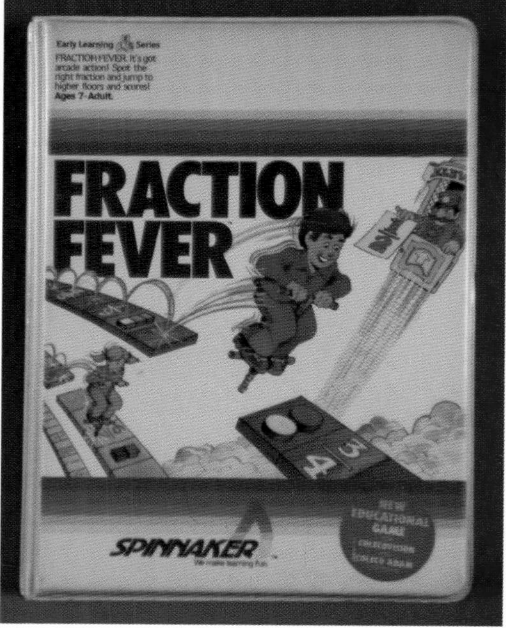

Fraction Fever by Spinnaker. $45 complete in box.

Frogger by Parker Brothers. $18 complete in box.

Heist by Micro Fun. $35 complete in box.

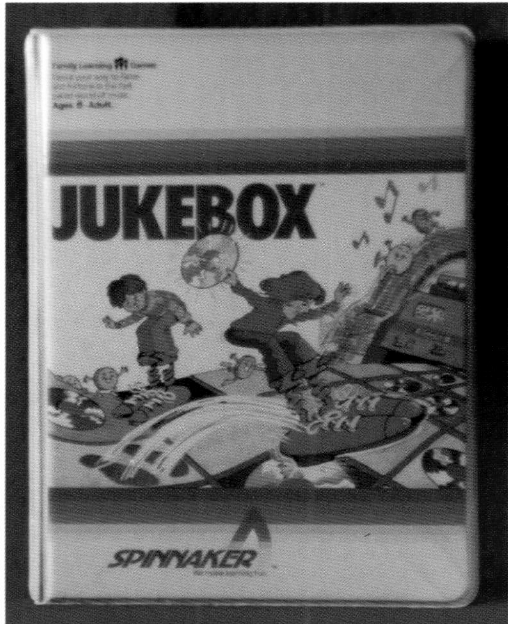

Jukebox by Spinnaker. $82 complete in box.

Keystone Kapers by Activision. $29 complete in box.

Miner 2049er by Micro Fun. $35 complete in box.

Montezuma's Revenge by Parker Brothers. $59 complete in box.

Pitfall by Activision. $19 complete in box.

Popeye by Parker Brothers. $25 complete in box.

Q*bert by Parker Brothers. $18 complete in box.

Q*bert's Qubes by Parker Brothers. $195 complete in box.

River Raid by Activision. $18 complete in box.

Super Cobra by Parker Brothers. $65 complete

Tutankham by Parker Brothers. $65 complete in box.

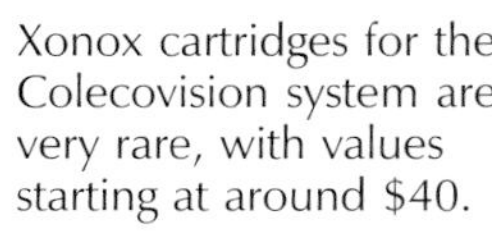

Xonox cartridges for the Colecovision system are very rare, with values starting at around $40.

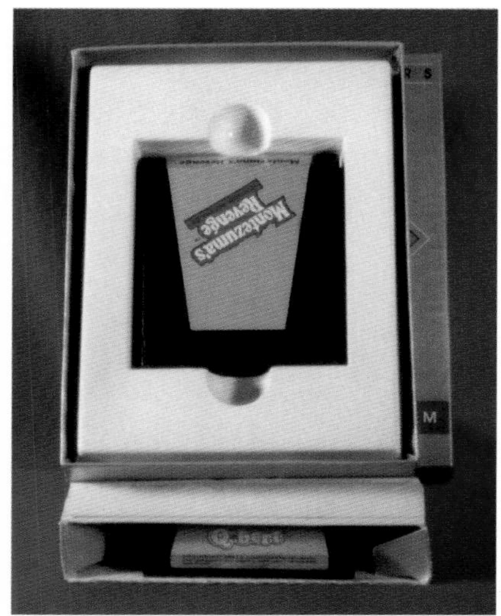

Parker Brothers games were released in two different styles of boxes: one was a two piece that had a removable front, while the other opened on the top. The second style (opening on the top) is harder to come by and will add 10% - 20% to the value of a boxed game.

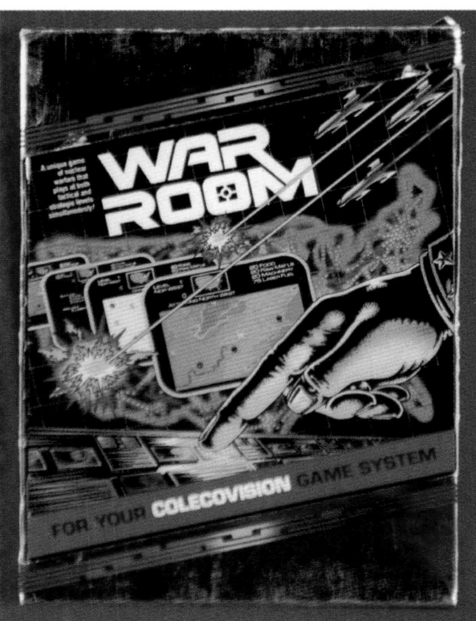

War Room by Probe 2000. $35 complete in box.

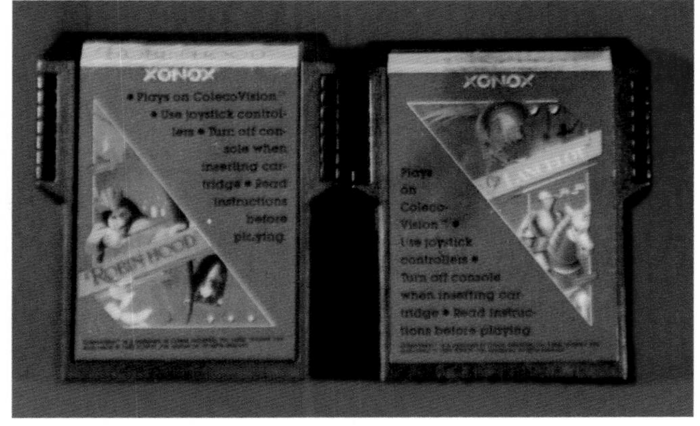

Assorted Colecovision Items

Roller Controller for the Colecovision system. $50 - $80 boxed.

Instructions for the Super Action Controllers are valued at $4 - $8, while a pair of the controllers themselves will bring $35 - $50.

Expansion module #2, the Driving controller. $25 - $35 loose.

Prostick III joystick for the Colecovision. $15 - $29.

Expansion module #1 allows you to play Atari 2600 cartridges on the Colecovision system. $25 - $35 loose.

Power Stick joystick for the Colecovision. $19 - $30.

Co-Stickler adaptor turns your Colecovision contoller into more of a joystick. $10 - $20 mint on card.

Third party joystick and keypad for the Colecovision. $25 - $40 for the pair.

Coleco vacation savings certificate. $2 - $5.

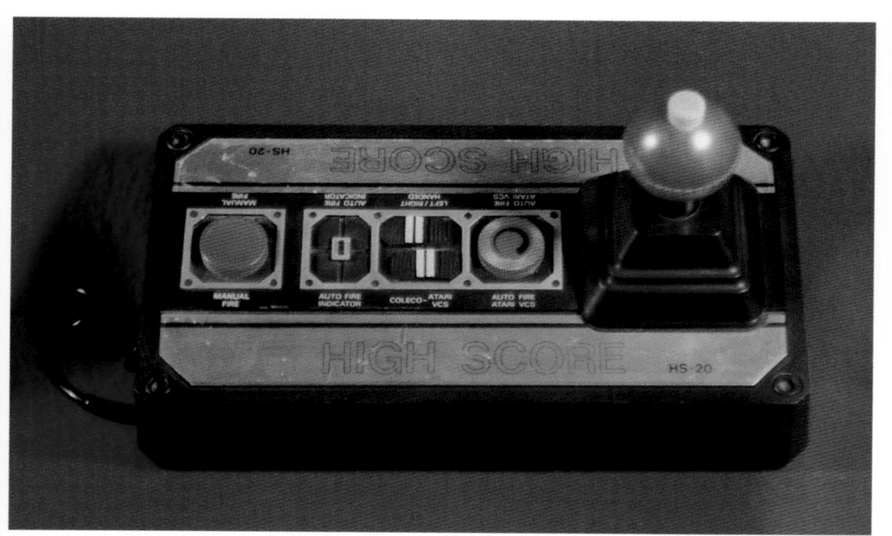

This High Score joystick features a rapid fire control and was made for use with both the Colecovision and the Atari 2600. $35 - $50.

Mattel Intellivision

Mattel's Intellivision System was second only to the Atari 2600 in its heyday. Sports titles, nearly all of which were licensed by national organizations, were considered by many to be the system's strength. When Mattel finally decided to pull the plug on the Intellivision system, it was sold off to INTV corp., which continued to release titles for the system for quite some time. When using an Intellivision system, do not leave it turned on when not in use as this system has a tendency to overheat, which may leave you with a non-working unit.

Intellivision Systems

Early version box for the Intellivision. $150 - $350 complete in box.

Rear view of the early version of the Intellivision box, picturing the extremely rare computer module.

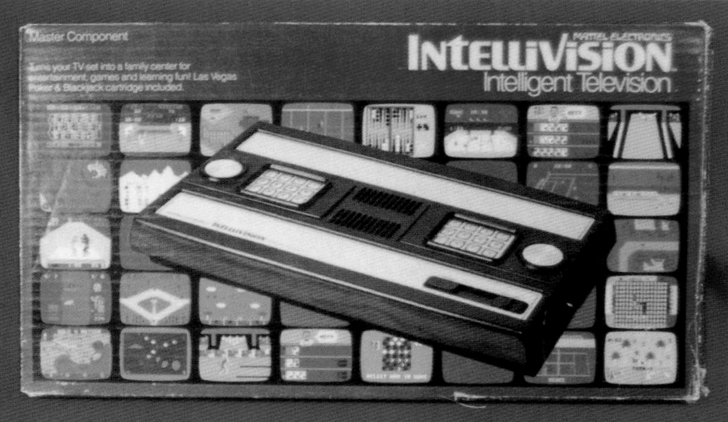

Later boxed version of the Mattel Intellivision. $100 - $250 complete in box.

Back side of the later Mattel issue Intellivision box.

Mattel Intellivision system. $50 - $75 complete and working.

The INTV system III. $100 - $250 complete in box.

The Radio Shack version of the Intellivision system — the Tandyvision One. $70 - $120 in excellent cosmetic and working condition.

Sears version of the Intellivision system — the Super Video Arcade. $100 - $250 complete in box.

The Sylvania version of the Intellivision system. $95 - $175 in excellent cosmetic and working condition.

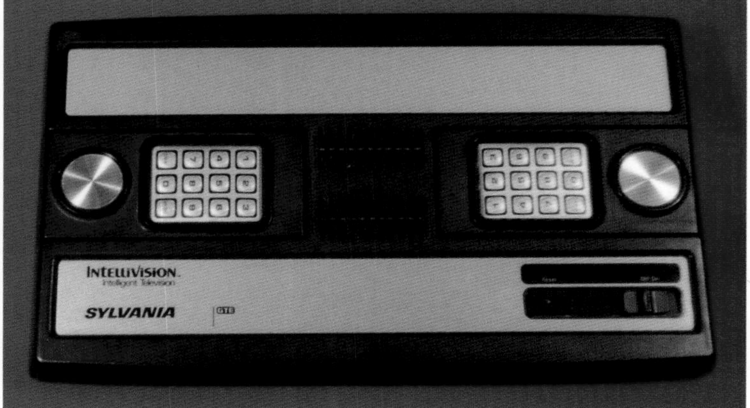

Intellivision II with computer adaptor. $50 - $75 for the system, and about the same for the computer add on.

Advanced Dungeons & Dragons — Treasure of Tarmin. $19 complete in box.

Intellivision Games

ABPA Backgammon. $15 complete in box.

Advanced Dungeons & Dragons. $14 complete in box.

Armor Battle. $10 complete in box.

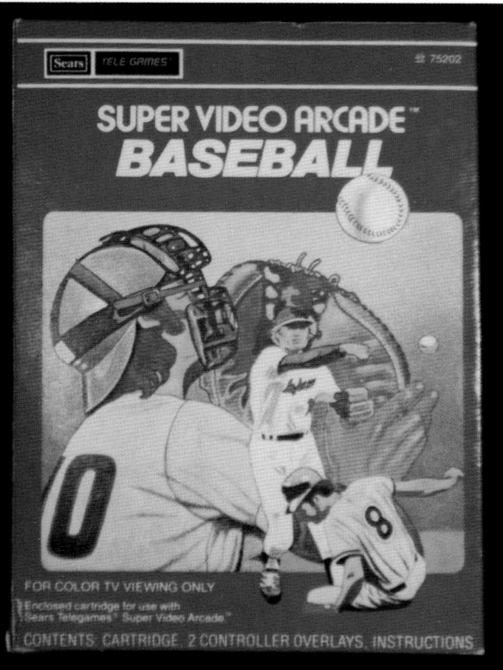

Clockwise from Top left:

Sears version of Armor Battle. $18 complete in box.

Astrosmash. $10 complete in box.

Sears version of Astrosmash. $19 complete in box.

Atlantis by Imagic. $19 complete in box.

Auto Racing. $14 complete in box.

B-17 Bomber. $14 complete in box.

Sears version of Backgammon. $31 complete in box.

Sears version of Baseball. $26 complete in box.

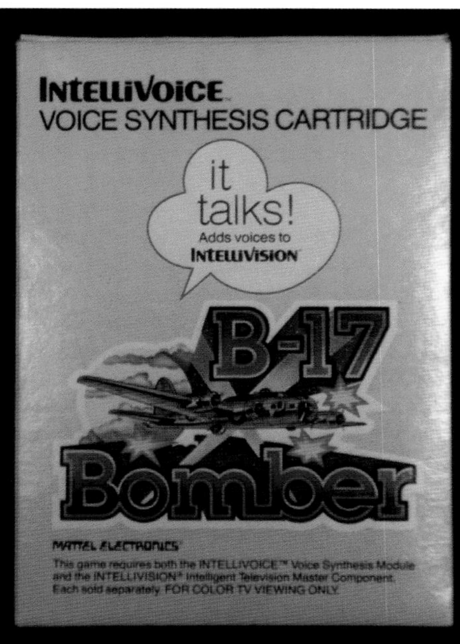

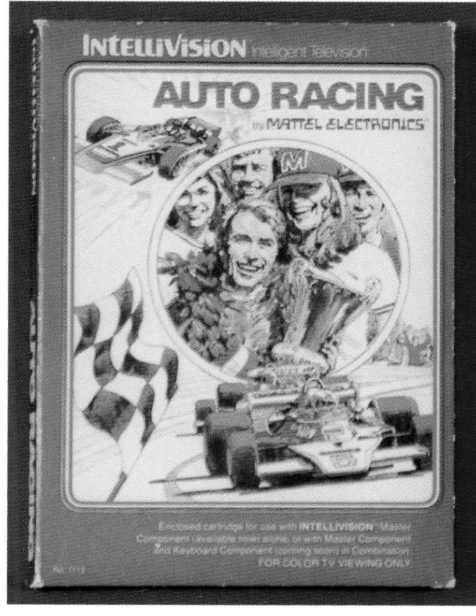

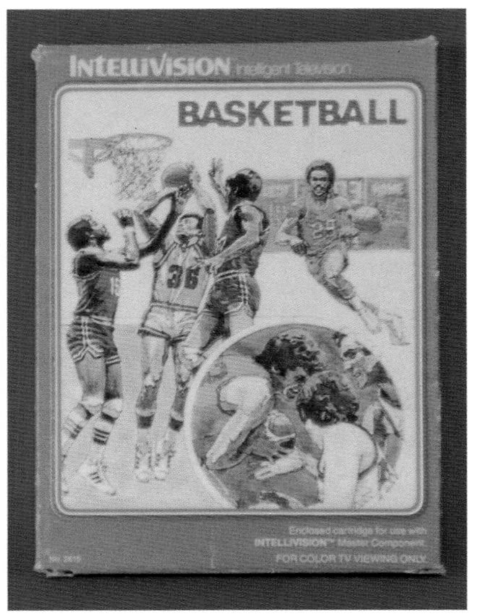

Clockwise from Top left:

INTV release of Basketball. $15 complete in box.

Sears version of Basketball. $26 complete in box.

Beamrider by Activision. $25 complete in box.

Beauty & the Beast by Imagic. $17 complete in box.

Big League Baseball from INTV. $25 complete in box.

Blockade Runner by Interphase. $36 complete in box.

INTV's Body Slam Super Pro Wrestling. $75 complete in box.

Bomb Squad. $19 complete in box.

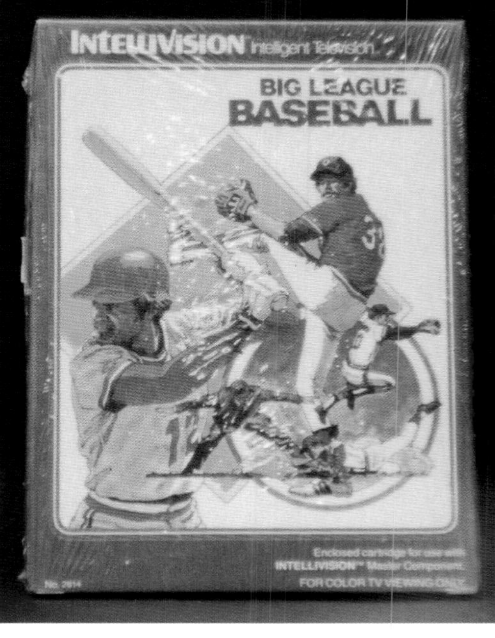

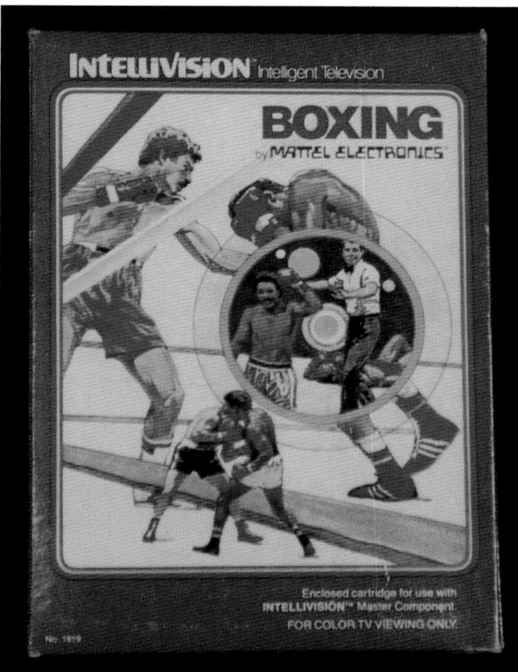

Clockwise from Top left:

Sears version of Bowling. $27 complete in box.

Boxing. $15 complete in box.

Bump 'n' Jump. $25 complete in box.

Burgertime. $12 complete in box.

Buzz Bombers. $27 complete in box.

Carnival by Coleco. $19 complete in box.

Later issue Carnival box from Coleco. $19 complete in box.

Centipede from Atarisoft. $25 complete in box.

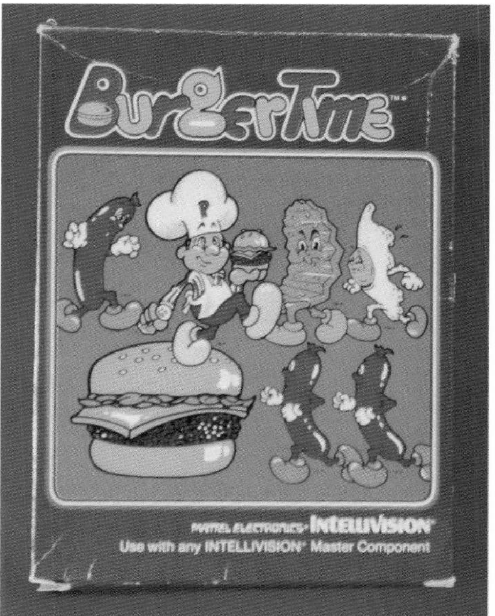

Clockwise from Top left:

Championship Tennis from INTV. $46 complete in box.

Checkers. $18 complete in box.

Sears version of Checkers. $29 complete in box.

Commando by INTV. $38 complete in box.

Congo Bongo from Sega. $165 complete in box.

Defender from Atarisoft. $35 complete in box.

Demon Attack by Imagic. $17 complete in box.

Another version of Demon Attack by Imagic. Also $17 complete in box.

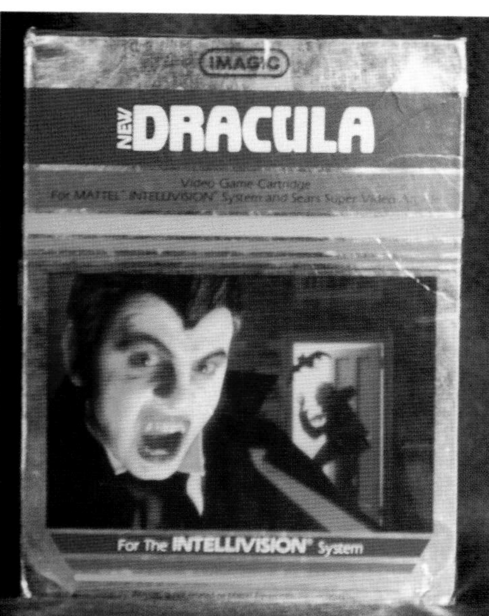

Clockwise from Top left:

This demonstration cartridge was never available to the general public. $100 complete in box.

Dig Dug by INTV. $65 complete in box.

INTV's Diner, the sequel to Burgertime. $65 complete in box.

Donkey Kong by Coleco. $12 complete in box.

The foreign release of Donkey Kong by CBS. $19 complete in box.

The foreign release of Donkey Kong Junior by CBS. $35 complete in box.

Dragonfire by Imagic. $19 complete in box.

Dracula by Imagic. $28 complete in box.

Clockwise from Top left:

Dreadnaught Factor by Activision. $35 complete in box.

Electric Company Math Fun. $22 complete in box.

Electric Company Word Fun. $22 complete in box.

Football by INTV. $15 complete in box.

Sears version of Football. $25 complete in box.

Frog Bog. $14 complete in box.

Frogger by Parker Brothers. $15 complete in box.

Golf from INTV. $15 complete in box.

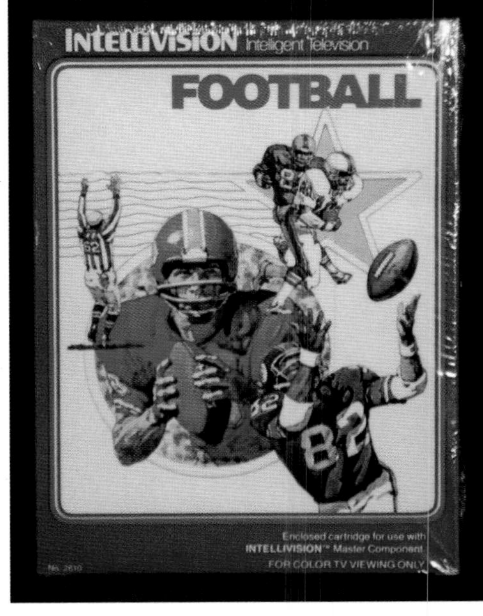

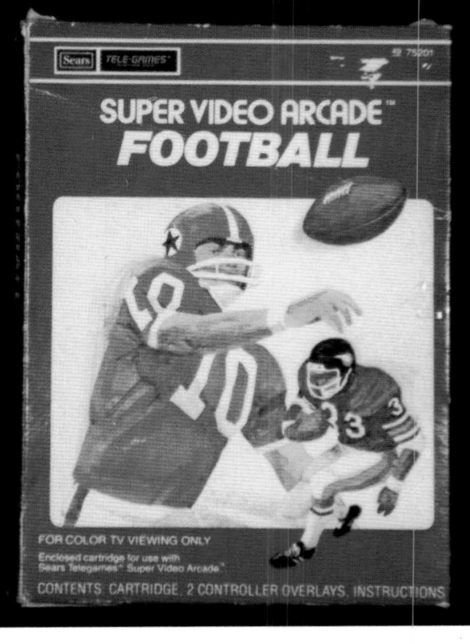

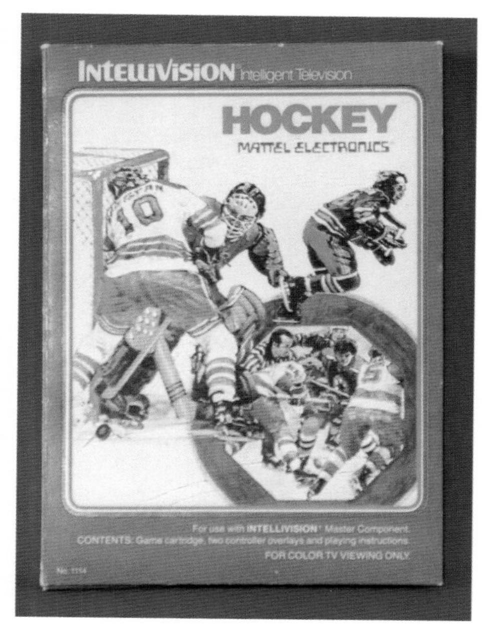

Clockwise from Top left:

Sears version of Golf. $22 complete in box.

Happy Trails by Activision. $32 complete in box.

Hockey from INTV. $17 complete in box.

Horse Racing. $17 complete in box.

Hover Force by INTV. $49 complete in box.

The Jetsons' Ways With Words. $95 complete in box.

Kool-Aid Man. $39 complete in box.

Lady Bug by Coleco. $25 complete in box.

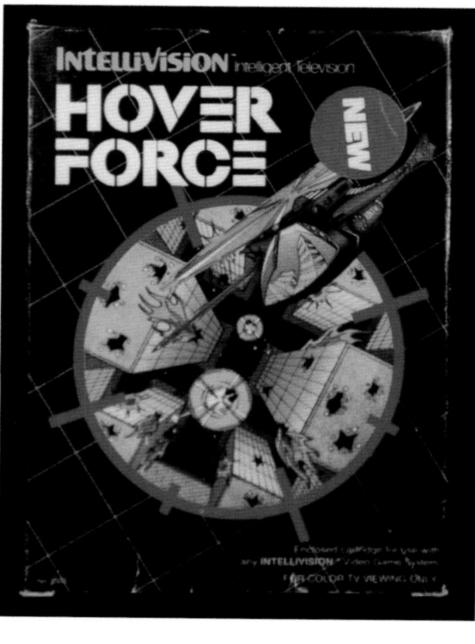

Las Vegas Poker & Blackjack was the original pack in game for the Intellivision system. $9 complete in box.

Sears version of Las Vegas Roulette. $22 complete in box.

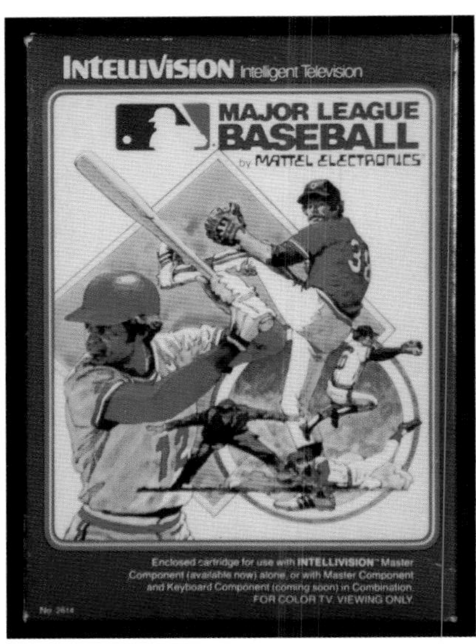

Major League Baseball. $10 complete in box.

Sears version of Las Vegas Poker & Blackjack. $15 complete in box.

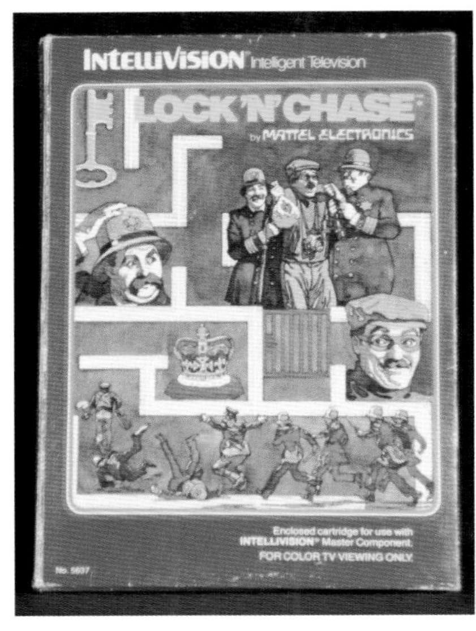

Lock 'N' Chase. $13 complete in box.

Masters of the Universe — the Power of He-Man. $35 complete in box.

Las Vegas Roulette. $14 complete in box.

Loco Motion. $25 complete in box.

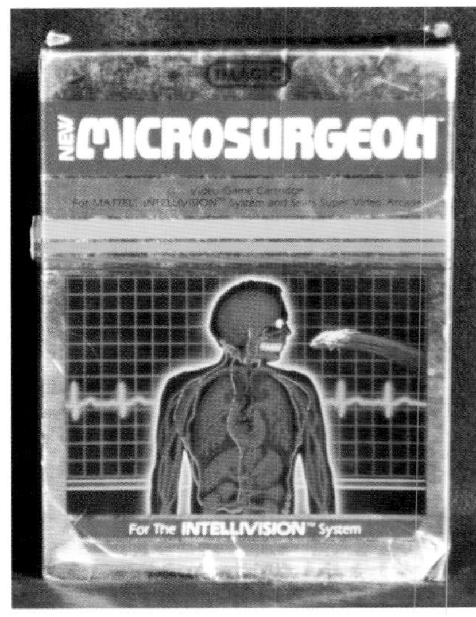

Microsurgeon by Imagic. $21 complete in box.

Melody Blaster is for use with the Intellivision music synthesizer. $70 complete in box.

Motocross. $35 complete in box.

INTV's Mountain Madness Super Pro Skiing. $70 complete in box.

Mind Strike is for use with the Intellivision computer keyboard. $65 complete in box.

Coleco version of Mouse Trap. $21 complete in box.

Mission-X. $25 complete in box.

CBS version of Mouse Trap. $25 complete in box.

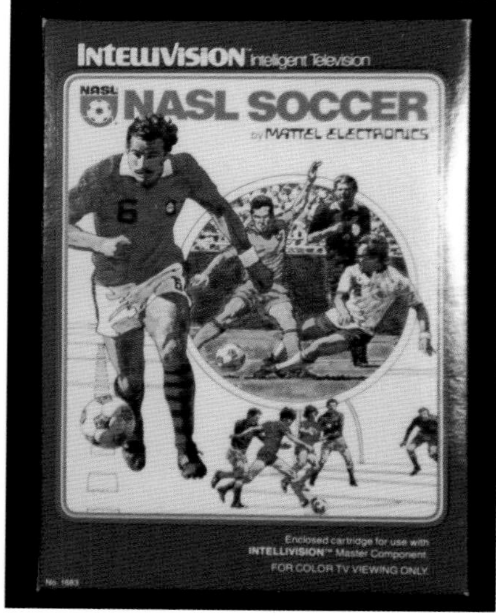

Mr. Basic Meets Bits 'N Bytes, for use with the Intellivsion computer keyboard. $55 complete in box.

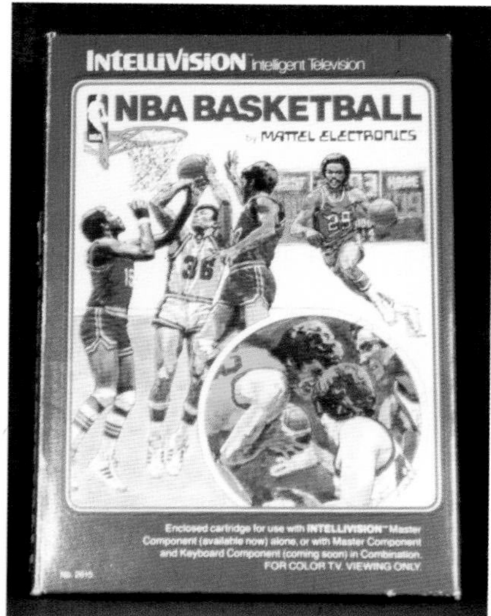

NASL Soccer. $14 complete in box.

NBA Basketball. $14 complete in box.

NFL Football. $13 complete in box.

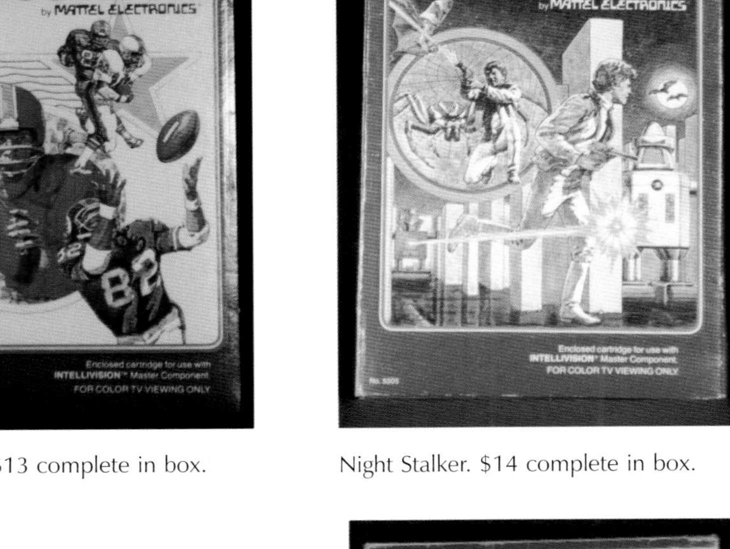

Night Stalker. $14 complete in box.

Pac-Man by Atarisoft. $39 complete in box.

NHL Hockey. $15 complete in box.

Sears version of Night Stalker. $23 complete in box.

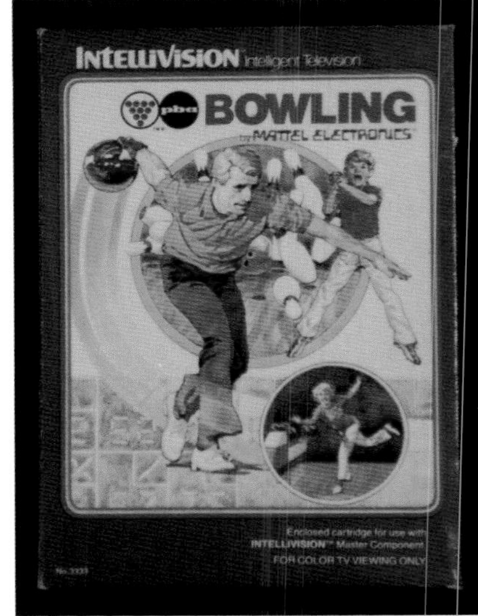

PBA Bowling. $15 complete in box.

This foreign released version of Hockey for the Intellivision features a box with slits on the back for the instruction manual. $25 - $40 complete in box.

Nova Blast by Imagic. $43 complete in box.

PGA Golf. $14 complete in box.

INTV release of Pinball. $31 complete in box.

Popeye by Parker Brothers. $30 complete in box.

River Raid by Activision. $49 complete in box.

Pitfall by Activision. $15 complete in box.

Q*bert by Parker Brothers. $37 complete in box.

Royal Dealer. $19 complete in box.

Pole Position by INTV. $70 complete in box.

Reversi. $19 complete in box.

Scooby Doo's Maze Chase. $95 complete in box.

Sea Battle. $10 complete in box.

Shark! Shark! $25 complete in box.

Sears version of Skiing. $25 complete in box.

Sears version of Sea Battle. $19 complete in box.

Sharp Shot. $21 complete in box.

Slam Dunk Super Pro Basketball from INTV. $70 complete in box.

Sewer Sam by Interphase. $39 complete in box.

Skiing by INTV. $16 complete in box.

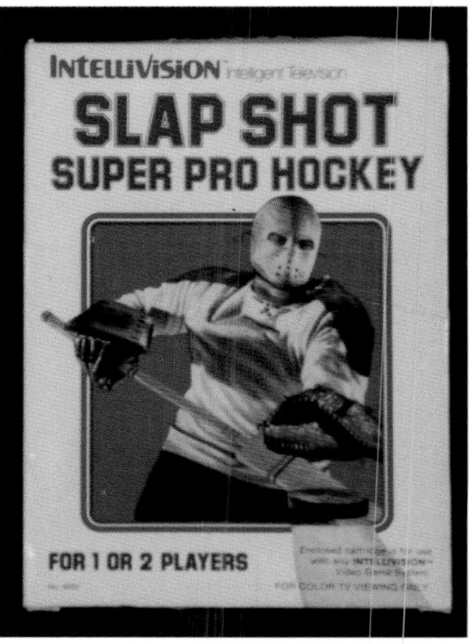

Slap Shot Super Pro Hockey from INTV. $75 complete in box.

SNAFU. $16 complete in box.

Space Armada. $10 complete in box.

Blue box version of Space Battle. $10 complete in box.

Sears version of SNAFU. $29 complete in box.

INTV version of Space Armada. $12 complete in box.

Red box version of Space Battle. $12 complete in box.

Sears version of Soccer. $24 complete in box.

Sears Version of Space Armada. $15 complete in box.

Sears version of Space Battle. $15 complete in box.

INTV version of Space Hawk. $13 complete in box.

Stampede by Activision. $26 complete in box.

Star Wars: The Empire Strikes Back by Parker Brothers. $55 complete in box.

Space Hawk. $12 complete in box.

Star Strike from INTV. $11 complete in box.

Sub Hunt. $17 complete in box.

Space Spartans. $15 complete in box.

Star Strike. $10 complete in box.

Super Pro Decathlon from INTV. $65 complete in box.

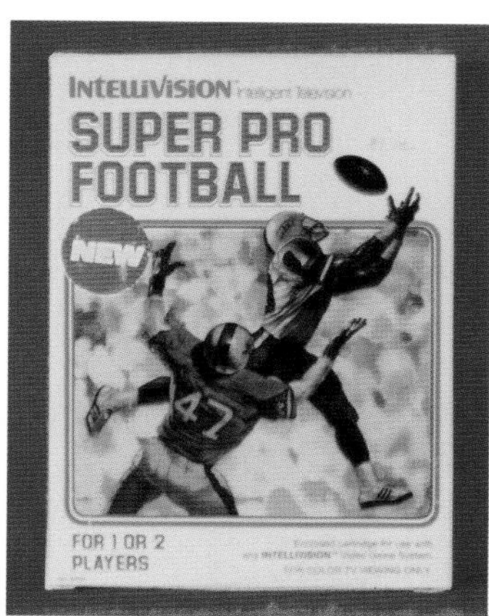

Super Pro Football from INTV. $55 complete in box.

Sears version of Tennis. $25 complete in box.

Tower of Doom from INTV. $50 complete in box.

Swords & Serpents by Imagic. $32 complete in box.

Thin Ice from INTV. $55 complete in box.

Triple Action. $15 complete in box.

INTV version of Tennis. $15 complete in box.

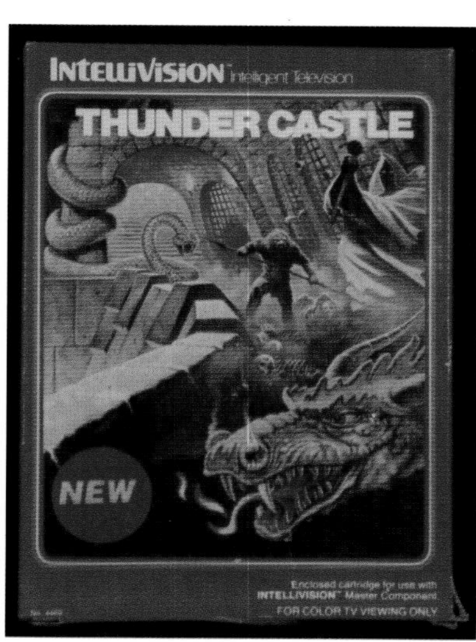

INTV version of Thunder Castle. $38 complete in box.

Tron Deadly Discs. $25 complete in box.

Tron Discos Mortais, a South American release of Tron Deadly Discs. $50 complete in box.

Tropical Trouble by Imagic. $51 complete in box.

Utopia. $15 complete in box.

Tron Maze-A-Tron. $25 complete in box.

US Ski Team Skiing. $15 complete in box.

Vectron. $19 complete in box.

Tron Solar Sailer. $29 complete in box.

USCF Chess. $50 complete in box.

White Water by Imagic. $55 complete in box.

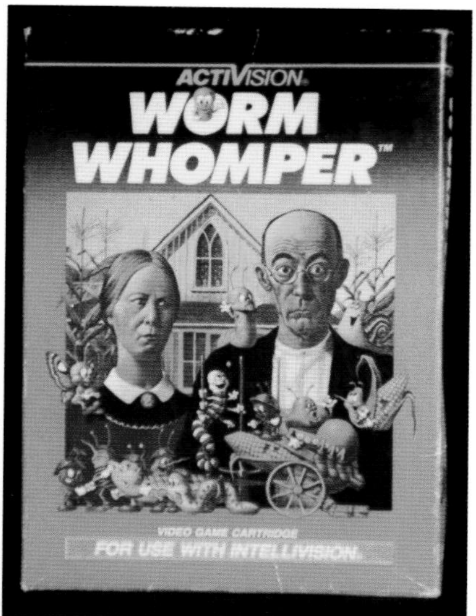

Worm Whomper by Activision. $35 complete in box.

Foreign release of Zaxxon by CBS. $50 complete in box.

Some INTV carts, which were all released with white labels.

Zaxxon by Coleco. $55 complete in box.

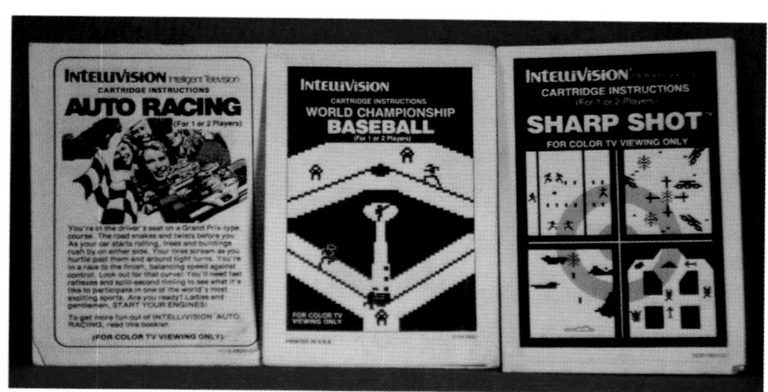

All INTV release instruction manuals were printed in black and white.

Miscellaneous Intellivision Items

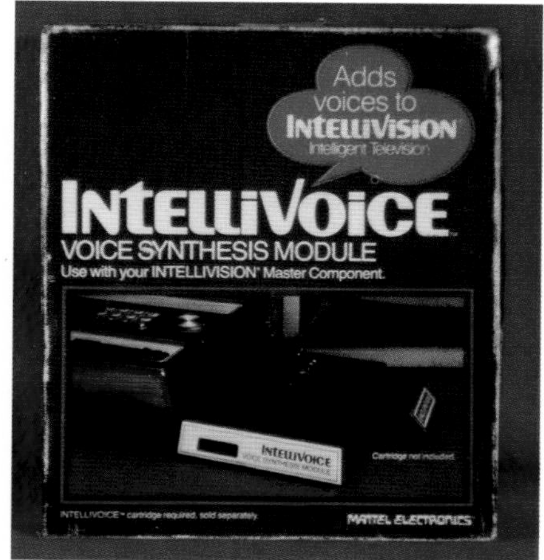

The Intellivoice Voice Synthesis Module allowed your Intellivision system to talk when used with special games made for this peripheral (quite a feat for 1981). $35 - $45 complete in box.

The Intellivision System Changer allowed you to play Atari 2600 games on your Intellivision system. $50 - $75 complete in box.

Intellivision Music Synthesizer. $150 - $200 complete in box.

Third party controllers for Intellivision systems are not often seen. These two are valued at $30 - $50 for the pair.

Scarce "Intellivision specific" book. $25 - $55.

1985 Intellivision catalog from Triton. $10 - $15.

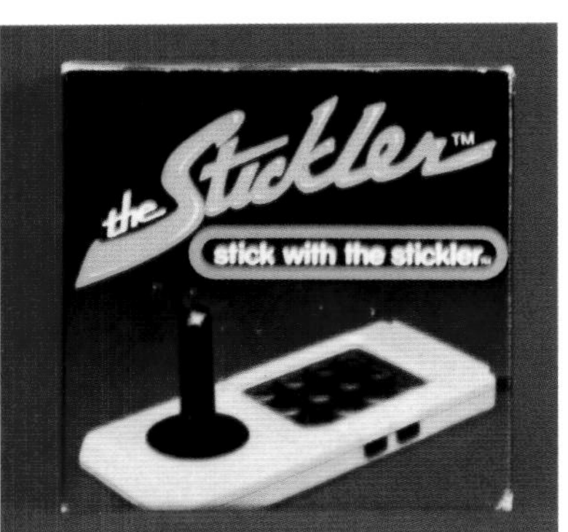

Stickler adaptors gave your Intellivsion controllers more of a joystick feel. $10 - $15 unused in box.

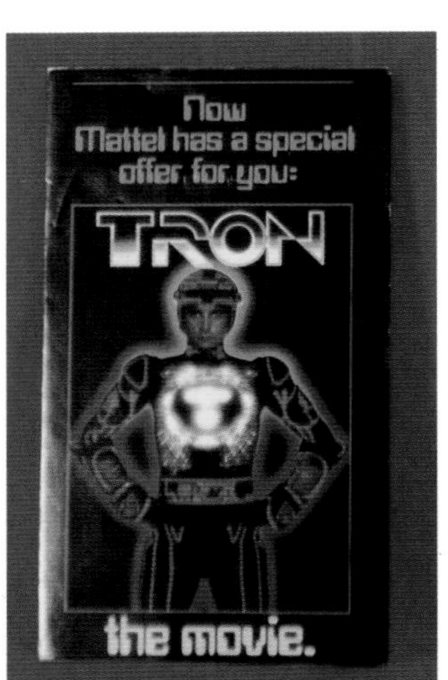

For a short time, this Tron offer was enclosed with Mattel titles. $5 - $10.

1988 INTV mail order catalog. $10 - $18.

Another variety of Intellivision joystick adaptors. $15 - $25 mint on card.

Other Home Video Game Systems from 1972 to 1982

Bally Astrocade

Originally released by Bally, but later sold (along with the Bally logo) to a company called Astrovision. This promising system doomed itself early on by releasing the Bally Basic cartridge. This cartridge allowed users to program their own games and download them to cassettes. After a while, there were so many public domain games floating around that software sales slowed to the point that the production of the system was discontinued. A cream version of this unit was also released and is considerably more rare than the standard version pictured here.

Typical packaging for an Astrocade cartridge. A sealed Galactic Invasion 2011 can bring up to $25.

Bally Astrocade, also know as the Bally Professional Arcade and the Bally Videocade. $200 - $300 complete in box.

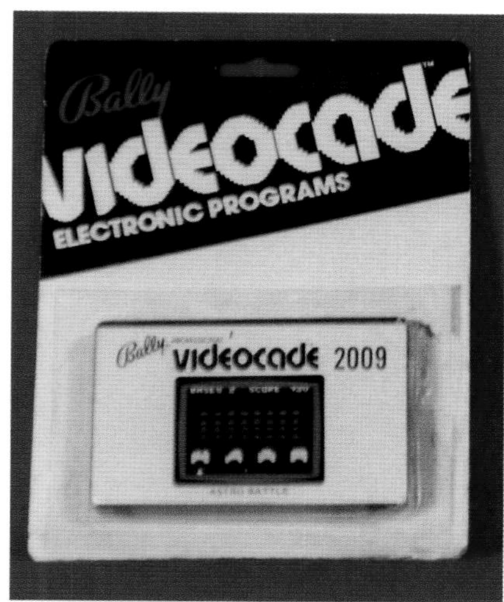

Typical cassette programs for the Astrocade are valued at $5-$25 each.

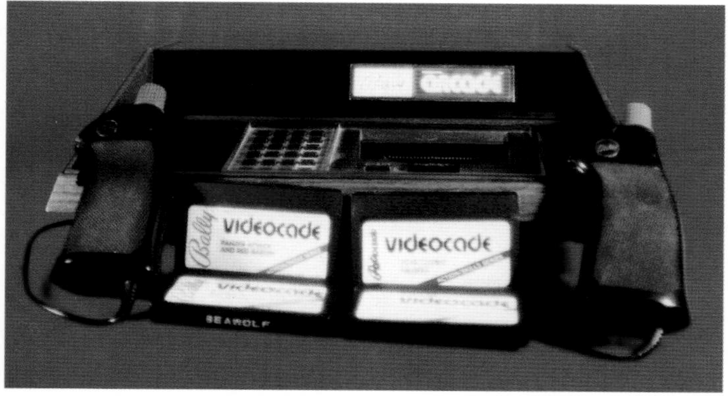

Bally Astrocade, pictured here with some of its cartridges. $100 - $175 complete and working.

Bally Basic, the cartridge that killed the system. $20 - $30 cartridge only.

Epoch Cassette Vision

The Japanese desire for newness, coupled with a lack of storage space for outdated items, makes pre-Famicom Japanese systems such as this one extremely difficult to find, even in Japan. It was the Japanese answer to the Atari 2600 and, as far as I know, was never released outside of Japan.

The very rare Japanese Cassette Vision system. $500 and up, complete in box.

Cartridges for the Cassette Vision system. $25 - $75 each.

Emerson Arcadia 2001

This system enjoyed much greater popularity in countries outside of the U.S. It was released by many different manufacturers the world over. Foreign released games and systems should all be considered rare (at least in the United States). While produced in somewhat low numbers, items for this system are not as hard to come by as one might expect due to lack of collector interest in this system.

Emerson Arcadia 2001 sans the screw in joysticks. $50 - $100 complete.

Alien Invaders. $20 complete in box.

Breakaway. $20 complete in box.

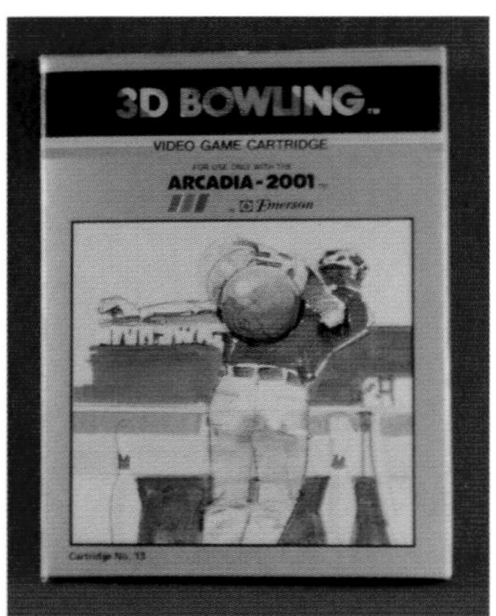

3D Bowling. $20 complete in box.

Baseball. $20 complete in box.

Cat Trax. $20 complete in box.

Escape. $20 complete in box.

Space Raiders. $20 complete in box.

Some Arcadia 2001 cartridges were released in long casings, while others were in shorter casings.

Soccer. $20 complete in box.

Tanks A Lot. $20 complete in box.

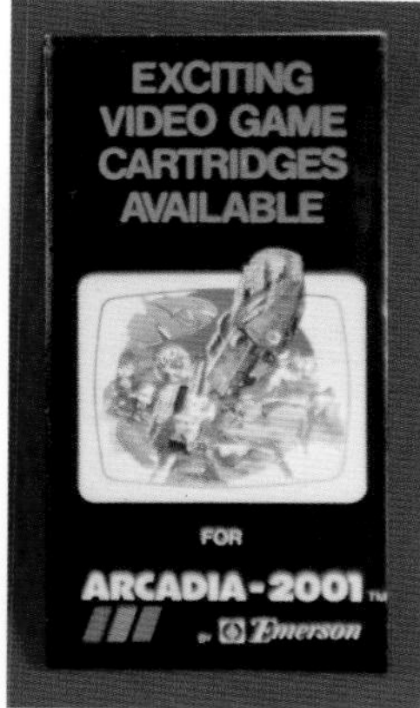

Emerson Arcadia 2001 catalog. $2 - $5.

Space Attack. Note the Star Wars inspired graphics. $20 complete in box.

Open box view of a complete Arcadia game.

Fairchild Channel F

One of the first systems for home use. Released even before the legendary Atari 2600. The Channel F was a rather dull system, prone to breakdowns and problems with its hardwired controllers. The Channel F II is a sturdier machine with detachable controllers. It is recommended to use the model II for actual game play. Cartridges for this system are pictured in numerical order, as they do have those big, bright numbers on the boxes.

First Version of the Fairchild Channel F. $150 - $250 complete in box.

More common boxed version of the Fairchild Channel F. $150 - $160 complete in box.

Channel F System II. $125 - $175 complete in box.

Spitfire. $23 complete in box.

Backgammon / Acey - Deucey. $25 complete in box.

Tic Tac Toe / Shooting Gallery / Doodle / Quadra Doodle. $15 complete in box.

Space War. $23 complete in box.

Sonar Search. $28 complete in box.

Desert Fox / Shooting Gallery. $15 complete in box.

Magic Numbers / Mindreader / Nim. $23 complete in box.

Video Blackjack. $20 complete in box.

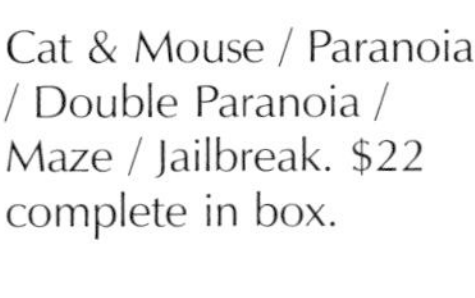
Cat & Mouse / Paranoia / Double Paranoia / Maze / Jailbreak. $22 complete in box.

GCE Vectrex

The unique and highly sought after Vectrex system was released in 1982, but unfortunately had a fairly short shelf life due to the high cost of manufacturing. It is the only vector based system ever released for home use. And not only that, it emits X-rays! Really, open one up and see the warning label inside. It is worth this risk of irradiation though, as this system is (in the author's opinion) the best of the era, and can still hold its own with some of today's systems. Color overlays that fit over the screen were originally included with each game, but are usually missing today. Milton Bradley, parent company of GCE, released the Vectrex in Europe, where it did not last much longer than it did in the United States. The Vectrex maintains a strong following today, with new games being produced by Vectrex enthusiasts.

An assortment of Vectrex cartridges. The lack of interesting labels is more than compensated for by the amazing game play.

The Vectrex system. $150 - $225.

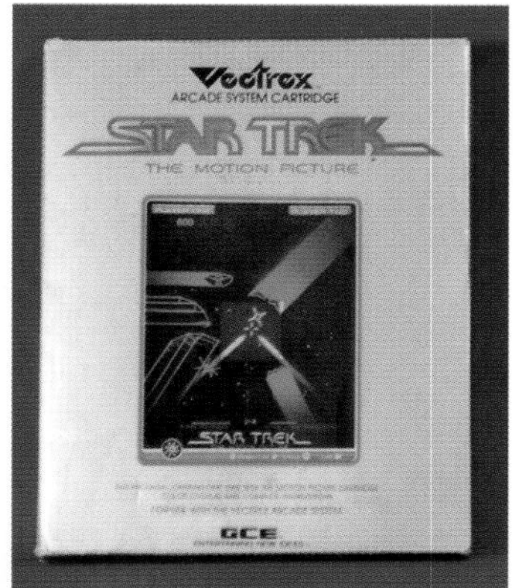

Trekkies will love this Star Trek: The Motion Picture game. $38 complete in box.

Vectrex Carrying Case

Now you can take your Vectrex Arcade System and your favorite game cartridges to a friend's house, on vacation, anywhere - with this handy carrying case.

- Holds Vectrex console, second control panel, and up to nine cartridges, screen overlays and game instruction manuals.
- Sturdy and attractive, easy-care nylon and vinyl with corrugated reinforced sides and bottom.
- Top closes with convenient fabric hook and loop fastener.
- Folds flat for easy storage.

Only $14.95

Vectrex Dust Cover

Keep your Vectrex Arcade System clean and dust-free with this attractive vinyl cover.

Only $5.95

Order Now!

Mail order form for the extremely rare Vectrex carrying case and dust cover. The order form itself is valued at $5 - $10, while either the case or cover will bring $200 - $400 each.

The excellent translation of the arcade hit Berzerk. $35 complete in box.

Vectrex Light Pen. $100 - $125.

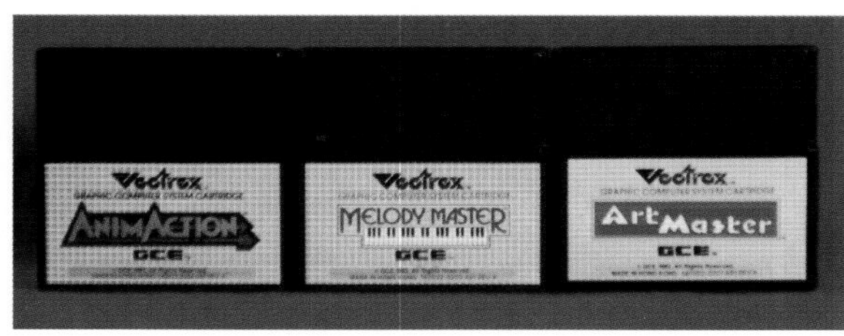

Cartridges for use with the Light Pen. $35 - $50 each.

Spike, the only talking game released for this system. $41 complete in box.

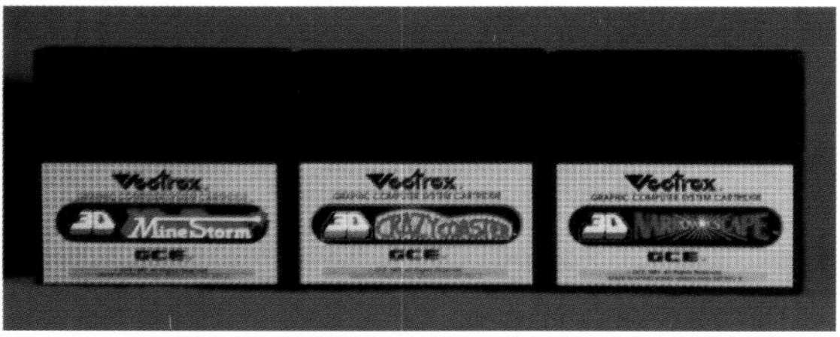

Cartridges for use with the 3D imager. $60 - $65 each.

The Vectrex Passport is the standard pack in catalog that was included with most games. $5 - $9

Magnavox Odyssey

The first home video game system by several years, the Magnavox Odyssey was released in 1972. It was a very primitive system with blocks of light moving behind colored overlays that fit over the television screen. The overlays came in large and small sizes for different TV sets. The system was a moderate success, but was soon discontinued as it did not meet the sales expectations of Magnavox. Magnavox Odysseys are extremely desirable to collectors due to the system' s historical significance and low production numbers.

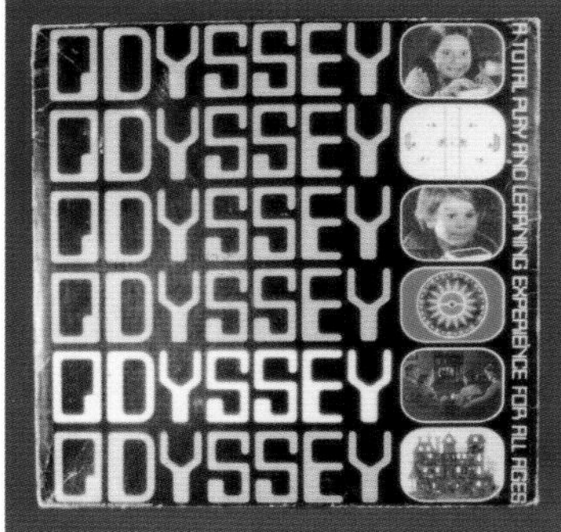

Magnavox Odyssey, the first home game system. $200 - $400 complete in box.

Bird's-eye view of the Magnavox Odyssey. This system included many, many extras. Be sure of completeness before purchasing one of these.

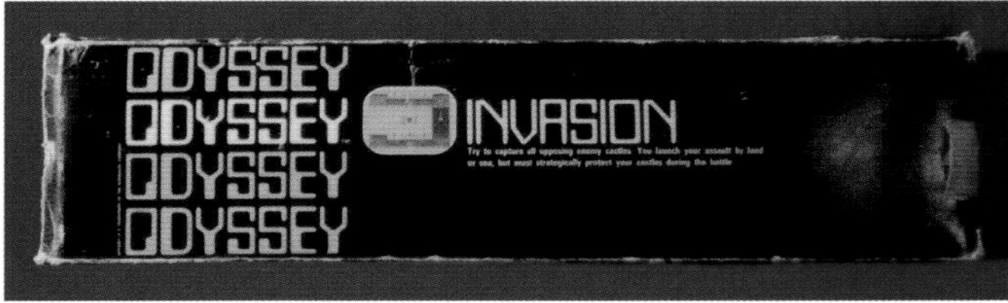

All boxed, complete (they came with playing pieces) games for the Odyssey are valued at $50 - $100 each.

The Shooting Gallery game included a large, realistic shotgun. This was the only peripheral produced for the Magnavox Odyssey. $250 - $350 complete in box.

Magnavox Odyssey 2

Bordering on a home computer system, the Odyssey 2 features a full keyboard, which many games for this system took full advantage of. Most games for the Odyssey 2, however, lacked the excitement and graphics of other systems, and it failed to spark the retail frenzy and collector interest of other systems. The Odyssey 2 fared far better in Europe though, where it was released as the Philips G 7000. There was much more third party support, and games were produced to a much later date than in the U.S. Another interesting note is that K. C. Munchkin, a game produced for the Odyssey 2, spawned one of the earliest video game related lawsuits. Atari felt it too closely mimicked their Pac-Man game. Apparently the judge agreed, as Magnavox was ordered to cease distribution of the game.

Magnavox Odyssey 2. $75 - $150 complete in box.

Inside view of a Magnavox Odyssey 2 box.

The Voice allowed speech capabilities for the Odyssey 2 which were quite impressive for the time. Expect to pay $35 - $60 for a working one.

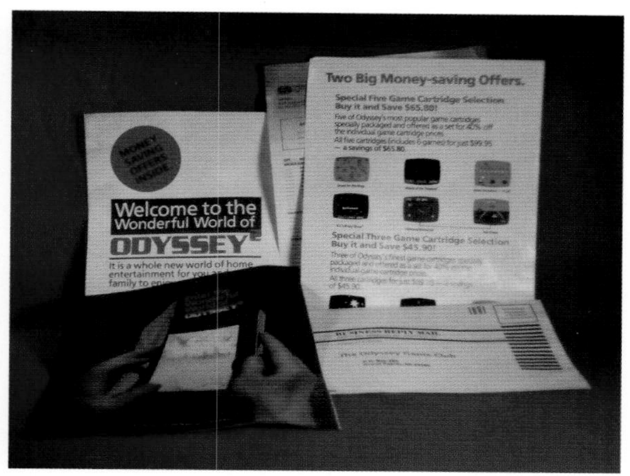

Odyssey Game Club packet. $30 - $75.

Armored Encounter / Sub Chase. $8 complete in box.

Computer Golf. $10 complete in box.

Alien Invaders Plus. $10 complete in box.

Baseball. $10 complete in box.

Bowling / Basketball. $10 complete in box.

Computer Intro. $17 complete in box.

Alpine Skiing. $10 complete in box.

Blockout / Breakdown. $9 complete in box.

Casino Slot Machine. $13 complete in box.

Instruction book for Computer Intro. $4 - $6 by itself.

Conquest of the World was designed, in part, by an ex-C.I.A. official. $50 complete in box.

Dynasty. $10 complete in box.

Freedom Fighters. $9 complete in box.

Invaders From Hyperspace. $9 complete in box.

Cosmic Conflict. $10 complete in box.

Electronic Table Soccer. $15 complete in box.

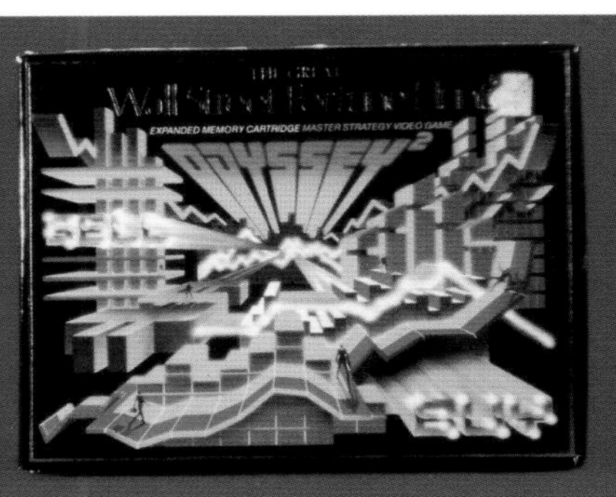

The Great Wall Street Fortune Hunt. $50 complete in box.

I've Got Your Number. $10 complete in box.

Demon Attack, one of only two Imagic releases for this system. $60 complete in box.

Football. $9 complete in box.

Hockey / Soccer. $9 complete in box.

K.C. Munchkin. $9 complete in box.

K.C.'s Krazy Chase. $12 complete in box.

Monkeyshines. $15 complete in box.

Pick Axe Pete. $18 complete in box.

Showdown in 2100 A.D. $9 complete in box.

Las Vegas Blackjack. $9 complete in box.

Out of This World / Helicopter Rescue. $10 complete in box.

Pocket Billiards. $12 complete in box.

Speedway / Spin-out / Crypto Logic. $8 complete in box.

Math A Magic / Echo. $9 complete in box.

Pachinko. $12 complete in box.

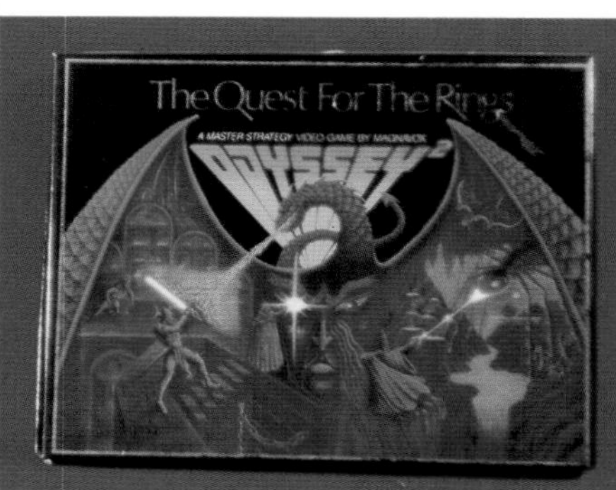

Quest For the Rings. $50 complete in box.

Take the Money and Run. $10 complete in box.

Thunderball. $10 complete in box.

Volleyball. $10 complete in box.

Typical Philips release of a Videopac game for the G 7000 system (the European version of the Odyssey 2). $30 - $75 each, complete in box.

UFO. $15 complete in box.

War of Nerves. $10 complete in box.

Philips release for the + series of Videopac games. $50 - $80 each, complete in box.

Parker Brothers only released games for the Odyssey 2 overseas. Frogger is valued at $95 complete in box.

Milton Bradley Microvision

This was the first handheld system with interchangeable cartridges, a predecessor to the Game Boy. The Microvision used LCD graphics and all of the controls, except for one knob, were built into the cartridges. While the Microvision did not provide the greatest game play, it was certainly a novel idea at the time and laid the groundwork for many portable systems in years to come.

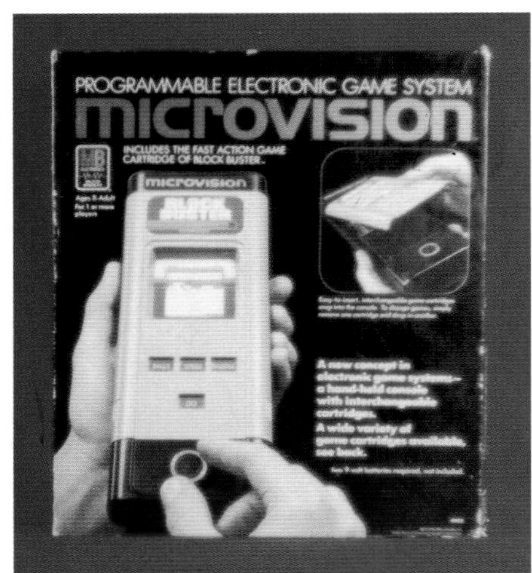

Milton Bradley's handheld Microvision. $75 - $150 complete in box.

A view of the Microvision without a cartridge. $25 - $50 as shown.

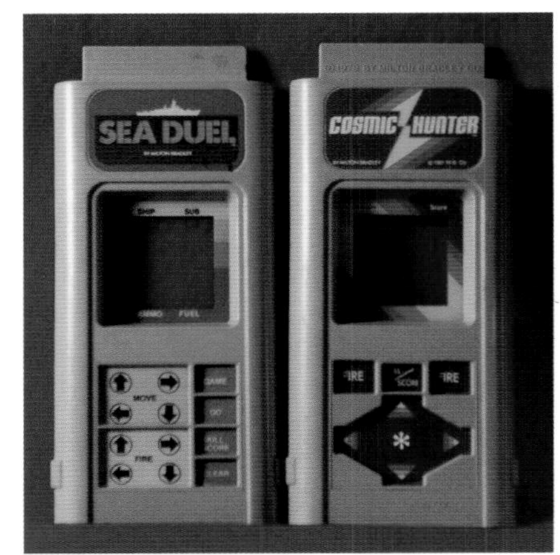

Loose Microvision cartridges are valued at $15 - $35 each.

Typical Microvision cartridge in opened box. $20 - $45 each.

Front view of an unused Microvision game. $25 - $55 each.

Rear view of the unused game.

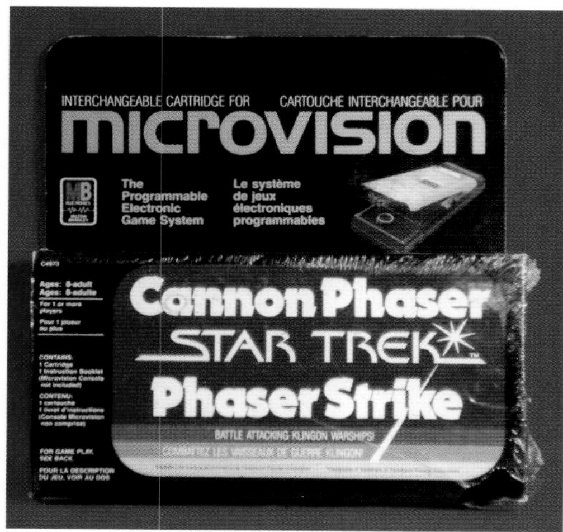

Bilingual release of Star Trek Phaser Strike for the Microvision. $40 - $50.

RCA Studio II

One of the earlier home systems, the RCA Studio II, also known as the RCA Home TV Programmer, had no joysticks. It featured two panels of buttons instead of joysticks. Unexciting to many gamers (due to lack of both joysticks and color graphics), this system had a short shelf life. The Studio II included an unusual RF adapter, which is also where the power supply connects. The system will not work and cannot be considered complete without this adapter.

RCA Studio II. $150 - $250.

Another style of RCA Studio II box.

An unpackaged RCA Studio II. $100 - $150.

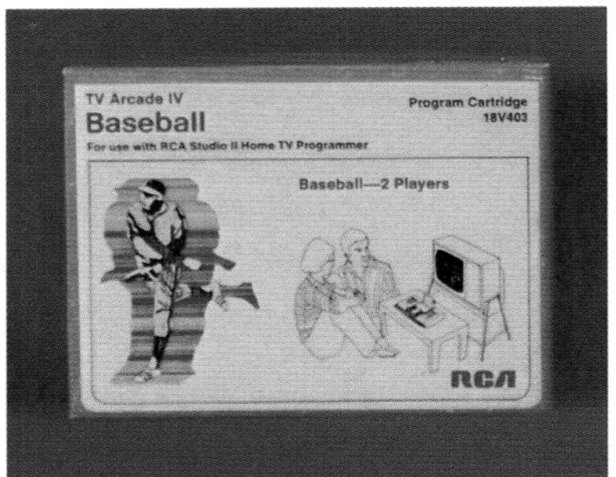

Baseball. $25 complete in box.

Space War. $35 complete in box.

TV Schoolhouse II — Math Fun. $45 complete in box.

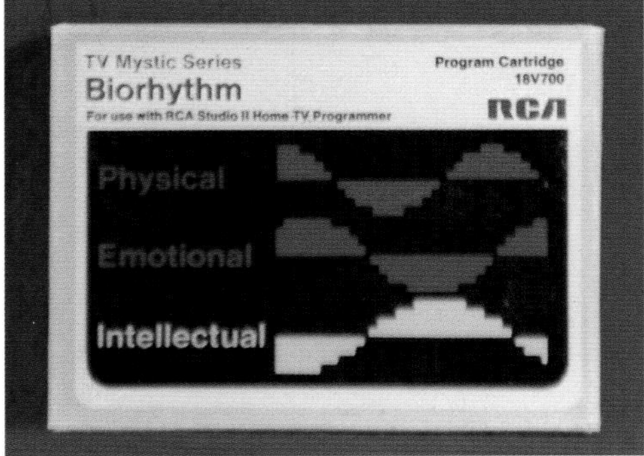

Biorhythm. $45 complete in box.

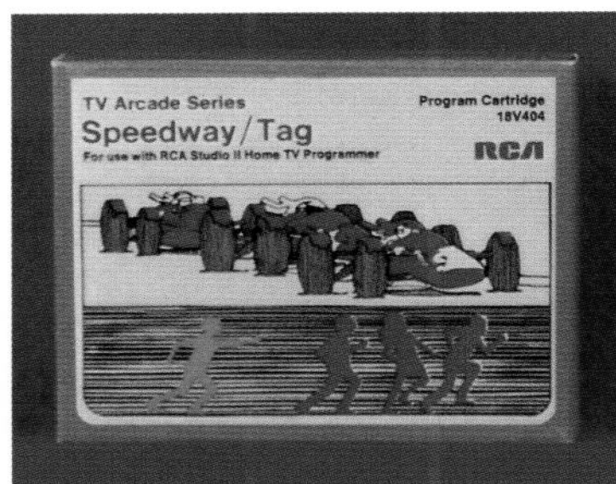

Speedway / Tag. $26 complete in box.

RCA Studio II cartridge with its accompanying instruction manual.

Blackjack. $21 complete in box.

Tennis / Squash. $20 complete in box.

RCA Studio II catalog. $3 - $6.

Gunfighter / Moonship Battle. $39 complete in box.

TV Schoolhouse I. $50 complete in box.

Handhelds, Tabletops, & Stand Alones

Stand alones are considered to be systems that do not use cartridges, but are still required to be attached to a television set for use. For the most part these will be Pong style games, but there are some exceptions. Hundreds of different stand alone consoles were produced over the years. In this chapter you will find a very brief overview of some of these.

Tabletop games are battery operated games that often resemble miniature arcade games in appearance. These were a popular alternative to cartridge based systems during the early 1980s as they freed up the family television set. Many of these were actually based on hit arcade games. Those tabletop games that were are very desirable to collectors today. There are many more tabletops and variations from around the world. Below you will find an outline of what is available.

These miniature portable games were a huge hit in the 1970s and 1980s and are still continuing strong today. Some of the earliest handhelds had a combination of both electronic and mechanical parts. Sports games were probably the most popular of all handheld games, particularly the Mattel Electronics series. Handheld games are sometimes difficult to differentiate from tabletop games. Sometimes it simply comes down to a matter of opinion.

Pong & Other Stand Alone Consoles

The Atari Pong, their first home release. $100 - $150.

Sears Pong Sports IV, their version of Atari's Ultra Pong. $80 - $150 complete in box.

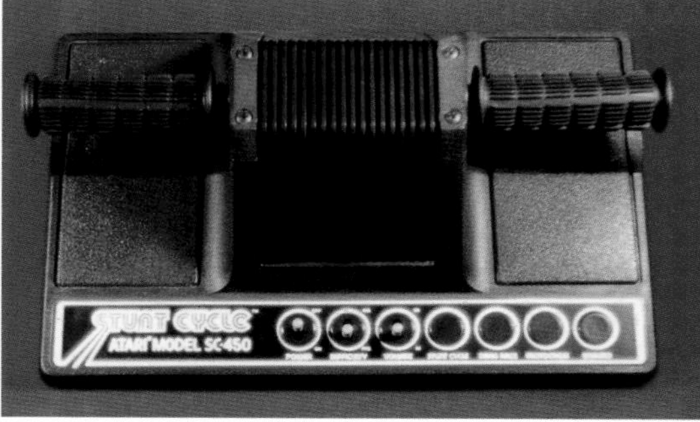

The Atari Pong Stunt Cycle, a tough to find stand alone game. $100 - $200.

The Atari Super Pong is somewhat easier to come by than its predecessor. $70 - $100.

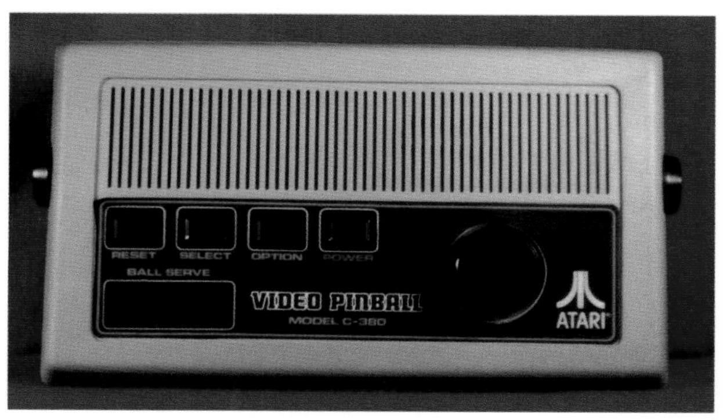

Atari's Video Pinball also allows you to play Breakout. $50 - $70.

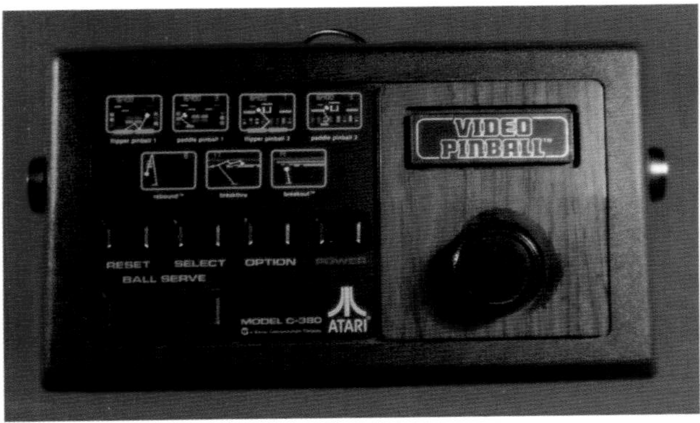

This brown version of Video Pinball by Atari is much more difficult to find than the previously pictured beige version. $75 - $125.

This instruction booklet for the Magnavox Odyssey 400 is valued at $5 - $9.

The Magnavox Odyssey 3000, one of their later Pong efforts. $20 - $50.

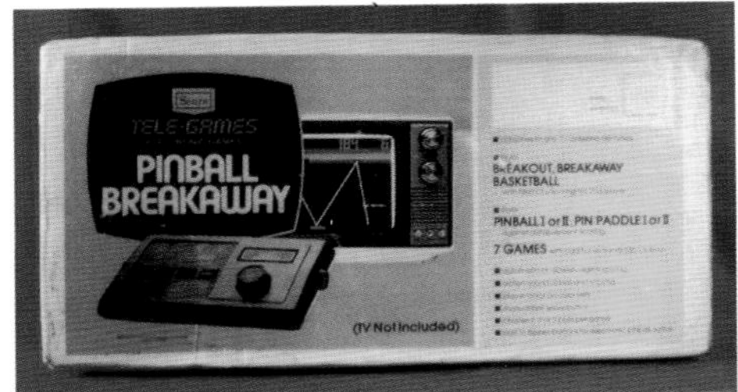

The brown Sears release of Video Pinball is much more common than the Atari version in the same color . $90 - $150 complete in box.

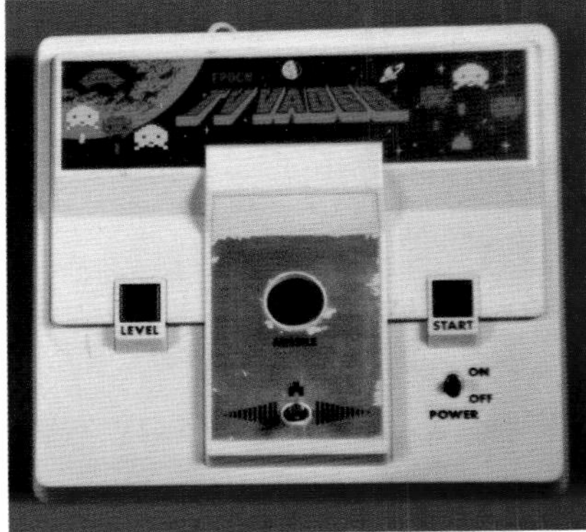

TV Vader by Epoch is a stand alone version of Space Invaders and is quite difficult to find . $75 - $100.

The Atari Video Music connects from your stereo to your television, and produces graphics in accordance to the music being played. It is as unusual as it is rare. $350 - $500.

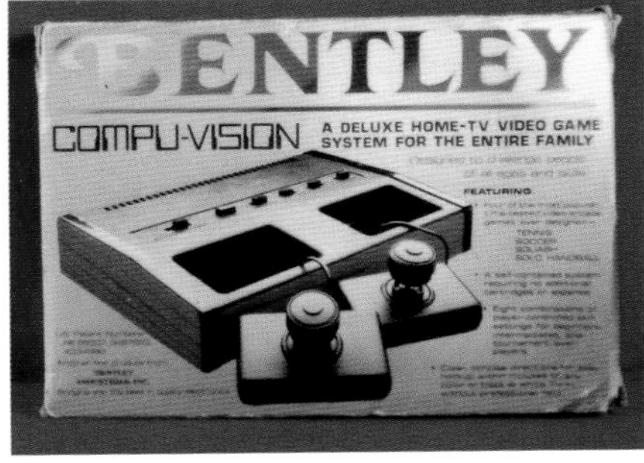

The Bentley Compu-Vision is one of a large number of fairly generic Pong style games that glutted the market in the late 1970s and early 1980s. $35 - $60 complete in box.

An early Pong release, the Magnavox Odyssey 400. $25 - $50.

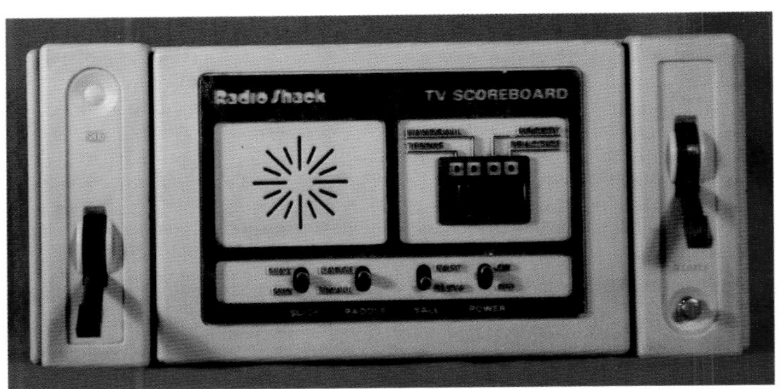

Radio Shack produced a seemingly endless variety of their version of Pong — the TV Scoreboard. $15 - $20.

Another version of the TV Scoreboard. $25 - $40 complete in box.

Yet another version of the TV Scoreboard from Radio Shack. Also $25 - $40 complete in box.

Coleco's Tabletop Games

Coleco tabletop games are somewhat difficult to find with the original boxes. This Pac-Man is valued at $125 - $200 complete in box.

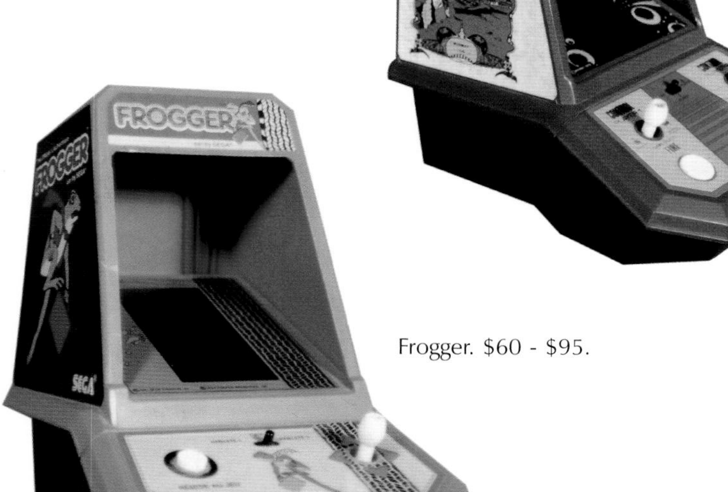

Galaxian. $75 - $125.

Frogger. $60 - $95.

COLECO Guide No 95197 A

The Official MS. PAC-MAN by BALLY MIDWAY

Plays and sounds like the MS. PAC-MAN™ arcade game!

INSTRUCTIONS AND GAME RULES

- Arcade-style joystick controls
- Multi-color display
- Two challenging skill levels
- Remembers best score earned in one-player Ms. Pac-Man™

Model No. 2396

AGES 6 TO ADULT

COLECO

Instruction manual for the Ms. Pac-Man tabletop game from Coleco. $10 - $15.

Donkey Kong, one of the more common Coleco tabeltops. $50 - $75.

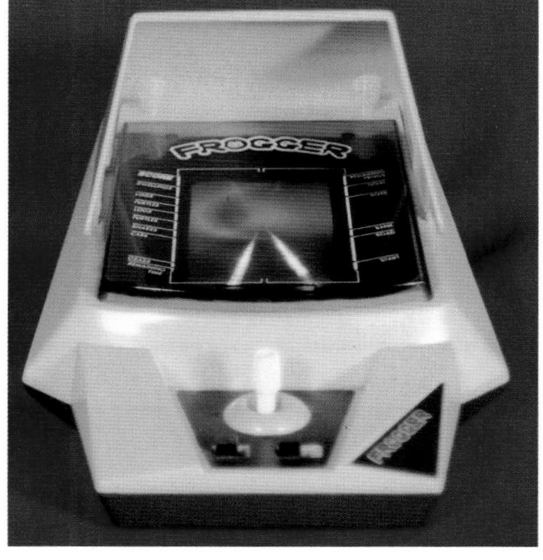

This European released CGL version of Frogger is identical to the Coleco release in every aspect except for the casing. $75 - $95.

Zaxxon. $80 - $145.

Donkey Kong Junior, licensed from Nintendo and manufactured by Coleco, featured a built in alarm clock. $200 - $300 complete in box.

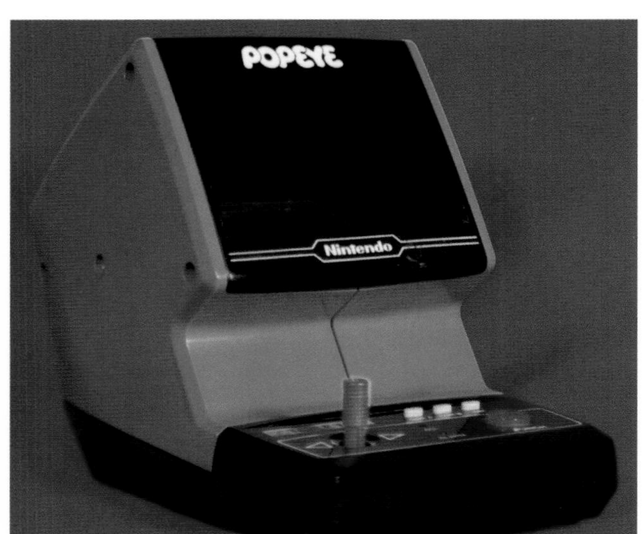

Popeye. $80 - $125.

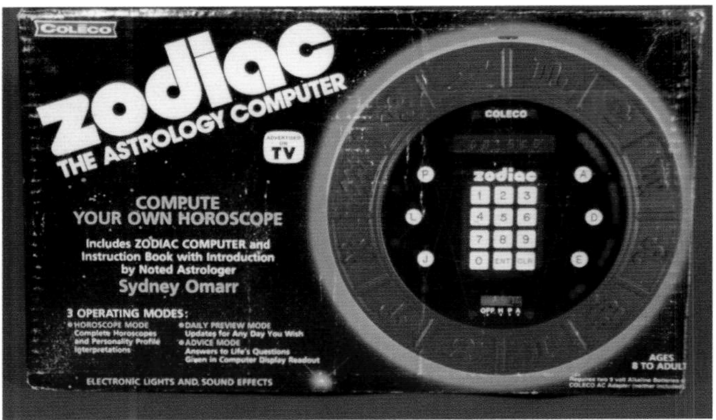

Coleco's Zodiac was capable of giving you a daily horoscope. $50 - $95 complete in box.

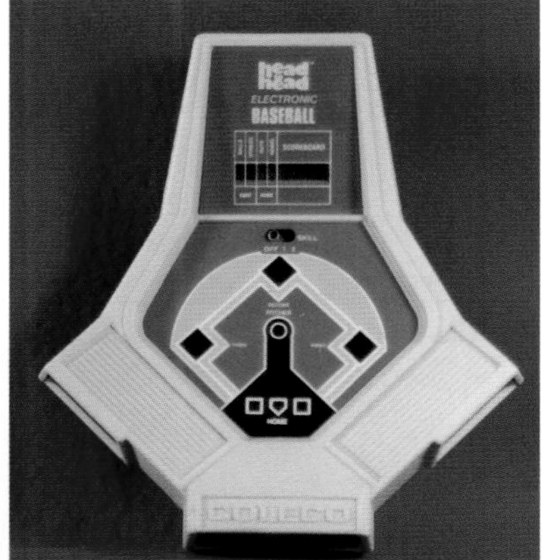

Coleco answered Mattel's line of handheld sports games with their own highly successful Head to Head sports game series. This Head to Head Baseball is valued at $25 - $45.

This Coleco adapter allowed handheld games to be powered with a 9 volt AC adapter rather than a battery. $10 - $15.

Catalog of electronic games from Coleco. $6 - $10.

Other Tabletop Games

Q*bert from Parker Brothers. $75 - $100.

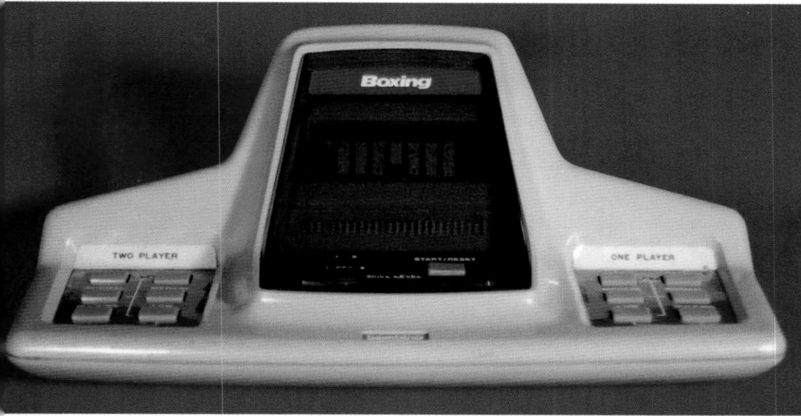

Bambino produced an interesting line of tabletop games ranging in value from $50 - $100 each.

Scramble from Grandstand. $70 - $95.

Mattel Electronics Games

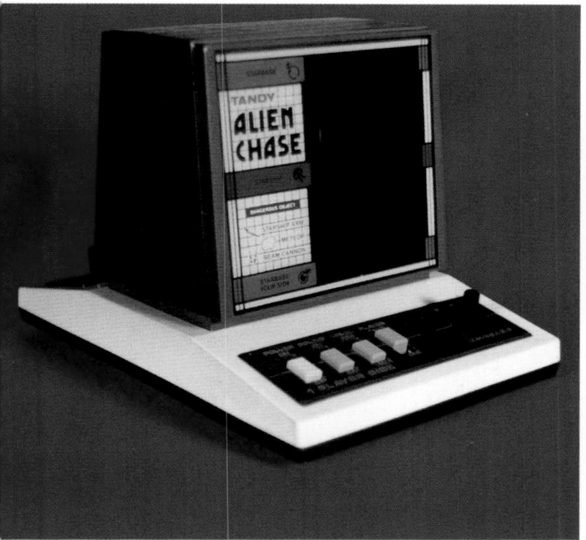

Alien Chase from Tandy features screens and controls on both sides for simultaneous two player use. $50 - $80.

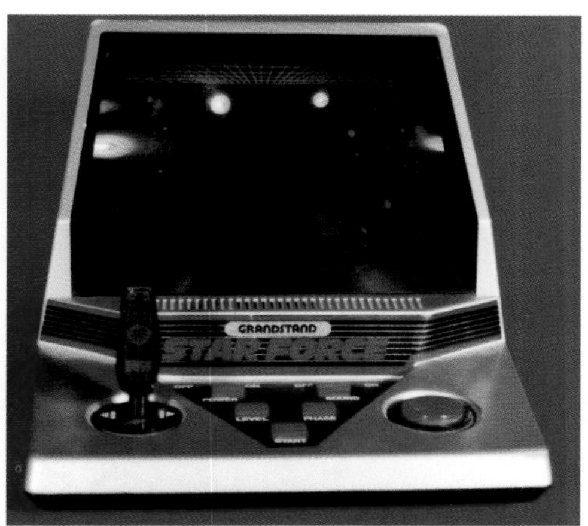

Star Force from Grandstand. $65 - $95.

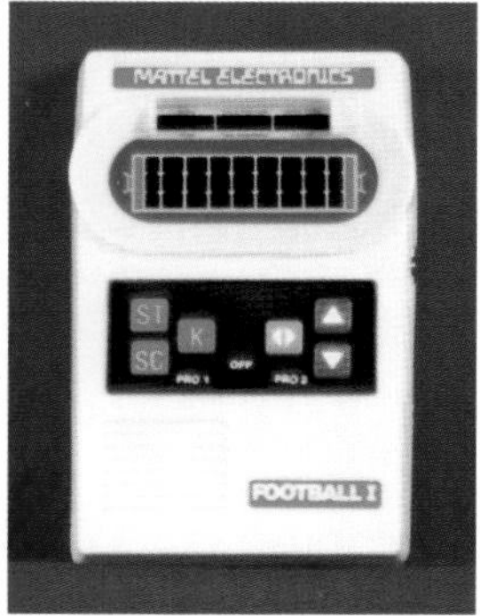

Though not a rare game, Mattel's Football I brings a high price due to its playability. People have fond memories of this game! $65 - $95.

Astro Command from Tandy. $60 - $85 complete in box.

Firefox F-7 from Grandstand. $65 - $95.

Japanese boxed version of Mattel's Football I. The sticker on the front, and the foreign language instructions inside, are the only difference between this and the American release, but this is a scarce variation that is highly desirable to collectors today. $200 - $295 complete in box.

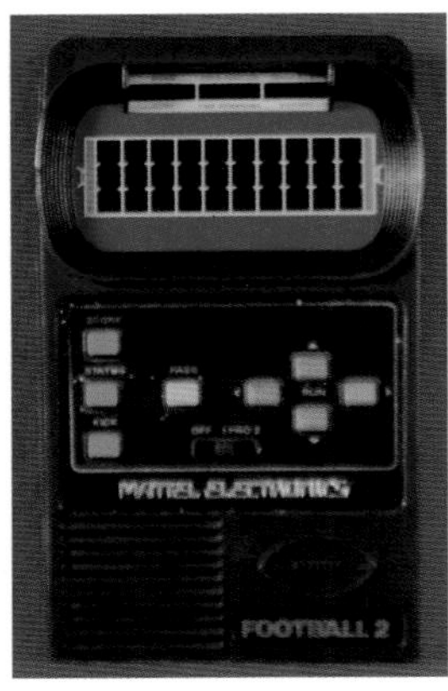

Football 2, though slightly more difficult to find, is not quite as in demand as its predecessor. $60 - $85.

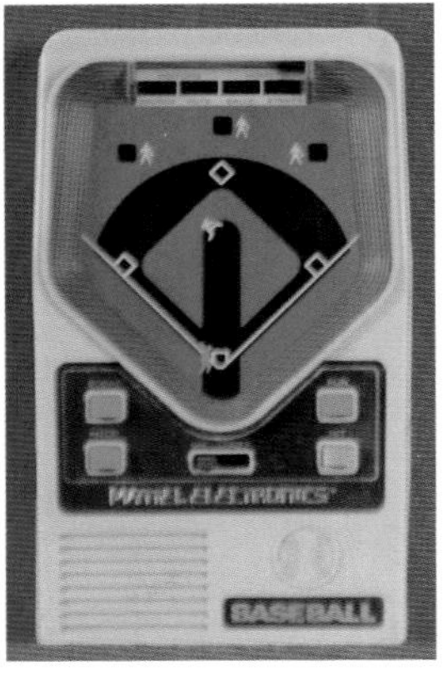

Baseball. $35 - $60.

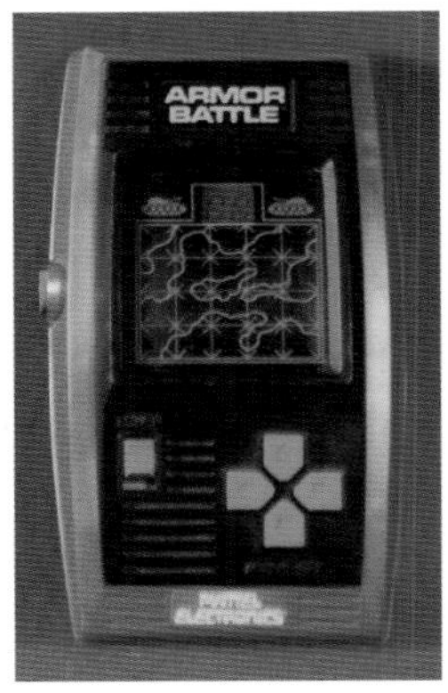

Armor Battle. $45 - $65.

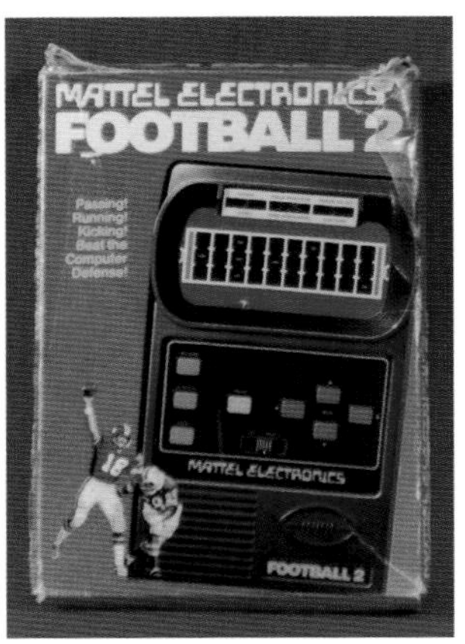

Football 2. $95 - $140 complete in box.

Auto Race. $40 - $65.

Mattel's Funtronics series of games were targeted at a very young audience. $35 - $75 each.

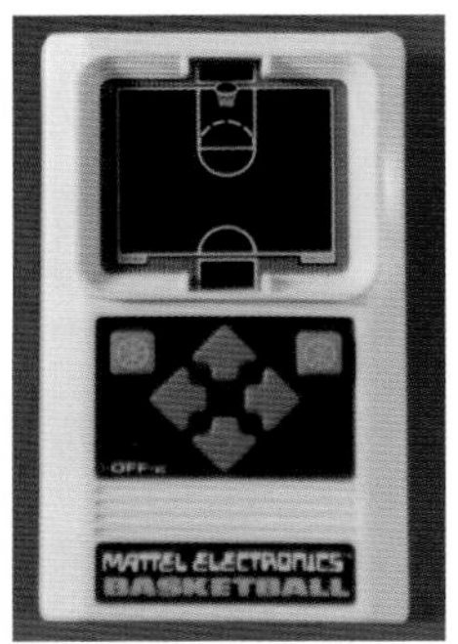

Basketball. $35 - $65.

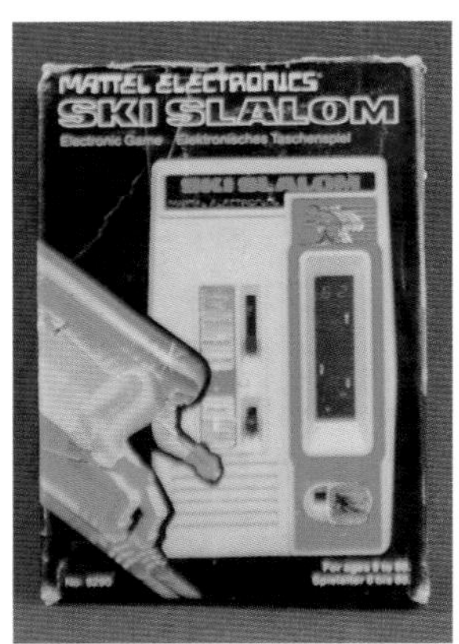

Ski Slalom. $75 - $135 complete in box.

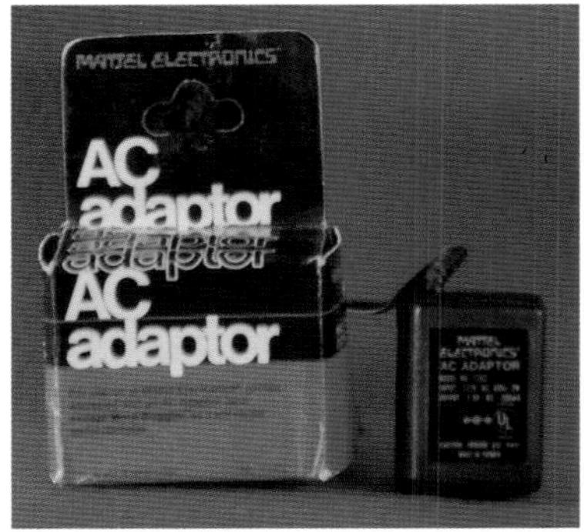

This AC adapter from Mattel eliminated the need for batteries. $25 - $35 with box.

Basketball 2. $75 - $135 complete in box.

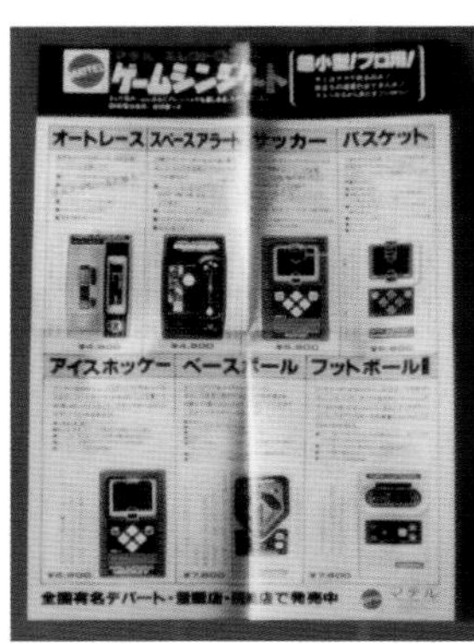

Japanese Catalog of Mattel handheld games. $10 - $20.

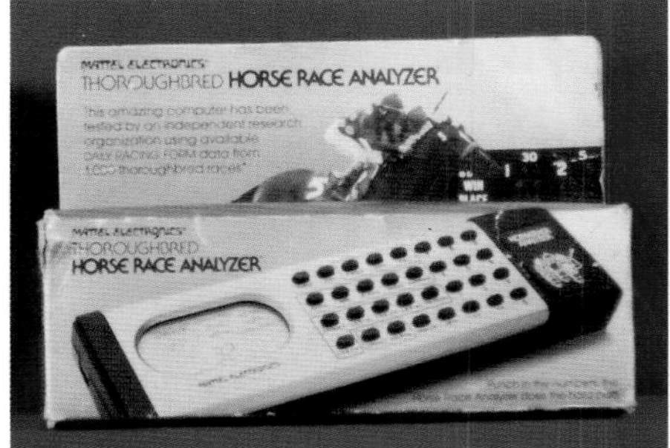

This Horse Race Analyzer advertised odds of winning at above 50%. $50 - $95 complete in box.

Dungeons & Dragons LCD game from Mattel's Action Arcade series. $65 - $95 complete in box.

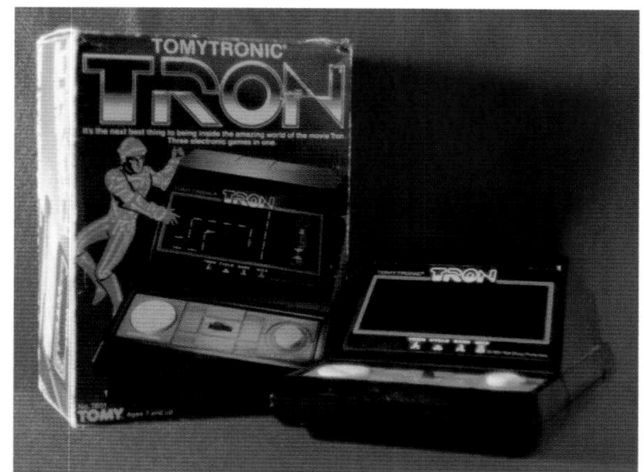

Tron. $150 - $250 complete in box.

Mattel's Dungeons & Dragons electronic board game. $50 - $95 complete in box.

The European tabletop game Munchman from Grandstand is an exact duplicate of Tomy's Pac-Man. $80 - $145 complete in box.

Tomy/Tomytronic Games

Blip, the *hugely* successful electro-mechanical game from Tomy. $35 - $55 complete in box.

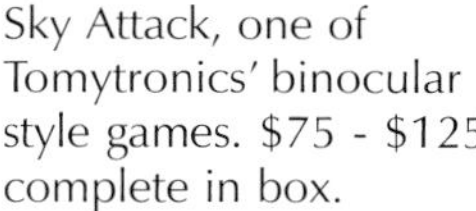
Sky Attack, one of Tomytronics' binocular style games. $75 - $125 complete in box.

Hit and Missile, another electro-mechanical game from Tomy. $40 - $75 complete in box.

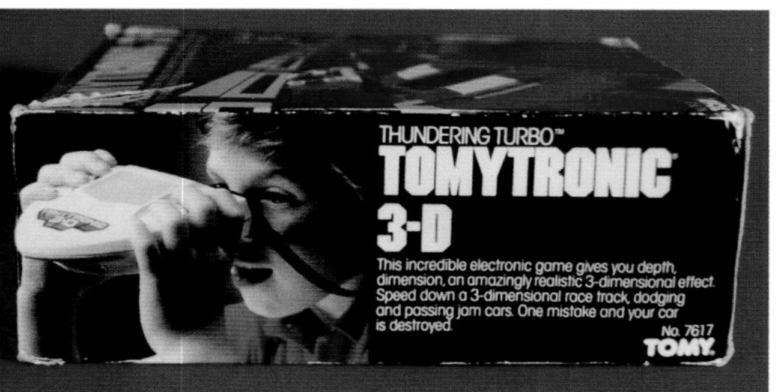

Thundering Turbo. $70 - $100 complete in box.

Jungle Fighter is one of the more difficult to find Tomy binocular style games. $150 - $225 complete in box.

3D Stereo Skyfighters features two built in speakers for stereo sound. $50 - $80.

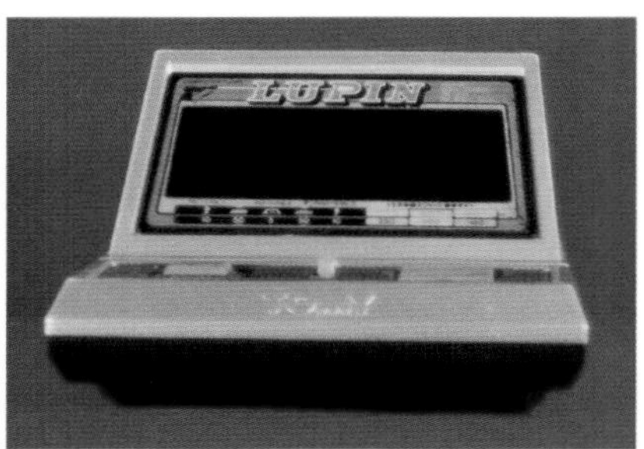

Lupin was one of many Tomy games that never saw release outside of Japan. $95 - $150.

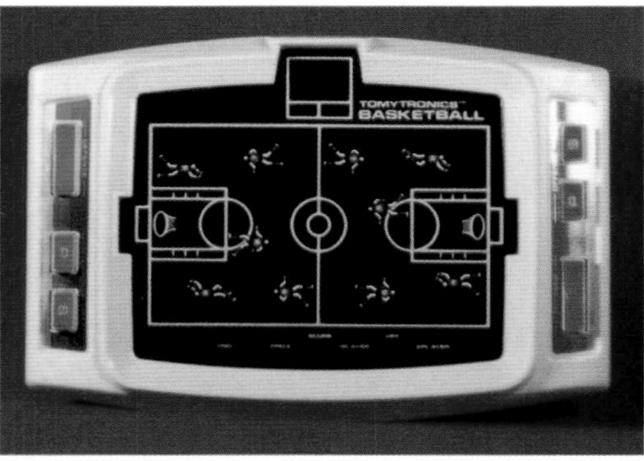

Tomytronics Basketball allowed simultaneous two player action. $25 - $40.

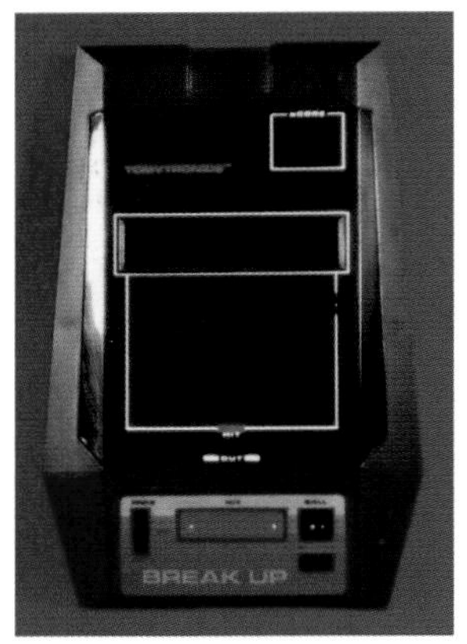

Break Up. $20 - $35.

Tomy's Technoboy series are all mechanical rather than electronic, but are of interest to some collectors of handheld games. $45 - $80 complete in box.

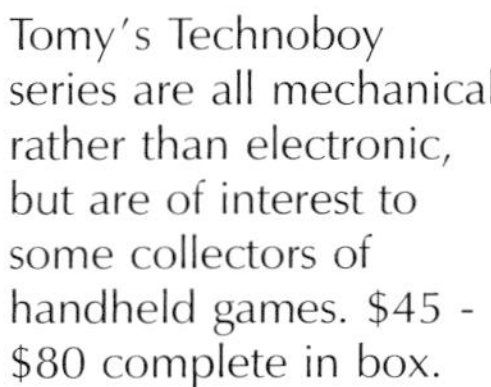

The mechanical Pocket Arcade series of games from Tomy are also of interest to handheld game collectors. $15 - $25 each.

Other Handheld Games

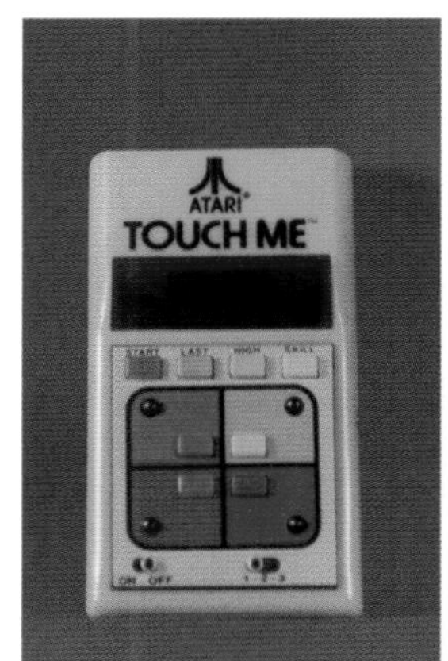

Touch Me was Atari's only attempt in the handheld market. $35 - $75.

Galaxian 2 from Entex. $85 - $140 complete in box.

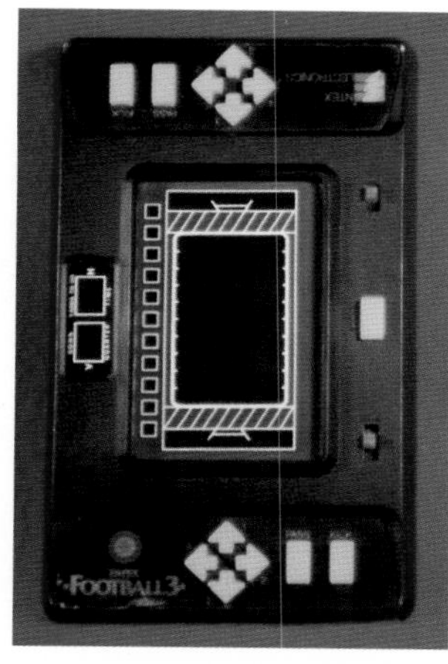

Entex Football 3. $25 - $40.

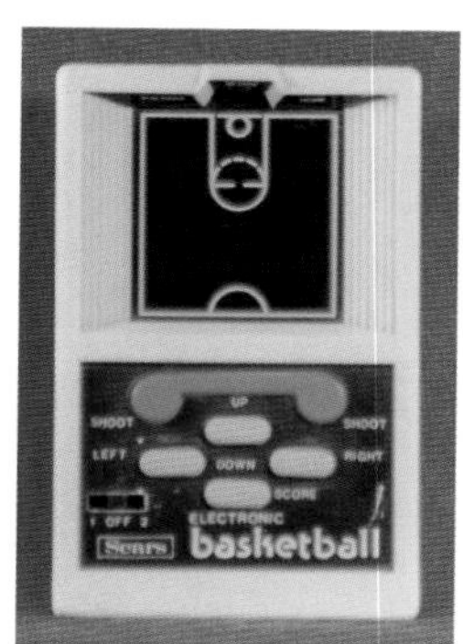

Sears Basketball. $25 - $45.

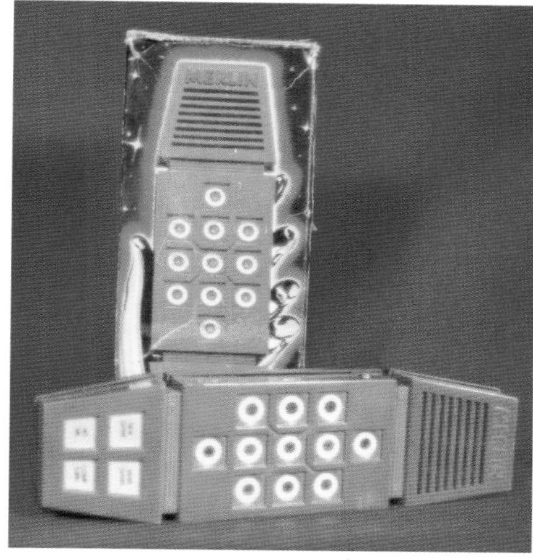

Merlin from Parker Brothers. $35 - $55 complete in box.

An unusual electro-mechanical version of Baseball from Entex. $45 - $85 complete in box.

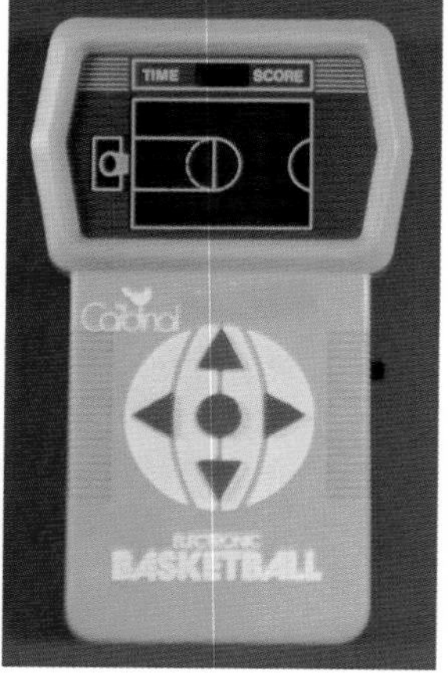

Basketball game by Cardinal. $20 - $35.

Bank Shot Electronic Pool from Parker Brothers. $30 - $55 complete in box.

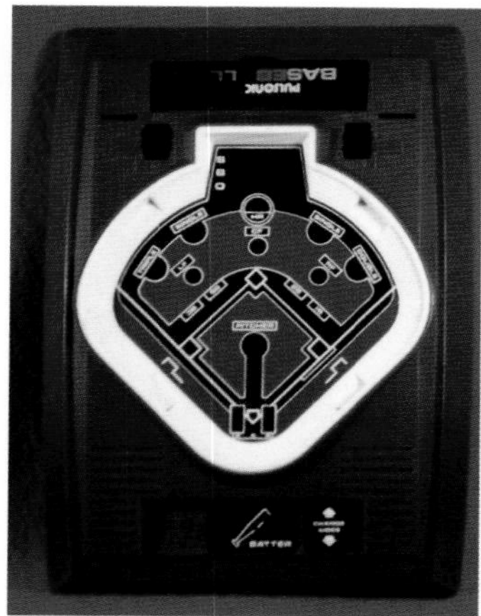

Even the legendary toy manufacturer Mego made an attempt at the handheld game market. This Mego Baseball is valued at $30 - $45.

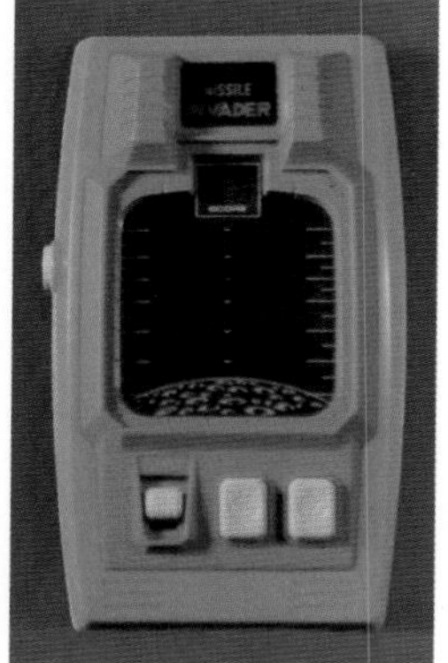

Missile Invader from Bandai. $35 - $65.

Split Second from Parker Brothers. $30 - $50 complete in box.

Bandai solar powered LCD games. Frankenstein (left) is valued at $75 - $100, while Evil Spirit House (right) is valued at $50 - $75.

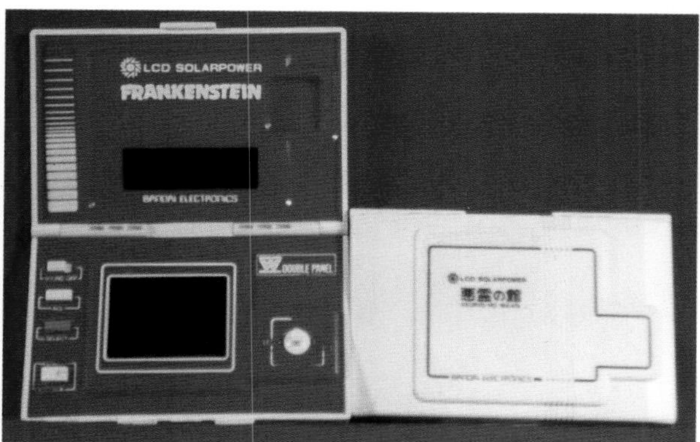

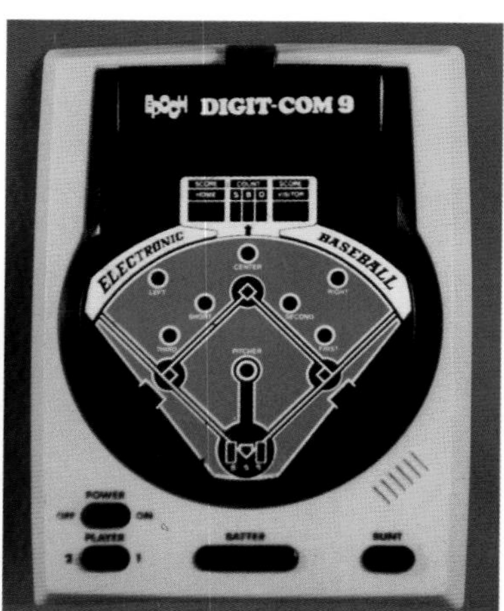

This Baseball game from Epoch is nearly identical to the previously pictured Mego version. $20 - $30.

Namco Pac-Land, LCD version of Pac-Man. $45 - $55.

The original release of the hugely popular Simon from Milton Bradley. $25 - $50 complete in box.

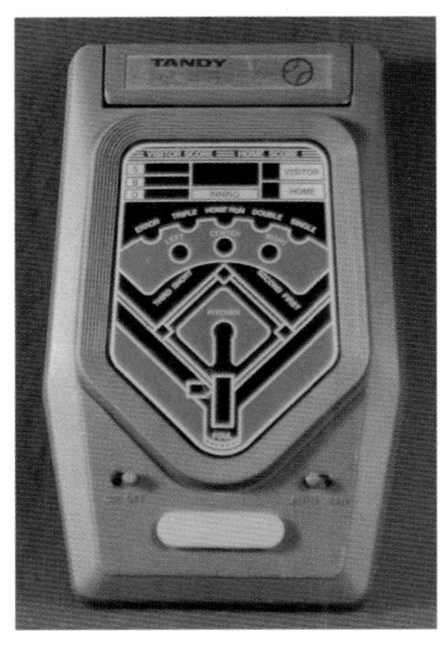

Baseball by Tandy. $15 - $25.

An LCD version of Scramble from Grandstand. $50 - $80 complete in box.

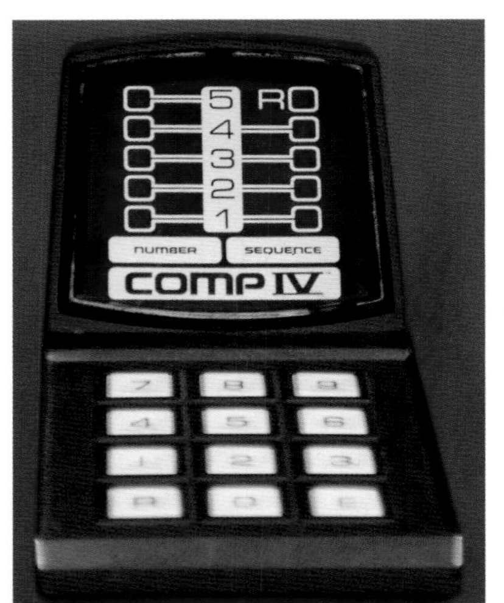

Comp IV from Milton Bradley. $20 - $40.

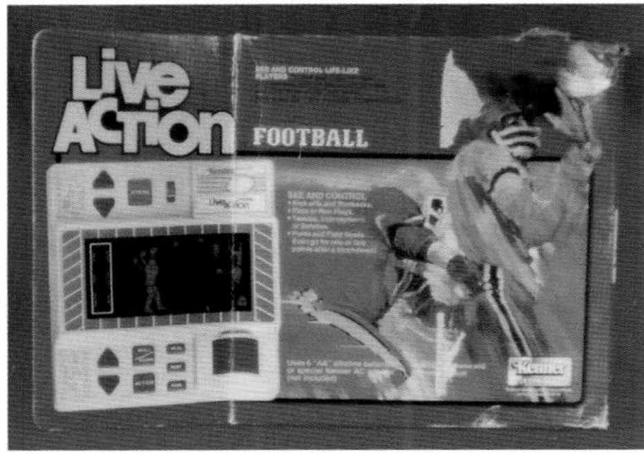

Kenner's Live Action Football. $50 - $75 complete in box.

Rocket Pinball from Tiger. $15 - $25.

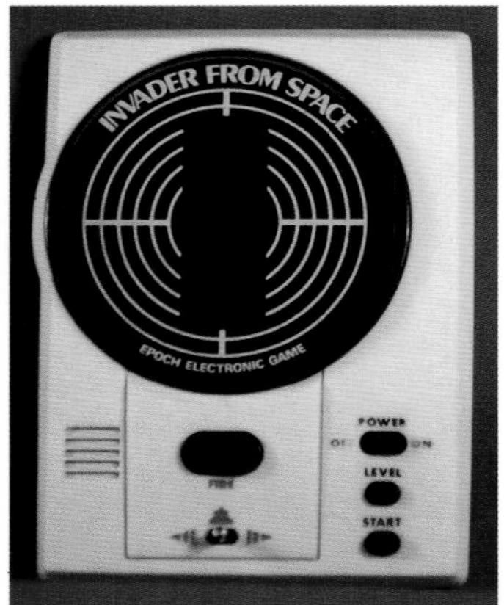

Invader From Space — a Space Invaders clone by Epoch. $35 - $55.

Football / Basketball / Soccer from Fonas. $30 - $60 complete in box.

Texas Instruments Math Marvel calculator style game. $20 - $40.

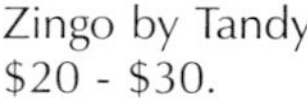

Zingo by Tandy. $20 - $30.

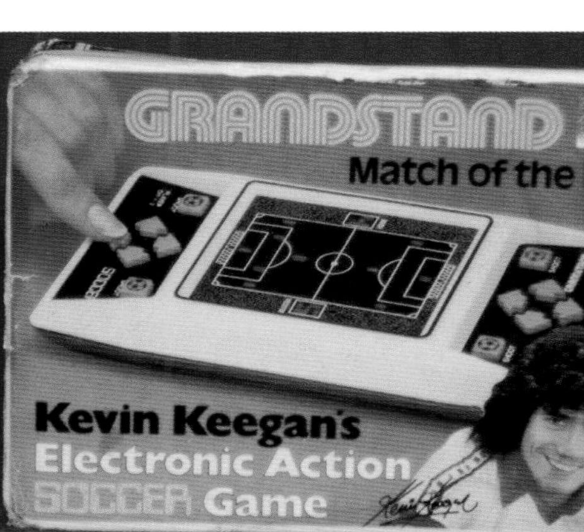

Grandstand's Match of the Day soccer game starring Kevin Keegan. $50 - $80 complete in box.

Electronic Bridge Challenger from Fidelity Electronics. $40 - $70.

Video Game Watches

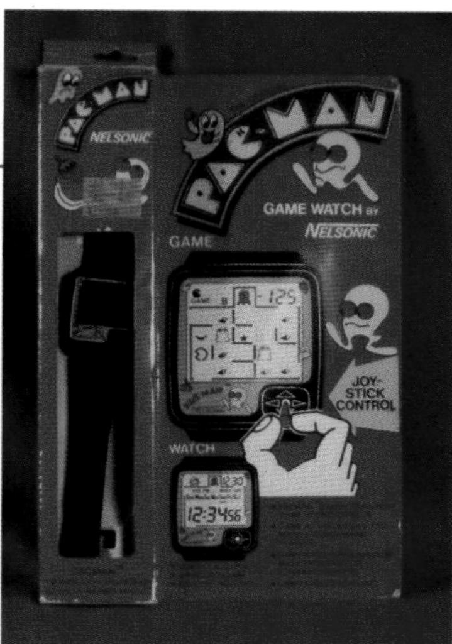

This version of Pac-Man watch by Nelsonic features a miniature joystick. $150 - $200 complete in box.

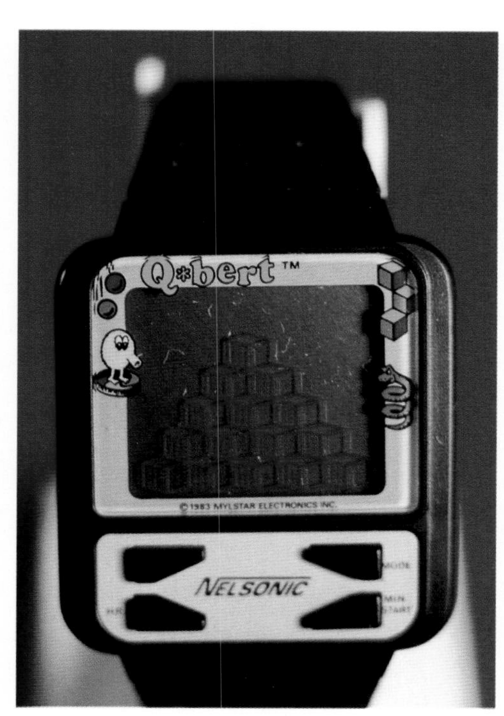

Q*bert watch by Nelsonic. $50 - $90.

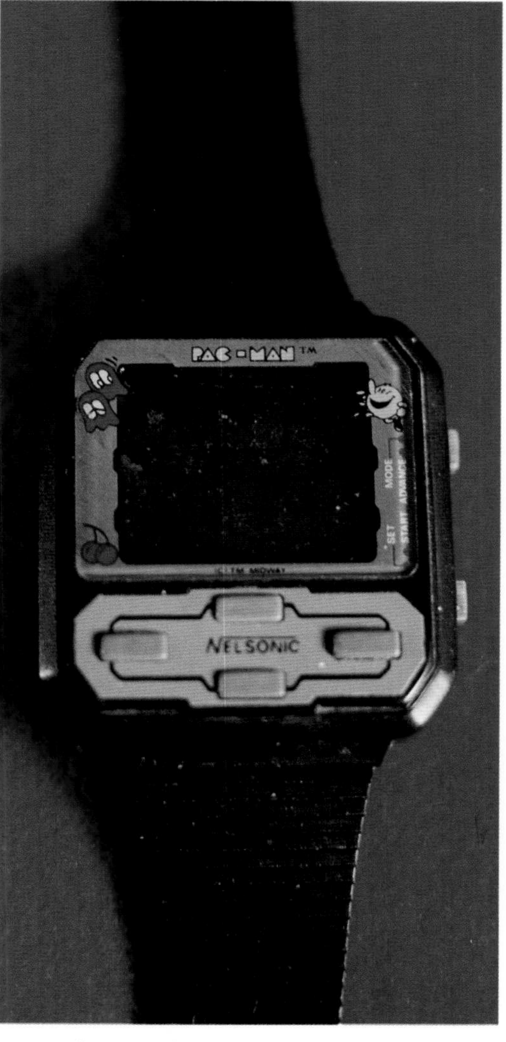

Pac-Man watch by Nelsonic. $70 - $95.

Sea Ranger game watch (manufacturer unknown). $45 - $95 complete in box.

Video Game Memorabilia

Some items in this section extend beyond the home video game realm, including a few items relating to popular arcade games. The reason that they are included here is that they often find their way into the collections of people who focus mostly on home gaming items. Many items listed here, as well as some other places in this book, are considered crossover collectibles — that is, things that are desired by collectors in more than one field of collecting.

Video Game Related Books

So What's Wrong With Playing Video Games? humor book. $8 - $15.

How To Master the Video Games. $8 - $15.

How To Win At Donkey Kong. $9 - $15.

How To Win Video Games. $8 - $15.

"Video Game" sheet music. $15 - $25.

Pac-Mania: The Official Pac-Man Joke Book. $10 - $15.

Secrets of the Video Game Super Stars. $8 - $15.

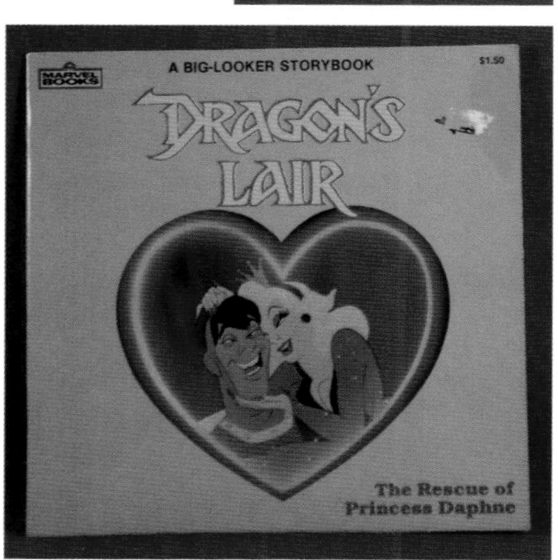

Dragon's Lair storybook. $10 -$18.

Scoring Big at Pac-Man. $9 - $15.

Mastering Pac-Man. $7 - $15.

How To Win At Pac-Man. $9 - $15.

Playing Ms. Pac-Man To Win. $10 - $15.

Video Game Related Magazines

Atari Connection —Fall 1984. $15 - $25.

Computer Games —February 1984. $10 - $20.

Electronic Games — November 1982. $10 - $20.

Joystik — November 1982. $10 - $20.

Videogaming Illustrated — August 1982. $20 - $35.

Electronic Games — December 1982. $10 - $20.

Electronic Fun — August 1983. $10 - $20.

Electronic Games — July 1982. $20 - $35.

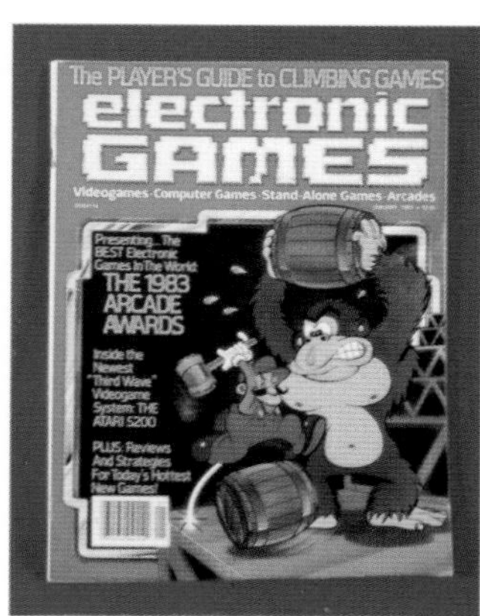

Electronic Games — January 1983. $10 - $20.

Video Games — August 1982. $10 - $20.

September 1982 issue of *MAD Magazine* featuring Pac-Man. $10 - $20.

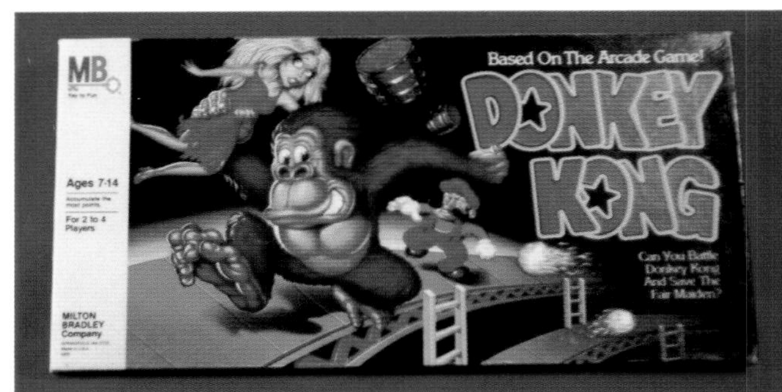

Donkey Kong board game from Milton Bradley. $20 - $35.

Video Game Board Games

Dragon's Lair board game from Milton Bradley. $35 - $75.

Video Games — December 1982. $10 - $20.

Berzerk board game from Milton Bradley. $25 - $39.

Centipede board game from Milton Bradley. $25 - $35.

Frogger board game from Milton Bradley. $25 - $35.

April 1982 issue of *MAD Magazine* featuring Space Invaders. $10 - $20.

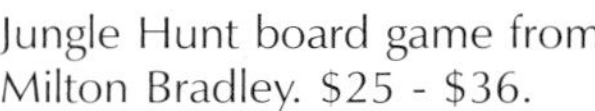

Jungle Hunt board game from Milton Bradley. $25 - $36.

Pac-Man board game from Milton Bradley. $15 - $30.

Pitfall board game from Milton Bradley. $25 - $39.

Turbo board game from Milton Bradley. $25 - $39.

Zaxxon board game from Milton Bradley. $15 - $30.

Q*bert board game from Parker Brothers. $29 - $39.

Popeye board game from Parker Brothers. $25 - $38.

Defender board game from Entex. $29 - $49.

Video Game Lunch Boxes

Atari lunch box. $40 - $60.

Q*bert lunch box. $35 - $50.

Dragon's Lair lunch box. $30 - $50.

Pac-Man puzzle game from Milton Bradley. $10 - $25.

Pac-Man portfolio folders are valued at $5 - $10 each.

Ms. Pac-Man portfolio folders are valued at $10 - $15 each.

Ms. Pac-Man activity book. $10 - $20.

Pac-Man jigsaw puzzle by Springbok. $20 - $35.

Plastic Pac-Man lunch box on the left ($35 - $50) is more difficult to locate than the Pac-Man metal box to the right ($15 - $35).

Pac-Man Memorabilia

Pac-Man card game from Milton Bradley. $10 - $20.

Pac-Man book and record sets are valued at $10 - $20 each.

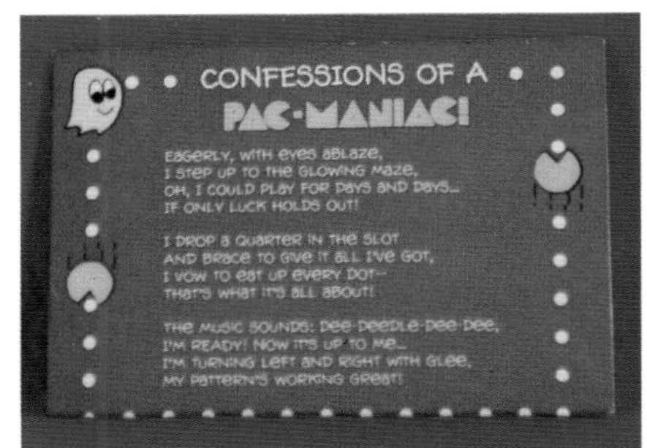

Pac-Man greeting card. $5 - $10.

Pac-Man wind up by Tomy. $30 - $50 mint on card.

Pac-Man PVC figurines by Coleco. $5 - $15 each.

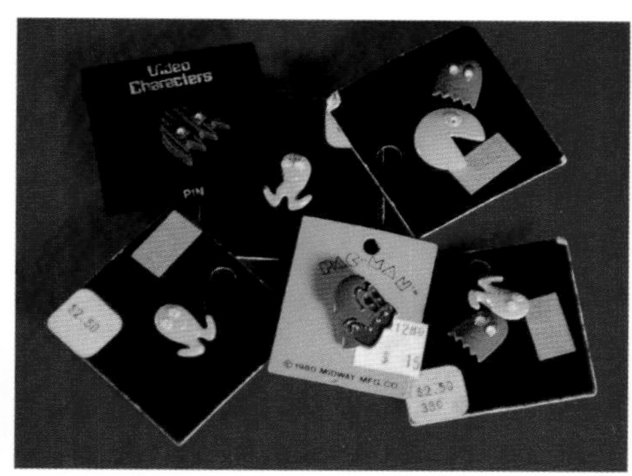

Assorted Pac-Man pins. $10 - $25 each.

Ms. Pac-Man figurines by Coleco. $15 - $35 each, mint on card.

This Pac-Man glass picture was most likely a prize from a carnival. $25 - $35.

Pac-Man and Ms. Pac-Man tooth-brushes. $15 - $25 each.

Ms. Pac-Man plush figures from Knickerbocker. $15 - $25 each.

Pac-Man watch. $40 - $60.

Pac-Man roller skates. $35 - $60.

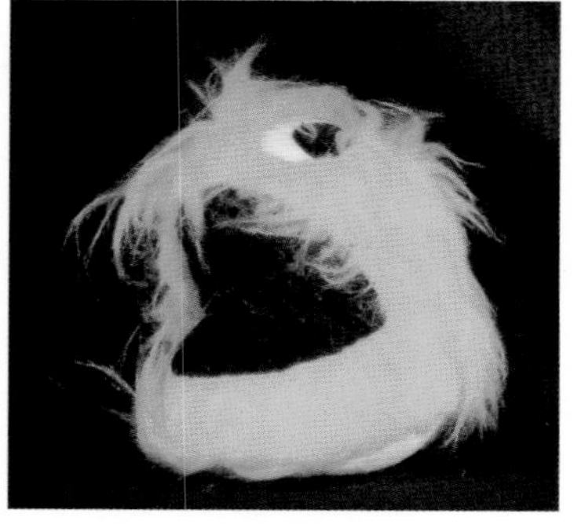

Unlicensed Pac-Man plush figure. $10 - $20.

Pac-Man vitamins. $25 - $50 unused in box.

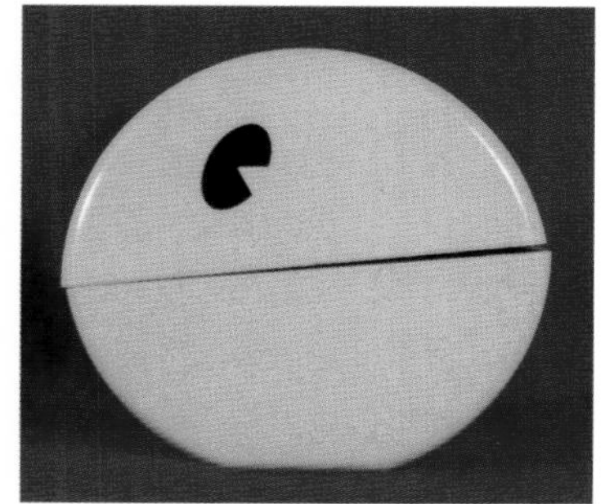

Pac-Man telephone. $40 - $75.

Pac-Man rubber figures by Ben Cooper. $15 - $30 each.

Pac-Men noodles from Japan. $25 - $45.

Pac-Man Panic game by Ideal. $35 - $65 mint in package.

Pac-Man tin container. $10 - $20.

Pac-Man championship mug / quarter holder. $20 - $35.

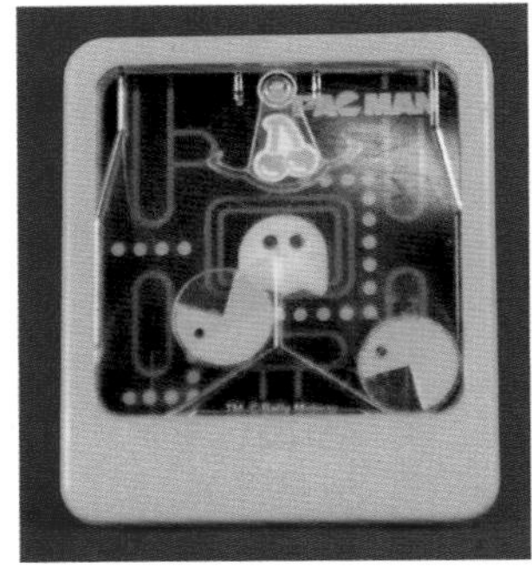

Pac-Man game by Tomy. $10 - $20.

Pac-Man plastic bowl by Deka. $15 - $35.

Baby Pac-Man Slurpee cup from 7-Eleven. $20 - $35.

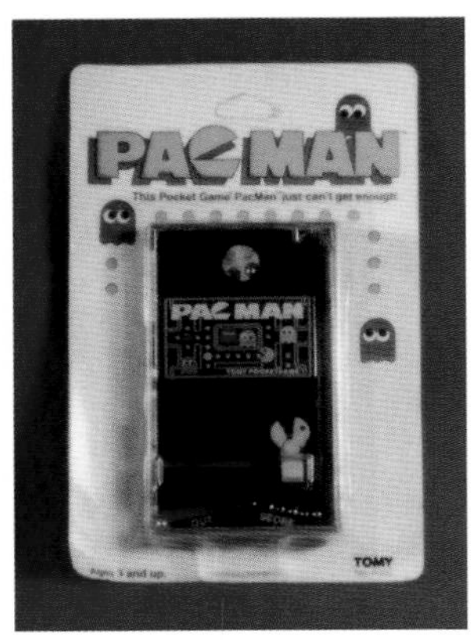

Mechanical Pac-Man game by Tomy. $25 - $45 mint on card.

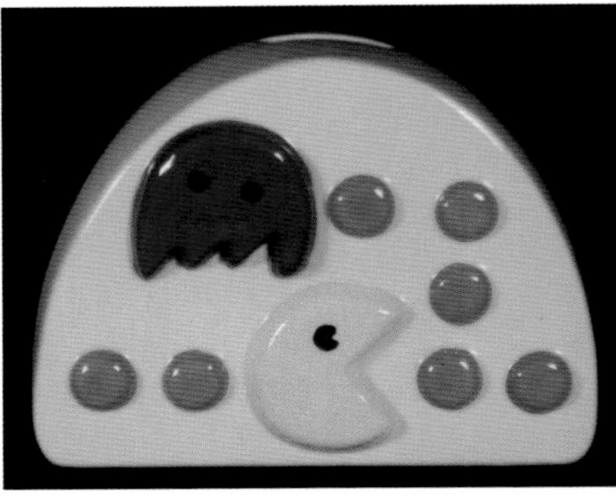

Unlicensed Pac-Man ceramic bank. $20 - $30.

Pac-Man mugs and glasses will generally fetch $10 - $15 each.

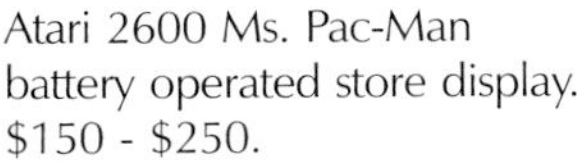

Atari 2600 Ms. Pac-Man battery operated store display. $150 - $250.

Donkey Kong Memorabilia

Donkey Kong card game by Milton Bradley. $15 - $25.

Donkey Kong puzzle by Milton Bradley. $15 - $25.

Donkey Kong mugs. $10 - $25 each.

Donkey Kong penny bank.
$25 - $35.

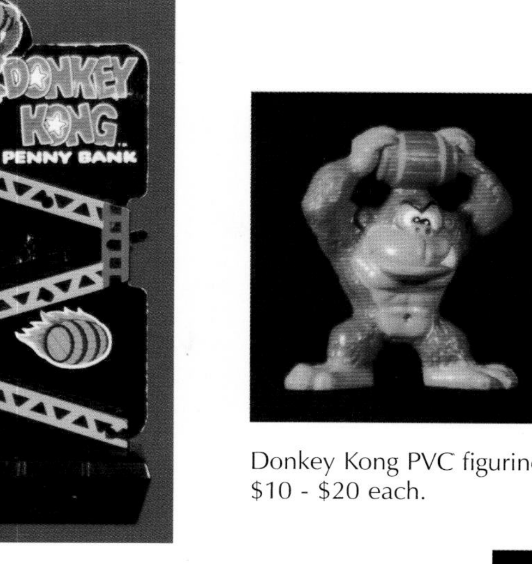

Donkey Kong PVC figurines by Coleco.
$10 - $20 each.

Plastic Donkey Kong plate. $15 - $25.

Donkey Kong PVC figurine by Coleco. $25 - $35 mint on card.

Donkey Kong plush toys. $15 - $35 each.

One style of Donkey Kong portfolio folder. $10 - $15 each.

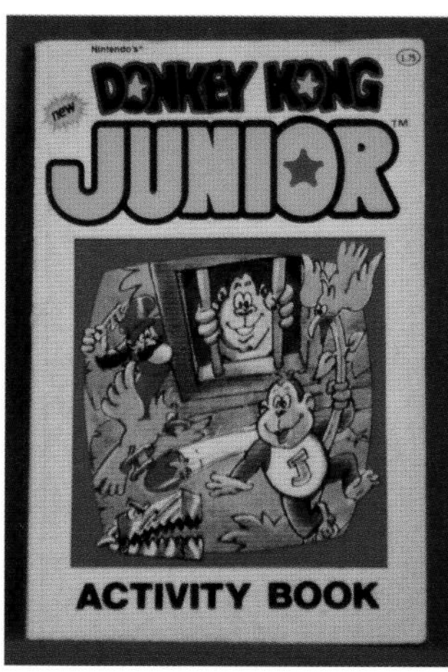

Donkey Kong Junior activity book. $10 - $20.

Large size Donkey Kong plush toy. $25 - $39.

Donkey Kong puffy stickers. $10 - $15.

Donkey Kong Junior cereal premiums. $30 - $50 each.

Q*bert Memorabilia

Q*bert puzzle by APC. $20 - $30.

Q*bert card sliding puzzle. $25 - $35 mint on card.

Q*bert wind up by Kenner. $35 - $55 mint on card.

Another Q*bert puzzle by APC. $20 - $30.

Q*bert card flying disc. $45 - $75 mint in package.

Q*bert PVC figurines by Kenner. $10 - $18 each.

Q*bert PVC figurine by Kenner. $20 - $40 mint on card.

Q*bert card game by Parker Brothers. $15 - $25.

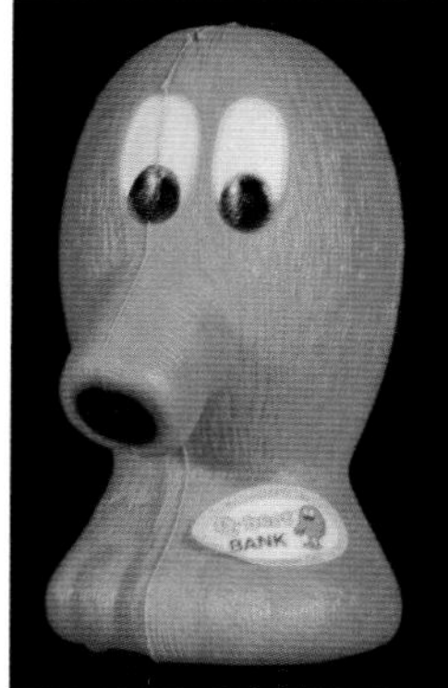

Plastic Q*bert bank. $25 - $35.

*The Adventures of Q*bert* book. $10 - $20.

Assorted Video Game Memorabilia

Various video game trading cards will bring $15 - $50 per complete set.

Frogger puzzle by Milton Bradley. $15 - $25.

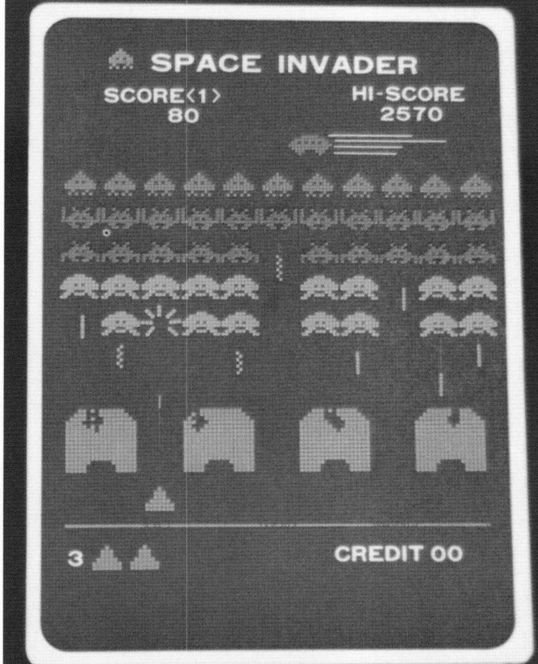

Space Invaders pencil board from Japan. $20 - $40.

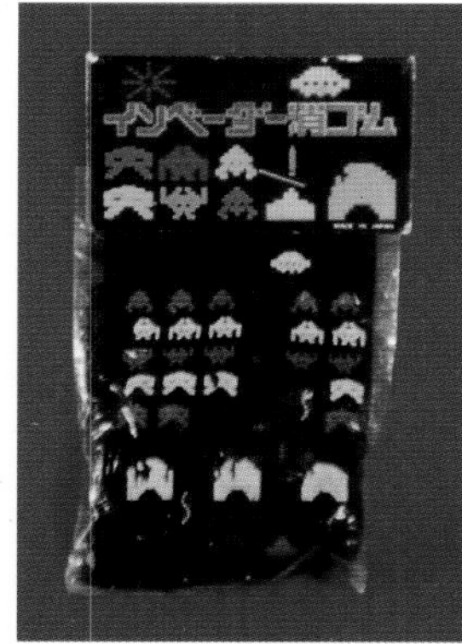

Space Invaders figural erasers from Japan. $25 - $40.

Party Invaders centerpiece. $15 - $25 unused.

Atari halloween decorations were made for several different games. $15 - $35 each.

Asteroids book and audio cassette set. $15 - $30.

Atari Olympic promotional pin. $15 - $40.

Activision promotional hockey puck. $50 - $90.

Gorf Space Cadet medal, similar to the Activision patch, was earned by photographing high scores. $25 - $40.

Imagic Numb Thumb Club membership card. $40 - $60.

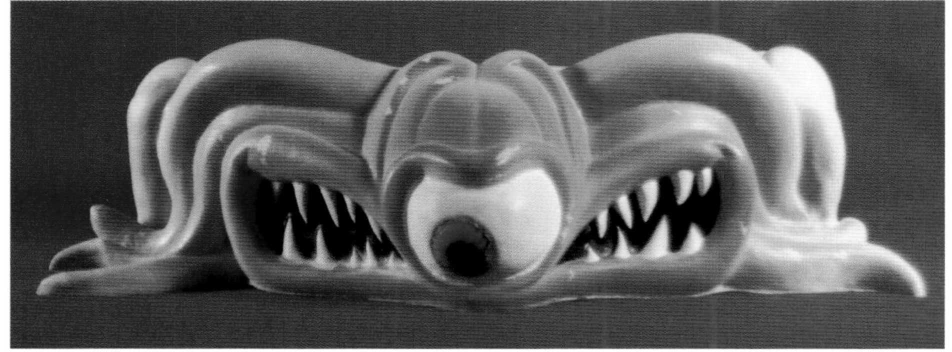

This ominous looking beast is actually a video game storage unit. $30 - $45.

Shirts and other clothing items related to classic video games will bring $20 - $50 today.

Robotron 2084 Rub N Play transfers from Colorforms. $18 - $35.

Tomy Tron Cine Sticker from Japan. $10 - $15.

Recommended Reading

Books

Digital Press Collector's Guide. Pompton Lakes, New Jersey. www.digitpress.com. An interesting and extensive book compiled by a number of prominent collectors. They also produce a bi-monthly fanzine.

Herman, Leonard. *Phoenix: The Rise and Fall of Video Games*. Springfield, New Jersey: Rolenta Press. www.rolentapress.com. Hands down the best book to date on the history of classic video games.

Websites

Arcade Village — Play classic arcade games on your own computer! www.arcadevillage.com
Atari Gaming Headquarters — Information on all things Atari. www.atarihq.com
Billy Galaxy's site — Correspond with the author! www.billygalaxy.com
Classic Gaming Expo — Organizers of the aforementioned event. www.cgexpo.com
Clint's Handheld Webpage — The best site around for handheld games! http://zappa.brainiac.com/cdyer
Hozer Video Games — Manufacturer of NEW titles for classic systems! www.netway.com/~hozervideo
Intellivision Exhibition — Nice looking site about Intellivision games. www.hotcom.com/intellivision
Magnavox Odyssey site — All about the first home gaming system ever. www.run.to/odyssey
Video Game Advertisement Archive — Tons of old video game advertisements. http://vgaa.cjb.net
Video Game Museum — Covers just about everything. www.vgmuseum.com

Price Guide

Atari 2600 Software

Game	Manufacturer	Notes	Cart Only	W/ Instructions	Complete in Box	New
32 in 1	Atari		$35	$40	n/a	n/a
3D Tic-Tac-Toe	Atari	Picture Label	$9	$13	$20	$30
3D Tic-Tac-Toe	Atari	Text Label	$7	$11	$18	$28
3D Tic-Tac-Toe	Sears		$15	$20	$35	$45
A Game of Concentration	Atari	Picture Label	$11	$15	$25	$32
Acid Drop	Salu		$15	$20	$27	$35
Action Force	Parker Bros.		$25	$33	$51	$65
Action Pak	Atari		n/a	n/a	$65	$95
Adventure	Atari	Picture Label	$8	$12	$40	$65
Adventure	Atari	Text Label	$8	$12	$40	$65
Adventure	Sears	Text Label	$8	$14	$45	$75
Adventure	Sears	Picture Label	$16	$22	$54	$75
Adventures of Tron	Mattel		$15	$21	$35	$49
Adventures on GX-12	Telegames		$10	$15	$20	$25
Air Raiders	Mattel		$8	$11	$16	$22
Air Raiders	INTV	White Label	$9	$12	$17	$25
Air Raiders	Telegames		$10	$15	$20	$25
Air-Sea Battle	Atari	Picture Label	$3	$5	$10	$15
Air-Sea Battle	Atari	Text Label	$3	$5	$10	$15
Air-Sea Battle	Atari	02 Label	$7	$10	$18	$27
Airlock	Data Age		$9	$13	$15	$19
Alien	20th Century Fox		$15	$20	$45	$65
Alpha Beam with Ernie	Atari		$10	$14	$20	$30
Amidar	Parker Bros.		$6	$9	$14	$19
Arcade Golf	Sears		$13	$19	$35	$50
Arcade Pinball	Sears		$6	$10	$20	$30
Armor Ambush	Mattel		$6	$8	$12	$15
Armor Ambush	Telegames		$10	$15	$20	$25
Artiller Duel	Xonox		$35	$40	$68	$85
Artillery Duel / Chuck Norris Superkicks	Xonox		$25	$35	$65	$75
Artillery Duel / Ghost Manor	Xonox		$45	$55	$85	$100
Artillery Duel / Spike's Peak	Xonox		$35	$45	$75	$95
Assault	Bomb		$125	$150	$200	$225
Asterix	Atari	Red Label	$35	$42	$58	$65
Asteroids	Atari	Picture Label	$3	$4	$9	$15
Asteroids	Atari	Red Label	$9	$12	$20	$24
Asteroids	Atari	Silver Label	$12	$14	$19	$20
Asteroids	Sears	64 Games	$4	$7	$15	$25
Asteroids	Sears	66 Games	$8	$12	$20	$30
Astroblast	Mattel		$4	$6	$9	$13
Atari Video Cube	Atari		$40	$48	$75	$110
Atlantis	Imagic	Blue Label	$9	$13	$20	$25
Atlantis	Imagic	Day Sky	$6	$9	$15	$22
Atlantis	Imagic	Night Sky	$5	$8	$14	$20
Atlantis	Imagic	Text Label	$5	$8	$14	$20
Bachelor Party	Mystique	Adult	$35	$40	$50	$60
Bachelor Party / Gigolo	Playaround	Adult	$50	$60	$75	$95
Bachelorette Party / Burning Desire	Playaround	Adult	$50	$60	$75	$95
Back to School Pak	Atari		n/a	n/a	$65	$95
Backgammon	Atari	Picture Label	$8	$11	$16	$25
Backgammon	Atari	Text Label	$6	$9	$14	$22
Backgammon	Sears	Text Label	$15	$22	$45	$68
Bank Heist	20th Century Fox		$25	$32	$45	$65
Barnstorming	Activision		$7	$10	$16	$20
Baseball	INTV	White Label	$5	$8	$12	$18
Baseball	Sears	Text Label	$5	$9	$19	$28
Baeball	Telegames		$10	$15	$20	$25
Basic Math	Atari	Text Label	$9	$13	$20	$30
Basic Programming	Atari	Picture Label	$9	$13	$20	$30
Basic Programming	Atari	Text Label	$8	$12	$19	$30
Basketball	Atari	Picture Label	$4	$6	$10	$15

Game	Manufacturer	Notes	Cart Only	W/ Instructions	Complete in Box	New
Basketball	Atari	Text Label	$3	$5	$9	$15
Basketball	Sears	Text Label	$6	$10	$18	$25
Battlezone	Atari		$5	$7	$9	$10
Beamrider	Activision		$25	$32	$45	$65
Beany Bopper	20th Century Fox		$10	$15	$25	$35
Beat 'Em & Eat 'Em	Mystique	Adult	$35	$40	$50	$60
Beat 'Em & Eat 'Em / Lady in Wading	Playaround	Adult	$50	$60	$75	$95
Berenstain Bears	Coleco		$100	$120	$250	$300
Bermuda Triangle	Data Age		$9	$13	$21	$28
Berzerk	Atari		$4	$6	$11	$15
Berzerk	Sears		$6	$10	$25	$39
Big Bird's Egg Catch	Atari		$10	$14	$20	$30
Black Jack	Atari	51 Label	$9	$12	$19	$25
Black Jack	Atari	Text Label	$7	$9	$15	$22
Black Jack	Sears	Picture Label	$10	$14	$22	$30
Black Jack	Sears	Text Label	$7	$10	$19	$30
Blueprint	CBS		$12	$16	$25	$35
BMX Airmaster	Atari		$150	$175	$220	$250
BMX Airmaster	TNT		$15	$20	$25	$35
Bogey Blaster	Telegames		$10	$15	$20	$25
Bowling	Atari	Picture Label	$5	$7	$11	$15
Bowling	Atari	Text Label	$4	$6	$10	$15
Bowling	Sears	Text Label	$9	$15	$36	$45
Boxing	Activision		$5	$7	$10	$15
Boxing	Activision	Blue Label	$7	$9	$12	$15
Brain Games	Atari	Picture label	$9	$13	$20	$29
Brain Games	Atari	Text Label	$7	$11	$19	$27
Brain Games	Sears		$18	$25	$35	$45
Breakaway IV	Sears	Picture Label	$6	$9	$23	$30
Breakaway IV	Sears	Text Label	$4	$7	$22	$30
Breakout	Atari	Picture Label	$5	$7	$10	$15
Breakout	Atari	Text Label	$5	$7	$10	$15
Breakout	Atari	Orange Label	$25	$27	$30	$35
Bridge	Activision		$9	$13	$21	$27
Buck Rogers - Planet of Zoom	Sega		$12	$17	$25	$35
Bugs	Data Age		$8	$11	$15	$20
Bump 'N Jump	INTV	White Label	$20	$23	$30	$35
Bump 'N Jump	Mattel		$15	$18	$25	$30
Bump 'N Jump	Telegames		$10	$15	$20	$25
Bumper Bash	Spectravision		$115	$140	$200	$235
Burgertime	Mattel		$10	$12	$18	$25
Burgertime	Telegames		$10	$15	$20	$25
Burning Desire	Mystique		$90	$95	$135	$150
Burning Desire / Bachelorette Party	Playaround	Adult	$50	$60	$75	$95
Cake Walk	Commavid		$150	$175	$265	$295
California Games	Epyx		$8	$11	$15	$20
Cannon Man	Sears	Text Label	$30	$40	$75	$98
Canyon Bomber	Atari	Picture Label	$6	$8	$12	$18
Canyon Bomber	Atari	Text Label	$6	$8	$12	$18
Canyon Bomber	Sears	Picture Label	$15	$20	$35	$47
Capture	Sears	Text Label	$9	$15	$25	$35
Carnival	Coleco		$6	$9	$16	$23
Casino	Atari	Picture Label	$6	$9	$15	$22
Casino	Atari	Text Label	$5	$8	$14	$22
Cathouse Blues / Philly Flasher	Playaround	Adult	$50	$60	$75	$95
Centipede	Atari		$5	$7	$10	$15
Challenge of Nexar	Spectravision		$13	$19	$29	$35
Championship Soccer	Atari		$5	$7	$12	$18
Chase	Sears	Picture Label	$15	$20	$35	$49
Chase	Sears	Text Label	$9	$14	$25	$35
Chase the Chuckwagon	Spectravision		$200	$225	$395	$415
Checkers	Activision		$15	$20	$35	$45
Checkers	Sears	Text Label	$10	$16	$30	$43
China Syndrome	Spectravision		$15	$20	$34	$39
Chopper Command	Activision		$6	$8	$13	$19
Chopper Command	Activision	Blue Label	$9	$11	$15	$19
Chopper Command	Salu	white label	$11	$13	$18	$20
Chuck Norris Superkicks / Artillery Duel	Xonox		$25	$35	$65	$75
Chuck Norris Superkicks / Spike's Peak	Xonox		$50	$60	$100	$130
Circus	Sears	Text Label	$6	$10	$17	$25
Circus Atari	Atari	Picture Label	$5	$7	$12	$16
Circus Atari	Atari	Text Label	$4	$6	$11	$16
Coconuts	Telesys		$9	$12	$19	$25
Codebreaker	Atari	Picture Label	$9	$13	$20	$26

Game	Manufacturer	Notes	Cart Only	W/ Instructions	Complete in Box	New
Codebreaker	Atari	Text Label	$7	$11	$18	$26
Codebreaker	Sears	Text Label	$10	$15	$25	$35
Combat	Atari	01 Label	$5	$7	$15	$20
Combat	Atari	Picture Label	$1	$2	$5	$9
Combat	Atari	Text Label	$1	$2	$5	$9
Commando	Activision		$10	$14	$20	$25
Commando Raid	US Games		$6	$9	$15	$22
Communist Mutants From Space	Starpath	Cassette	$9	$12	$15	$22
Condor Attack	Ultravision		$150	$175	$250	$295
Congo Bongo	Sega		$10	$14	$25	$32
Cookie Monster Munch	Atari		$10	$14	$20	$30
Cosmic Ark	Imagic	Text Label	$5	$7	$12	$19
Cosmic Ark	Imagic	Picture Label	$6	$8	$13	$19
Cosmic Commuter	Activision		$25	$31	$45	$50
Cosmic Corridor	Zimag		$35	$43	$70	$95
Cosmic Creeps	Telesys		$10	$15	$25	$32
Cosmic Swarm	Commavid		$65	$75	$110	$145
Crackpots	Activision		$10	$14	$25	$35
Crash Dive	20th Century Fox		$15	$22	$34	$39
Crazy Climber	Atari		$170	$190	$275	$325
Cross Force	Spectravision		$25	$30	$45	$60
Crossbow	Atari	red label	$10	$14	$25	$30
Cruise Missile	Froggo		$10	$13	$15	$18
Crypts of Chaos	20th Century Fox		$25	$32	$45	$65
Crystal Castles	Atari	w/ Bentley Bear logo	$7	$10	$15	$20
Crystal Castles	Atari	no Bentley Bear logo	$15	$20	$25	$35
Custer's Revenge	Mystique	Adult	$50	$55	$65	$75
Dare Diver	Sears		$25	$35	$50	$70
Dark Cavern	Mattel		$6	$9	$12	$15
Dark Chambers	Atari	Red Label	$6	$8	$9	$10
Deadly Disk	Telegames		$15	$20	$25	$30
Deadly Duck	20th Century Fox		$9	$13	$20	$29
Death Trap	Avalon Hill		$75	$85	$110	$130
Decathlon	Activision		$5	$7	$12	$17
Defender	Atari		$3	$4	$9	$13
Defender	Sears	Picture Label	$4	$7	$18	$25
Defender II	Atari		$8	$11	$15	$17
Demolition Herby	Telesys		$75	$95	$165	$195
Demon Attack	Imagic	Blue Label	$10	$12	$15	$17
Demon Attack	Imagic	Picture Label	$4	$6	$10	$15
Demon Attack	Imagic	Text Label	$5	$7	$11	$15
Demons to Diamonds	Atari	Picture Label	$5	$7	$12	$14
Demons to Diamonds	Sears	Picture Label	$13	$20	$40	$65
Desert Falcon	Atari	Red Label	$9	$12	$15	$19
Dice Puzzle	Panda		$50	$65	$95	$120
Dig Dug	Atari		$7	$7	$9	$10
Dishaster	Zimag		$35	$43	$70	$95
Dodge 'Em	Atari	Picture Label	$6	$8	$12	$16
Dodge 'Em	Atari	Text Label	$5	$7	$11	$16
Dodger Cars	Sears	Text Label	$10	$15	$29	$39
Dolphin	Activision		$9	$13	$20	$25
Donkey Kong	Atari	Red Label	$6	$9	$15	$20
Donkey Kong	Coleco		$3	$4	$9	$15
Donkey Kong Jr.	Atari	Red Label	$7	$10	$15	$20
Donkey Kong Jr.	Coleco		$6	$9	$15	$25
Double Dragon	Activision		$10	$14	$20	$25
Double Dunk	Atari	Red Label	$9	$13	$19	$22
Dragonfire	Imagic	Picture Label	$6	$9	$15	$20
Dragonfire	Imagic	Text Label	$7	$10	$16	$20
Dragon Stomper	Starpath	Cassette	$15	$20	$27	$35
Dragster	Activision		$4	$6	$12	$19
E.T.	Atari		$5	$7	$10	$15
Earth Dies Screaming	20th Century Fox		$35	$45	$65	$79
Eggomania	US Games		$10	$15	$20	$25
Encounter at L-5	Data Age		$9	$13	$18	$22
Enduro	Activision		$5	$7	$12	$15
Enduro	Activision	Blue Label	$8	$10	$15	$19
Entombed	US Games		$16	$20	$29	$35
Escape From the Mindmaster	Starpath		$15	$19	$25	$29
Espial	Tigervision		$50	$60	$95	$115
Exocet	Panda		$50	$65	$95	$120
Fantastic Voyage	20th Century Fox		$15	$20	$35	$47
Fast Eddie	20th Century Fox		$10	$15	$25	$35
Fast Food	Telesys		$8	$12	$16	$20

Game	Manufacturer	Notes	Cart Only	W/ Instructions	Complete in Box	New
Fatal Run	Atari		$25	$30	$40	$50
Fathom	Imagic		$15	$21	$29	$39
Final Approach	Apollo		$16	$21	$29	$39
Fire Fighter	Imagic		$8	$11	$16	$20
Fire Fly	Mythicon		$9	$15	$39	$49
Fireball	Starpath	Cassette	$10	$13	$18	$20
Fishing Derby	Activision		$6	$9	$15	$20
Flag Capture	Atari	Text Label	$7	$11	$20	$29
Flash Gordon	20th Century Fox		$15	$22	$39	$55
Football	Atari	Picture Label	$3	$5	$9	$14
Football	Atari	Text Label	$3	$5	$9	$14
Football	INTV	White Label	$6	$9	$15	$19
Football	Sears	Text Label	$5	$9	$25	$32
Franeknstein's Monster	Data Age		$29	$35	$59	$75
Freeway	Activision		$4	$6	$12	$16
Frogger	Parker Brothers		$5	$7	$15	$20
Frogger	Starpath	Cassette	$45	$55	$75	$85
Frogger 2	Parker Brothers		$35	$45	$65	$85
Frogs & Flies	Mattel		$6	$9	$15	$20
Frogs & Flies	Telegames		$10	$15	$20	$25
Front Line	Coleco		$12	$17	$29	$45
Frostbite	Activision		$11	$16	$28	$36
Frostbite	Activision	White Label	$13	$16	$25	$31
Fun with Numbers	Atari	Picture Label	$15	$20	$29	$35
G.I. Joe	Parker Brothers	Black & White Label	$7	$12	$19	$29
G.I. Joe	Parker Brothers	Full Color Label	$16	$21	$28	$29
Galaxian	Atari		$5	$7	$9	$10
Gangster Alley	Spectravision		$12	$16	$22	$32
Gas Hog	Spectravision		$100	$115	$165	$190
Ghost Manor / Artillery Duel	Xonox		$45	$55	$85	$100
Ghost Manor / Spike's Peak	Xonox		$15	$25	$45	$65
Ghostbusters	Activision		$16	$22	$35	$40
Ghostbusters	Activision	Blue Label	$19	$25	$38	$40
Ghostbusters II	Activision		$25	$30	$35	$40
Gigolo / Bachelor Party	Playaround	Adult	$50	$60	$75	$95
Glacier Patrol	Sunrise		$45	$55	$85	$110
Glacier Patrol	Telegames		$15	$20	$25	$35
Glib	Selchow & Righter		$150	$175	$250	$295
Golf	Atari	Picture Label	$5	$8	$15	$21
Golf	Atari	Text Label	$5	$8	$15	$21
Golf	Sears	Text Label	$7	$12	$21	$35
Gopher	U.S. Games		$12	$16	$25	$29
Gorf	CBS		$7	$11	$22	$29
Grand Prix	Activision		$5	$7	$13	$16
Grand Prix	Activision	Blue Label	$9	$11	$15	$16
Gravitar	Atari	Red Label	$6	$8	$9	$10
Gravitar	Atari	Silver Label	$75	$85	$150	$175
Great Escape	Bomb		$85	$100	$165	$190
Gremlins	Atari		$35	$45	$75	$95
Guardian	Apollo		$65	$75	$120	$150
Gunslinger	Sears	Text Label	$5	$9	$18	$27
Gyruss	Parker Bros.		$15	$21	$35	$45
Halloween	Wizard Video		$125	$150	$350	$450
Hangman	Atari	Picture Label	$10	$15	$25	$35
Harbor Escape	Panda		$50	$65	$95	$120
Haunted House	Atari	Picture Label	$5	$7	$12	$18
Haunted House	Sears	Picture Label	$15	$20	$35	$42
H.E.R.O.	Activision		$19	$25	$35	$41
Homerun	Atari	one word title	$9	$12	$17	$19
Home Run	Atari	Picture Label	$3	$5	$9	$14
Home Run	Atari	Text Label	$4	$6	$10	$14
Human Cannonball	Atari	Picture Label	$5	$8	$15	$22
Human Cannonball	Atari	Text Label	$5	$8	$15	$22
Hunt & Score	Atari	Text Label	$9	$14	$21	$29
I Want My Mommy	Zimag		$35	$43	$70	$95
Ice Hockey	Activision		$4	$6	$12	$15
Ice Hockey	Activision	Blue text label	$9	$11	$17	$18
Ikari Warriors	Atari		$60	$70	$90	$100
Indy 500	Atari	Picture Label	$5	$7	$12	$16
Indy 500	Atari	Text Label	$4	$6	$11	$16
Infiltrate	Apollo	Blue Label	$8	$13	$19	$25
Infiltrate	Apollo	Red Label	$12	$17	$25	$29
International Soccer	Mattel		$10	$14	$19	$24

Game	Manufacturer	Notes	Cart Only	W/ Instructions	Complete in Box	New
James Bond 007	Parker Bros.		$35	$45	$75	$95
Jawbreaker	Tigervision		$35	$44	$75	$95
Journey Escape	Data Age		$9	$13	$18	$20
Joust	Atari		$5	$7	$9	$10
Jr. Pac-Man	Atari	Red Label	$5	$7	$9	$10
Jungle Fever / Knight on the Town	Playaround	Adult	$50	$60	$75	$95
Jungle Hunt	Atari		$5	$7	$9	$10
Kaboom	Activision		$5	$7	$12	$14
Kaboom	Activision	Blue Label	$9	$11	$16	$17
Kangaroo	Atari		$5	$7	$9	$10
Karate	Froggo		$9	$11	$15	$17
Karate	Ultravision		$150	$170	$250	$285
Keystone Kapers	Activision		$6	$8	$12	$14
Keystone Kapers	Activision	Blue Label	$9	$11	$15	$17
Killer Satellites	Starpath	Cassette	$10	$13	$18	$21
King Kong	Tigervision		$35	$45	$75	$95
Klax	Atari		$40	$49	$65	$75
Knight on the Town / Jungle Fever	Playaround	Adult	$50	$60	$75	$95
Kool Aid Man	Mattel		$15	$22	$35	$50
Krull	Atari		$10	$15	$25	$35
Kung Fu Master	Activision		$12	$16	$21	$25
Kung Fu Superkicks	Telegames		$15	$20	$25	$30
Lady in Wading / Beat 'Em & Eat 'Em	Playaround	Adult	$50	$60	$75	$95
Laser Blast	Activision		$4	$6	$10	$14
Laser Gates	Imagic		$35	$43	$65	$75
Lochjaw	Apollo		$95	$120	$190	$215
Lock 'N Chase	Mattel		$5	$7	$12	$15
Lock 'N Chase	Telegames		$10	$15	$20	$25
London Blitz	Avalon Hill		$65	$77	$110	$135
Lost Luggage	Apollo	Blue Label	$9	$13	$22	$31
Lost Luggage	Apollo	Green Label	$9	$13	$22	$31
M.A.D.	U.S. Games		$13	$18	$29	$38
Magicard	Commavid		$750	$850	n/a	n/a
Mangia	Specctravision		$100	$120	$180	$195
Marauder	Tigervision		$50	$60	$95	$110
Marine Wars	Gakken		$39	$47	$85	$105
Marine Wars	Konami		$35	$45	$75	$95
Mario Bothers	Atari		$6	$8	$13	$15
MASH	20th Century Fox		$8	$13	$25	$35
Masters of the Universe	Mattel		$15	$21	$35	$50
Math	Sears	Text Label	$10	$16	$29	$45
Math Gran Prix	Atari	Text Label	$8	$12	$25	$34
Maze	Sears	Picture Label	$7	$12	$28	$45
Maze	Sears	Text Label	$9	$15	$32	$45
Maze Craze	Atari	Picture Label	$6	$8	$15	$20
Maze Craze	Atari	Text Label	$6	$8	$15	$20
Maze Mania	Sears	Text Label	$8	$15	$35	$49
Mega Force	20th Century Fox		$10	$17	$45	$70
Megamania	Activision		$5	$7	$12	$21
Megamania	Activision	Blue Label	$15	$18	$23	$25
Memory Match	Sears	Text Label	$11	$18	$35	$55
Midnight Magic	Atari	Red Label	$6	$8	$12	$14
Millipede	Atari		$8	$11	$15	$16
Miner 2049er	Tigervision		$25	$32	$49	$65
Miner 2049er 2	Tigervision		$75	$90	$155	$180
Mines of Minos	Commavid		$50	$60	$100	$140
Miniature Golf	Atari	Text Label	$13	$19	$35	$55
Missile Command	Atari	Picture Label	$3	$4	$8	$10
Missile Command	Sears	Text Label	$4	$6	$15	$25
Mogul Maniac	Amiga		$11	$17	$29	$35
Montezuma's Revenge	Parker Bros.		$30	$38	$65	$80
Moon Patrol	Atari		$6	$8	$10	$12
Moonsweeper	Imagic		$9	$14	$21	$30
Moonsweeper	Imagic	Blue Label	$18	$25	$35	$39
Motocross Racer	Xonox		$45	$52	$85	$100
Motorodeo	Atari		$100	$118	$180	$210
Mountain King	CBS		$15	$22	$36	$54
Mouse Trap	Atari	Red Label	$7	$10	$14	$15
Mouse Trap	Coleco		$5	$7	$12	$15
Mr. Do	Coleco		$25	$35	$50	$65
Mr. Do's Castle	Parker Bros.		$95	$115	$180	$215
Ms. Pac-Man	Atari		$5	$7	$9	$10
Music Machine	Sparrow		$500	$560	$690	$700
My Golf	HES		$25	$30	$45	$50

Game	Manufacturer	Notes	Cart Only	W/ Instructions	Complete in Box	New
Name This Game	US Games		$9	$14	$25	$39
Night Driver	Atari	Picture Label	$4	$6	$14	$19
Night Driver	Atari	Text Label	$3	$5	$13	$19
No Escape	Imagic		$14	$20	$36	$48
Obelix	Atari		$55	$65	$86	$105
Off the Wall	Atari	Red Label	$15	$20	$29	$35
Ocean City Defender	Taiwan		$15	$16	$20	$25
Oink	Activision		$10	$15	$25	$35
Omega Race	CBS		$10	$16	$39	$50
Oscar's Trash Race	Atari		$15	$20	$35	$50
Othello	Atari	Picture Label	$6	$9	$19	$35
Othello	Atari	Text Label	$7	$10	$20	$35
Othello	Sears	Text Label	$18	$25	$49	$65
Outer Space	Sears	Picture Label	$7	$11	$26	$39
Outer Space	Sears	Text Label	$6	$10	$25	$39
Outlaw	Atari	Picture Label	$4	$6	$12	$25
Outlaw	Atari	Text Label	$3	$5	$11	$25
Pac-Man	Atari		$3	$4	$9	$15
Pac-Man	Sears	Picture Label	$4	$7	$20	$35
Party Mix	Starpath		$49	$59	$85	$95
Pele's Soccer	Atari	Picture Label	$6	$10	$20	$35
Pengo	Atari		$35	$45	$75	$95
Pete Rose Baseball	Absolute		$15	$20	$25	$30
Phaser Patrol	Starpath	Cassette	$10	$15	see "Supercharger"	
Philly Flasher / Cathouse Blues	Playaround	Adult	$50	$60	$75	$95
Phoenix	Atari		$5	$7	$9	$10
Pick N' Pile	Ubi Soft		$20	$25	$30	$35
Picnic	US Games		$19	$25	$35	$43
Piece o' Cake	US Games		$15	$21	$35	$50
Pigs in Space	Atari		$25	$32	$50	$70
Pitfall	Activision		$6	$8	$18	$25
Pitfall	Activision	Blue Text Label	$10	$12	$20	$25
Pitfall II	Activision		$15	$20	$25	$30
Plaque Attack	Activision		$12	$17	$28	$37
Poker Plus	Sears	Text Label	$7	$12	$30	$45
Polaris	Tigervision		$40	$50	$85	$110
Pole Position	Atari		$5	$7	$9	$10
Pole Positn	Atari	Label Error	$15	$17	$19	$20
Pong Sports	Sears	Text Label	$5	$9	$21	$35
Pooyan	Gakken		$39	$47	$75	$95
Pooyan	Konami		$35	$42	$65	$85
Popeye	Parker Bros.		$12	$18	$35	$55
Porky's	20th Century Fox		$12	$18	$29	$45
Pressure Cooker	Activision		$15	$20	$35	$49
Private Eye	Activsion		$15	$20	$25	$30
Q*bert	Atari	Red Label	$6	$8	$12	$15
Q*bert	Parker Bros.		$6	$8	$15	$25
Q*bert's Qubes	Parker Bros.		$190	$215	$300	$340
Quadrun	Atari		$200	$230	$350	$380
Quest For Quintana Roo	Telegames		$20	$25	$30	$35
Quick Step	Imagic		$15	$21	$35	$49
Rabbit Transit	Starpath	Cassette	$49	$59	$85	$95
Race	Sears	Text Label	$5	$9	$25	$35
Racing Pak	Atari		n/a	n/a	$65	$95
Racquetball	Apollo		$10	$15	$25	$35
Radar Lock	Atari		$10	$15	$20	$25
Raft Rider	US Games		$29	$37	$49	$65
Raiders Lost Ark	Atari	Label Error	$15	$19	$30	$35
Raiders of the Lost Ark	Atari		$6	$11	$22	$34
Ram It	Telesys		$45	$55	$90	$110
Rampage	Activision		$15	$20	$25	$30
Reactor	Parker Bros.		$6	$9	$16	$25
RealSports Baseball	Atari		$4	$6	$10	$15
RealSports Boxing	Atari		$8	$11	$15	$19
RealSports Football	Atari		$4	$8	$11	$15
RealSports Soccer	Atari		$6	$9	$15	$22
Realsports Tennis	Atari		$5	$8	$12	$18
RealSports Volleyball	Atari		$6	$9	$13	$16
Rescue Terra I	Venture Vision		$140	$160	$240	$270
Revenge of the Beefsteak Tomatoes	20th Century Fox		$15	$21	$34	$49
Riddle of the Sphynx	Imagic		$6	$9	$15	$22
River Raid	Activision		$6	$9	$14	$19

Game	Manufacturer	Notes	Cart Only	W/ Instructions	Complete in Box	New
River Raid	Activision	Blue Text Label	$9	$12	$15	$19
River Raid 2	Activision		$15	$20	$29	$35
Road Runner	Atari	Red Label	$15	$20	$35	$45
Robin Hood	Xonox		$50	$56	$95	$115
Robin Hood / Sir Lancelot	Xonox		$85	$112	$150	$175
Robin Hood / Super Kung Fu	Xonox		$55	$70	$130	$150
Robot Tank	Activision		$7	$10	$15	$19
Robot Tank	Activision	Blue Text Label	$14	$17	$19	$21
Roc'N Rope	Coleco		$25	$30	$39	$49
Room of Doom	Commavid		$50	$60	$110	$150
Rubik's Cube	Atari		$85	$100	$175	$195
Scuba Diver	Panda		$50	$65	$95	$120
Sea Hawk	Froggo		$10	$13	$16	$18
Sea Hawk	Panda		$50	$65	$95	$120
Sea Hunt	Froggo		$10	$13	$16	$18
Seaquest	Activision		$6	$9	$19	$25
Secret Quest	Atari	Red Label	$12	$16	$25	$29
Sentinel	Atari	Red Label	$10	$14	$22	$27
Shark Attack	Apollo		$15	$20	$29	$45
Shooting Gallery	Imagic		$21	$27	$49	$60
Shuttle Orbiter	Avalon Hill		$80	$100	$170	$195
Sir Lancelot	Xonox		$60	$65	$95	$115
Sir Lancelot / Robin Hood	Xonox		$85	$112	$150	$175
Skate Boardin'	Absolute		$10	$15	$20	$25
Skeet Shoot	Apollo		$19	$25	$35	$50
Skiing	Activision		$5	$7	$12	$15
Sky Diver	Atari	Picture Label	$6	$10	$20	$30
Sky Diver	Atari	Text Label	$5	$9	$19	$30
Sky Jinks	Activision		$6	$9	$15	$19
Slot Machine	Atari	Text Label	$15	$20	$35	$45
Slot Racers	Atari	Picture Label	$6	$9	$18	$25
Slot Racers	Atari	Text Label	$5	$8	$17	$25
Slots	Sears	Text Label	$25	$35	$55	$70
Smurfs	Coleco		$15	$20	$35	$50
Smurfs Save the Day	Coleco		$100	$120	see "Kid Vid" controller	
Sneak N' Peek	US Games		$7	$10	$19	$26
Snoopy & the Red Baron	Atari		$35	$45	$75	$89
Soccer	Sears	Text Label	$10	$17	$30	$42
Solar Fox	CBS		$8	$13	$29	$39
Solar Storm	Imagic		$15	$21	$35	$49
Solaris	Atari	Red Label	$5	$7	$9	$10
Sorcerer	Mythicon		$10	$18	$39	$50
Sorcerer's Apprentice	Atari		$18	$25	$49	$65
Space Attack	Mattel		$4	$6	$10	$12
Space Canyon	Panda		$50	$65	$95	$120
Space Cavern	Apollo	Blue Label	$9	$14	$20	$25
Space Cavern	Apollo	Red Label	$10	$15	$21	$25
Space Chase	Apollo		$10	$15	$20	$25
Space Combat	Sears	Picture Label	$9	$15	$35	$50
Space Combat	Sears	Text Label	$8	$14	$34	$60
Space Invaders	Atari	Picture Label	$3	$4	$8	$12
Space Invaders	Atari	Text Label	$3	$4	$8	$12
Space Invaders	Sears	Picture Label	$5	$9	$19	$28
Space Invaders	Sears	Text Label	$4	$8	$18	$28
Space Jockey	US Games		$5	$9	$14	$18
Space Shuttle	Activision		$10	$15	$20	$22
Space Shuttle	Activision	Blue Label	$13	$17	$22	$23
Space War	Atari	Picture Label	$5	$8	$15	$25
Space War	Atari	Text Label	$5	$8	$15	$25
Spacemaster X-7	20th Century Fox		$50	$65	$95	$120
Speedway II	Sears	Picture Label	$9	$13	$25	$35
Speedway II	Sears	Text Label	$4	$8	$20	$35
Spelling	Sears	Text Label	$15	$22	$45	$68
Spider Fighter	Activision		$7	$10	$18	$24
Spiderdroid	Froggo		$9	$11	$15	$17
Spiderman	Parker Bros.		$6	$10	$25	$35
Spike's Peak / Artillery Duel	Xonox		$35	$45	$75	$95
Spike's Peak / Chuck Norris Superkicks	Xonox		$50	$60	$100	$130
Spike's Peak / Ghost Manor	Xonox		$15	$25	$45	$65
Spitfire Attack	Milton Bradley		$15	$21	see "Flight Commander" controller	
Sprintmaster	Atari	Red Label	$15	$19	$29	$35

Game	Manufacturer	Notes	Cart Only	W/ Instructions	Complete in Box	New
Spy Hunter	Sega		$35	$44	$75	$95
Squeeze Box	US Games		$12	$16	$29	$38
Sssnake	Data Age		$9	$14	$22	$28
Stampede	Activision		$5	$8	$15	$23
Star Fox	Mythicon		$10	$18	$39	$49
Star Raiders	Atari		$3	$6	$10	$12
Star Raiders	Sears	Picture Label	$5	$9	$25	$39
Star Ship	Atari	03 Label	$9	$13	$25	$35
Star Ship	Atari	Text Label	$10	$14	$25	$35
Star Strike	INTV	White Label	$30	$36	$65	$85
Star Strike	Mattel		$35	$42	$75	$95
Star Trek	Sega		$16	$21	$31	$36
Star Voyager	Imagic		$5	$9	$15	$27
Star Wars, Arcade Game	Parker Bros.		$50	$70	$125	$175
Star Wars, Empire Strike Back	Parker Bros.		$7	$11	$19	$28
Star Wars, Jedi Arena	Parker Bros.		$13	$20	$35	$50
Star Wars, ROTJ Death Star Battle	Parker Bros.		$15	$23	$41	$59
Stargate	Atari		$8	$11	$14	$15
Stargunner	Telesys		$55	$70	$110	$135
Starmaster	Activision		$4	$7	$15	$22
Steeplechase	Sears	Text Label	$25	$35	$65	$85
Stellar Track	Sears	Text Label	$22	$29	$55	$75
Strategy X	Gakken		$39	$47	$75	$95
Strategy X	Konami		$35	$43	$69	$85
Strawberry Shortcake	Parker Bros.		$13	$20	$45	$65
Street Racer	Atari	12 Label	$7	$10	$20	$35
Street Racer	Atari	Picture Label	$4	$6	$12	$19
Street Racer	Atari	Text Label	$4	$6	$12	$19
Stronghold	Commavid		$150	$175	$250	$275
Stuntman	Panda		$50	$65	$95	$120
Sub Scan	Sega		$25	$33	$56	$67
Submarine Commander	Sears	Text Label	$45	$57	$95	$125
Subterrania	Imagic	Silver Label	$55	$65	$95	$115
Subterrania	Imagic	White Label	$35	$43	$65	$75
Suicide Mission	Starpath	Cassette	$10	$14	$19	$12
Summer Games	Epyx		$8	$11	$15	$18
Super Breakout	Atari	Picture Label	$5	$7	$15	$18
Super Breakout	Sears	Text Label	$7	$12	$26	$39
Super Challenge Baseball	Mattel		$4	$6	$10	$14
Super Challenge Baseball	Telegames		$10	$15	$20	$25
Super Challenge Football	Mattel		$4	$6	$10	$14
Super Challenge Football	Telegames		$10	$15	$20	$25
Super Cobra	Parker Bros.		$9	$14	$25	$35
Super Football	Atari	Red Label	$5	$7	$9	$10
Super Kung Fu / Robin Hood	Xonox		$55	$70	$130	$150
Superman	Atari	Picture Label	$6	$10	$25	$40
Superman	Atari	Text Label	$5	$9	$27	$43
Superman	Sears		$15	$25	$50	$70
Surfer's Paradise	Video Gems		$90	$105	$190	$225
Surround	Atari	41 text Label	$9	$12	$25	$37
Surround	Atari	Picture Label	$5	$8	$15	$25
Survival Island	Starpath	Cassette	$90	$110	n/a	n/a
Survival Run	Milton Bradley		$15	$21	see "Cosmic Command" controller	
Sword of Saros	Starpath	Cassette	$90	$110	n/a	n/a
Swordquest - Earthworld		Atari	$5	$8	$15	$25
Swordquest - Fireworld	Atari		$8	$12	$25	$35
Swordquest - Waterworld	Atari		$150	$215	$350	$450
Tac-Scan	Sega		$10	$17	$28	$35
Tank Brigade	Panda		$50	$65	$95	$120
Tank Plus	Sears	Text label	$5	$10	$23	$32
Tanks But No Tanks	ZiMag		$39	$47	$79	$95
Tape Worm	Spectravision		$13	$18	$29	$35
Tapper	Sega		$45	$54	$75	$88
Target Fun	Sears	Text Label	$4	$8	$15	$23
Task Force	Froggo		$9	$11	$15	$17
Tax Avoiders	American Videogame		$17	$24	$35	$39
Taz	Atari		$15	$22	$37	$49
Tennis	Activision		$5	$8	$15	$25
Texas Chainsaw Massacre	Wizard Video		$125	$150	$350	$450
Threshold	Tigervision		$29	$38	$55	$75
Thunderground	Sega		$18	$25	$42	$60

Game	Manufacturer	Notes	Cart Only	W/ Instructions	Complete in Box	New
Time Pilot	Coleco		$18	$24	$40	$58
Title Match Pro Wrestling	Absolute		$10	$15	$20	$25
Tomarc the Barbarian	Xonox		$60	$70	$100	$120
Tomcat F-14 Fighter Simulator	Absolute		$10	$15	$20	$25
Tooth Protectors	DSD / Camelot		$150	$185	n/a	n/a
Towering Inferno	US Games		$8	$12	$25	$35
Track & Field	Atari		$25	$33	see "Track & Field" controller	
Treasure Below	Video Gems		$90	$105	$190	$225
Trick Shot	Imagic		$12	$17	$29	$45
Tron Deadly Discs	Mattel		$15	$21	$35	$49
Tunnel Runner	CBS		$19	$26	$45	$65
Turmoil	20th Century Fox		$12	$17	$28	$37
Tutankham	Parker Bros.		$7	$11	$19	$28
Universal Chaos	Telegames		$15	$20	$25	$30
Up N Down	Sega		$65	$79	$125	$155
Vanguard	Atari		$5	$7	$12	$16
Venture	Atari	Red Label	$6	$8	$9	$10
Venture	Coleco		$6	$9	$17	$25
Video Checkers	Atari	Text Label	$7	$11	$18	$26
Video Chess	Atari	Picture Label	$6	$9	$18	$25
Video Chess	Atari	Text Label	$6	$9	$18	$25
Video Jogger	Exus		$120	$135	see "Foot Craz" controller	
Video Life	Commavid		$400	$475	n/a	n/a
Video Olympics	Atari	Picture Label	$4	$6	$10	$16
Video Olympics	Atari	Text Label	$4	$6	$10	$16
Video Pinball	Atari	Picture Label	$4	$6	$11	$16
Video Reflex	Exus		$120	$135	see "Foot Craz" controller	
Wabbit	Apollo		$17	$23	$35	$49
Wall Ball	Avalon Hill		$50	$65	$95	$120
Wall Defender	Bomb		$85	$100	$165	$190
Warlords	Atari	Picture Label	$4	$6	$10	$15
Warlords	Sears	Text Label	$6	$11	$25	$38
Warplock	Data Age		$9	$13	$20	$27
Wing War	Imagic	Silver Label	$55	$65	$95	$115
Wing War	Imagic	White Label	$35	$43	$65	$75
Winter Games	Epyx		$10	$13	$19	$23
Wizard of Wor	CBS		$9	$14	$25	$35
Word Zapper	US Games		$5	$9	$16	$22
Worm War I	20th Century Fox		$10	$15	$25	$35
X-man	Gamex	Adult	$200	$215	$250	$295
Xenophobe	Atari	Red Label	$15	$19	$26	$31
Yar's Revenge	Atari	Picture Label	$4	$6	$10	$14
Yar's Revenge	Sears	Picture Label	$8	$14	$28	$42
Z-Tack	Bomb		$85	$100	$165	$190
Zaxxon	Coleco		$9	$14	$27	$36

Atari 2600 Hardware, Etc. . . .

Item	Manufacturer	Notes	Loose	Complete in Box	New in Box
Atari 2600 system	Atari	4 switch - black	$60	$90	$195
Atari 2600 system	Atari	4 switch - woodgrain	$65	$95	$250
Atari 2600 system	Atari	6 switch	$75	$150	$350
Atari 2600 system	Atari	6 switch - early model	$100	$250	$500
Atari 2600 Jr. system	Atari	large rainbow	$60	$95	$175
Atari 2600 Jr. system	Atari	small rainbow	$50	$85	$150
Atari 2800 system	Atari	Japanese release	$280	$450	$590
Atari test console	Atari		$100	$150	$175
Columbia Home Arcade	Columbia House		$250	$350	$500
Compumate	Spectravision		$250	$400	$500
Compumate	Universum		$85	$150	$195
Cosmic Command Controller	Milton Bradley	includes cartridge	$95	$150	$195
Driving Controllers	Atari	pair	$15	$25	$35
Flight Commander Controller	Milton Bradley	includes cartridge	$95	$150	$195
Foot Craz Controller	Exus	includes 2			

Item	Manufacturer	Notes	Loose	Complete in Box	New in Box
Game Holder	Atari	cartridges	$350	$450	$495
Game Library	Atari	book style	$10	n/a	$20
Gameline Master Module	CVC		$25	$45	$60
Gemini system	Coleco	modem	$180	$300	$350
Joyboard Controller	Amiga		$75	$125	$195
Joystick	Atari	includes cartridge	$75	$125	$150
Keyboard Controllers	Atari		$12	$25	$35
Kid's Controller	Atari	pair	$22	$34	$41
Kid Vid Controller	Coleco		$15	$28	$39
Paddle Controllers	Atari	includes cartridge	$250	$350	$395
Supercharger	Starpath		$15	$25	$34
Telegames Video Arcade	Sears	includes game	$35	$55	$70
Telegames Video Arcade	Sears	4 switch	$85	$175	$335
Video Arcade II	Sears	6 Switch	$70	$145	$295
Touch Pad Controller	Atari		$95	$195	$350
Track & Field Controller	Atari	for "Star Raiders"	$10	$20	$28
Trackball Controller	Atari		$28	$49	$60
			$25	$40	$50

Atari 5200

Game	Manufacturer	Cart Only	W/ Instructions	Complete in Box	New
Astrochase	Parker Bros.	$20	$26	$35	$45
Ballblazer	Atari	$15	$20	$30	$35
Beamrider	Activision	$18	$24	$35	$39
Berzerk	Atari	$5	$7	$12	$16
Blueprint	CBS	$25	$32	$55	$75
Bounty Bob Strikes Back	Big 5	$175	$200	$275	$325
Buck Rogers - Planet of Zoom	Sega	$15	$21	$35	$41
Centipede	Atari	$4	$6	$11	$15
Choplifter	Atari	$9	$13	$21	$30
Congo Bongo	Sega	$15	$20	$30	$35
Countermeasure	Atari	$7	$10	$16	$21
Decathlon	Activision	$12	$16	$25	$33
Defender	Atari	$4	$6	$11	$15
Dig Dug	Atari	$5	$7	$12	$16
Dreadnaught Factor	Activision	$15	$20	$30	$35
Frogger	Parker Bros.	$5	$7	$14	$19
Frogger 2	Parker Bros.	$45	$57	$95	$115
Galaxian	Atari	$4	$6	$11	$15
Gorf	CBS	$22	$30	$50	$68
Gremlins	Atari	$35	$45	$65	$75
Gyruss	Parker Bros.	$20	$26	$35	$45
H.E.R.O.	Activision	$22	$30	$45	$52
James Bond 007	Parker Bros.	$30	$40	$65	$80
Joust	Atari	$5	$7	$12	$16
Jungle Hunt	Atari	$5	$7	$12	$16
K-Razy Shootout	CBS	$55	$65	$100	$135
Kaboom	Activision	$9	$13	$25	$31
Kangaroo	Atari	$4	$6	$11	$15
Keystone Kapers	Activision	$12	$16	$27	$35
Mario Brothers	Atari	$10	$14	$25	$35
Megamania	Activision	$12	$16	$28	$35
Meteorites	Electra Concepts	$175	$195	$255	$295
Miner 2049er	Big 5	$29	$36	$57	$68
Missile Command	Atari	$4	$6	$11	$15
Montezuma's Revenge	Parker Bros.	$35	$43	$70	$90
Moon Patrol	Atari	$5	$7	$12	$16
Mountain King	CBS	$32	$40	$65	$75
Mr. Do's Castle	Parker Bros.	$70	$82	$130	$155
Ms. Pac-Man	Atari	$4	$6	$11	$15
Pac-Man	Atari	$2	$3	$8	$13
Pengo	Atari	$20	$26	$37	$45
Pitfall	Activision	$6	$10	$18	$22
Pitfall II	Activision	$15	$20	$30	$35
Pole Position	Atari	$4	$6	$11	$15
Popeye	Parker Bros.	$9	$13	$25	$35
Q*bert	Parker Bros.	$6	$9	$16	$21
Qix	Atari	$4	$6	$11	$15
Quest for Quintana Roo	Sunrise	$38	$45	$70	$90
Realsports Baseball	Atari	$5	$7	$12	$16

Game	Manufacturer	Cart Only	W/ Instructions	Complete in Box	New
Realsports Football	Atari	$4	$6	$11	$15
Realsports Soccer	Atari	$5	$7	$12	$16
Realsports Tennis	Atari	$5	$7	$12	$16
Rescue on Fractalus	Atari	$30	$37	$65	$74
River Raid	Activision	$8	$11	$19	$24
Robotron 2084	Atari	$10	$14	$35	$45
Space Dungeon	Atari	$10	$14	$35	$45
Space Invaders	Atari	$4	$6	$11	$15
Space Shuttle	Atari	$12	$17	$27	$35
Star Raiders	Atari	$4	$6	$11	$15
Star Trek	Sega	$20	$26	$40	$50
Star Wars - Death Star Battle	Parker Bros.	$70	$85	$130	$150
Star Wars - Arcade Game	Parker Bros.	$35	$45	$85	$110
Super Breakout	Atari	$2	$3	$8	$13
Super Cobra	Parker Bros.	$16	$21	$35	$39
Vanguard	Atari	$6	$8	$14	$18
Wizard of Wor	CBS	$18	$25	$45	$68
Zaxxon	Sega	$60	$70	$95	$115
Zenji	Activision	$30	$37	$50	$60
Zone Ranger	Activision	$25	$31	$45	$50

Atari 7800

Game	Manufacturer	Cart Only	W/ Instructions	Complete in Box	New
Ace of Aces	Atari	$6	$9	$15	$22
Alien Brigade	Atari	$6	$9	$15	$22
Asteroids	Atari	$4	$6	$9	$10
Ballblazer	Atari	$5	$7	$13	$19
Barnyard Blaster	Atari	$4	$6	$9	$10
Basketbrawl	Atari	$6	$9	$15	$22
Centipede	Atari	$4	$6	$9	$10
Choplifter	Atari	$6	$9	$15	$22
Commando	Atari	$10	$14	$25	$32
Crack'ed	Atari	$6	$9	$15	$22
Crossbow	Atari	$6	$9	$15	$22
Dark Chambers	Atari	$4	$6	$9	$10
Desert Falcon	Atari	$4	$6	$9	$10
Dig Dug	Atari	$4	$6	$9	$10
Donkey Kong	Atari	$4	$6	$9	$10
Donkey Kong Jr.	Atari	$4	$6	$9	$10
Double Dragon	Activision	$15	$20	$30	$39
Fatal Run	Atari	$12	$16	$25	$32
F-18 Hornet	Absolute	$20	$26	$35	$42
Fight by Night	Atari	$6	$9	$15	$22
Food Fight	Atari	$4	$6	$9	$10
Galaga	Atari	$4	$6	$9	$10
Hat Trick	Atari	$4	$6	$9	$10
Ikari Warriors	Atari	$20	$26	$39	$45
Impossible Mission	Atari	$10	$14	$25	$30
Jinks	Atari	$4	$6	$9	$10
Joust	Atari	$4	$6	$9	$10
Karateka	Atari	$6	$9	$15	$22
Kung Fu Master	Activision	$20	$26	$35	$42
Mario Brothers	Atari	$6	$9	$15	$22
Mat Mania Challenge		$10	$14	$25	$30
Mean 18 Ultimate Golf	Atari	$20	$26	$39	$45
Meltdown	Atari	$10	$14	$25	$30
Midnight Mutants	Atari	$10	$15	$25	$35
Motorpsycho	Atari	$12	$16	$25	$32
Ms. Pac-Man	Atari	$4	$6	$9	$10
Ninja Golf	Atari	$10	$14	$25	$29
One on One Basketball	Atari	$4	$6	$9	$10
Pete Rose Baseball	Absolute	$20	$26	$35	$45
Planet Smashers	Atari	$15	$20	$30	$35
Pole Position 2	Atari	$2	$3	$7	$9
Rampage	Activision	$15	$20	$30	$39
Realsports Baseball	Atari	$4	$6	$9	$10
Robotron 2084	Atari	$4	$6	$9	$10
Scrapyard Dog	Atari	$4	$6	$9	$10
Sentinel	Atari	$30	$38	$50	$59
Summer Games	Atari	$6	$9	$15	$22
Super Huey UH-IX	Atari	$6	$9	$15	$20

Game	Manufacturer	Cart Only	W/ Instructions	Complete in Box	New
Super Skateboardin'	Absolute	$20	$26	$35	$42
Tank Command	Froggo	$65	$75	$98	$115
Title Match Pro Wrestling	Absolute	$20	$26	$35	$42
Tomcat F-14 Fighter Simulator	Absolute	$20	$26	$35	$42
Touchdown Football	Atari	$6	$9	$15	$20
Tower Toppler	Atari	$4	$6	$9	$10
Water Ski	Froggo	$50	$60	$90	$100
Winter Games	Atari	$4	$6	$9	$10
Xenophobe	Atari	$6	$9	$15	$22
Xevious	Atari	$4	$6	$9	$10

Bally Astrocade / Home Arcade

Game	Manufacturer	Cart Only	W/ Instructions	Complete in Box	New
280 Zzzap / Dodge Em	Bally	$10	$15	$20	$25
Amazin' Maze / Tic Tac Toe	Bally	$10	$15	$20	$25
Artillery Duel	Bally	$10	$15	$20	$25
Astro Battle	Astrovision	$12	$17	$25	$35
Astrocade Pinball	Bally	$10	$15	$20	$25
Bally Basic	Bally	$29	$40	$75	$89
Bally Pin	Bally	$10	$15	$20	$25
Basketball	Bally	$12	$17	$25	$32
Biorhythm	Bally	$13	$20	$29	$35
Blackjack / Poker / Acey Deucey	Bally	$10	$15	$20	$25
Blast Droid	Esoterica	$50	$60	$85	$105
Bowling	Bally	$50	$60	$80	$95
Checkers / Backgammon	Bally	$15	$21	$30	$38
Clowns / Brickyard	Bally	$10	$15	$20	$25
Coloring Book (w/ Lightpen)	Bally	$150	$170	$220	$260
Cosmic Raiders	Astrovision	$25	$32	$45	$60
Creative Canyon	Bally	$160	$180	$225	$270
Dogpatch	Bally	$13	$19	$27	$35
Drag Race / Desert Fox	$25	$33	$50	$65	
Elementary Math / Bingo Math	Bally	$12	$17	$25	$32
Football	Bally	$10	$15	$20	$25
Galactic Invasion	Astrovision	$10	$15	$20	$25
Galaxian	Bally	$15	$20	$30	$39
Grand Prix	Bally	$12	$17	$25	$32
ICBM Attack	Spectre Software	$90	$105	$140	$155
Incredible Wizard	Astrovision	$15	$20	$30	$39
Letter Match / Spell N Score / Crossword	Bally	$10	$15	$20	$25
Ms. Candyman	L&M Software	$50	$60	$90	$105
Muncher	Esoterica	$30	$40	$65	$79
Music Maker (w/ Tape Interface)	Bally	$125	$145	$195	$250
New Bally Basic	Bally	$25	$35	$65	$79
Panzer Attack / Red Baron	Bally	$10	$15	$20	$25
Pirate's Chase	Bally	$10	$15	$20	$25
Sea Devil	L&M Software	$62	$74	$105	$130
Sea Wolf / Bombadier	Bally	$10	$15	$20	$25
Sea Wolf / Missile	Bally	$10	$15	$20	$25
Soccer / Shootout	Bally	$60	$70	$95	$110
Solar Conqueror	Astrovision	$15	$21	$30	$38
Songs	Bally	$35	$42	$65	$79
Space Fortress	Bally	$10	$15	$20	$25
Space Invaders	Bally	$10	$15	$20	$25
Star Battle	Astrovision	$12	$17	$25	$32
Test Cartridge	Bally	$65	$75	$90	$100
Tornado / Baseball / Tennis / Hockey / Handball	Bally	$10	$15	$20	$25
Treasure Cove	Esoterica	$50	$60	$85	$100

Colecovision

Game	Manufacturer	Cart Only	W/ Instructions	Complete in Box	New
2010 Graphic Action Game	Coleco	$15	$20	$29	$35
Alcazar: Forgotten Fortress	Telegames	$25	$30	$35	$40
Alphabet Zoo	Spinnaker	$20	$27	$45	$59
Antarctic Adventure	Coleco	$14	$18	$35	$50
Aquattack	Interphase	$50	$60	$90	$115

Game	Manufacturer	Cart Only	W/ Instructions	Complete in Box	New
Artillery Duel	Xonox	$28	$35	$59	$75
Artillery Duel / Chuck Norris Superkicks	Xonox	$180	$195	$300	$350
B.C.'s Quest for Tires	Sierra Online	$15	$20	$39	$50
B.C. II Grog's Revenge	Coleco	$19	$25	$40	$50
Beamrider	Activision	$13	$17	$25	$29
Blockade Runner	Interphase	$30	$37	$55	$80
Boulder Dash	Telegames	$25	$30	$35	$40
Brain Strainers	Coleco	$15	$20	$35	$45
Buck Rogers: Planet of Zoom	Coleco	$12	$17	$35	$50
Bump N Jump	Coleco	$15	$20	$35	$45
Burgertime	Coleco	$15	$20	$25	$30
Cabbage Patch Kids: Adventures in the Park	Coleco	$12	$17	$25	$30
Cabbage Patch Kids: Picture Show	Coleco	$20	$25	$30	$35
Campaign '84	Sunrise	$35	$43	$70	$90
Carnival	Coleco	$5	$7	$15	$20
Centipede	Atarisoft	$10	$14	$23	$26
Choplifter	Coleco	$25	$30	$45	$50
Chuck Norris Superkicks	Xonox	$35	$42	$65	$79
Congo Bongo	Coleco	$13	$18	$32	$36
Cosmic Avenger	Coleco	$6	$9	$21	$25
Cosmic Crisis	Bit Corp.	$100	$125	$200	$245
Cosmic Crisis	Telegames	$20	$25	$30	$35
Dam Busters	Coleco	$20	$25	$37	$49
Dance Fantasy	Fisher Price	$35	$42	$65	$85
Decathlon	Activision	$10	$15	$25	$33
Defender	Atarisoft	$10	$14	$23	$26
Destructor	Coleco	$12	$17	$25	$29
Donkey Kong	Coleco	$3	$5	$15	$25
Donkey Kong Jr.	Coleco	$6	$9	$19	$25
Dr. Seuss' Fix Up the Mix Up Puzzler	Coleco	$25	$33	$55	$75
Dragonfire	Imagic	$13	$19	$35	$50
Dukes of Hazzard	Coleco	$20	$25	$45	$55
Evolution	Sydney	$20	$25	$39	$52
Facemaker	Spinnaker	$20	$26	$45	$55
Fathom	Imagic	$20	$25	$35	$45
Flipper Slipper	Spectravision	$20	$25	$45	$55
Fortune Builder	Coleco	$15	$21	$35	$50
Fraction Fever	Spinnaker	$20	$27	$45	$59
Frantic Freddy	Spectravision	$35	$43	$65	$90
Frenzy	Coleco	$12	$16	$25	$35
Frogger	Parker Bros.	$6	$9	$18	$25
Frogger II	Parker Bros.	$35	$45	$75	$95
Front Line	Coleco	$8	$12	$23	$32
Galaxian	Atarisoft	$15	$20	$29	$35
Gateway to Apshai	Epyx	$25	$32	$53	$70
Gorf	Coleco	$7	$10	$19	$26
Gust Buster	Sunrise	$38	$47	$76	$94
Gyruss	Parker Bros.	$15	$20	$35	$50
H.E.R.O.	Activision	$15	$20	$29	$37
Heist	Micro Fun	$15	$20	$35	$49
Illusions	Coleco	$26	$34	$55	$75
It's Only Rock n' Roll	Xonox	$40	$50	$85	$100
James Bond 007	Parker Bros.	$25	$34	$59	$75
Jukebox	Spinnaker	$38	$46	$82	$98
Jumpman Jr.	Epyx	$12	$16	$30	$43
Jungle Hunt	Atarisoft	$25	$31	$45	$50
Ken Uston's Blackjack & Poker	Coleco	$10	$14	$25	$35
Keystone Kapers	Activision	$12	$16	$29	$35
Kung Fu Superkicks	Telegames	$10	$15	$20	$25
Ladybug	Coleco	$8	$11	$19	$26
Learning with Leeper	Sierra Online	$29	$35	$55	$70
Linking Logic	Fisher Price	$35	$42	$65	$85
Logic Levels	Fisher Price	$35	$42	$65	$85
Looping	Coleco	$8	$11	$19	$26
Memory Manner	Fisher Price	$35	$42	$65	$85
Meteoric Shower	Bit Corp.	$130	$150	$230	$260
Miner 2049'er	Micro Fun	$12	$17	$35	$49
Monkey Academy	Coleco	$25	$31	$55	$75
Montezuma's Revenge	Parker Bros.	$25	$32	$59	$75
Moonsweeper	Imagic	$15	$20	$38	$54
Motocorss Racer	Telegames	$10	$15	$20	$25
Motocross Racer	Xonox	$42	$52	$88	$105
Motocross Racer / Tomarc the Barbarian		$195	$215	$325	$360

Game	Manufacturer	Cart Only	W/ Instructions	Complete in Box	New
Mountain King	Sunrise	$30	$38	$59	$75
Mouse Trap	Coleco	$5	$7	$15	$25
Mr. Do	Coleco	$15	$20	$35	$50
Mr. Do's Castle	Parker Bros.	$50	$60	$90	$112
Nova Blast	Imagic	$15	$21	$36	$50
Oil's Well	Sierra Online	$30	$37	$58	$75
Omega Race	Coleco	$10	$14	$25	$35
One on One Basketball	Micro-Fun	$30	$37	$55	$70
Pepper II	Coleco	$8	$11	$19	$27
Pitfall	Activision	$8	$12	$19	$25
Pitfall II	Activision	$15	$20	$30	$35
Pitstop	Epyx	$15	$20	$35	$49
Popeye	Parker Bros.	$9	$13	$25	$35
Q*bert	Parker Bros.	$6	$9	$18	$26
Q*bert's Qubes	Parker Bros.	$110	$129	$195	$245
Quest for Qunitana Roo	Sunrise	$20	$25	$35	$40
River Raid	Activision	$7	$10	$18	$25
Robin Hood	Xonox	$49	$58	$90	$112
Robin Hood / Sir Lancelot	Xonox	$125	$143	$210	$245
Roc N' Rope	Coleco	$10	$14	$25	$35
Rock N' Bolt	Telegames	$10	$15	$20	$25
Rocky Super Action Boxing	Coleco	$10	$15	$30	$45
Rolloverture	Sunrise	$45	$55	$80	$95
Sammy Lightfoot	Sierra Online	$50	$60	$90	$110
Sector Alpha	Spectravision	$55	$68	$95	$115
Sewer Sam	Interphase	$25	$32	$55	$70
Sir Lancelot	Xonox	$40	$49	$75	$95
Skiing	Telegames	$15	$20	$25	$30
Slither	Coleco	$7	$10	see Roller Controller	
Slurpy	Xonox	$50	$60	$95	$120
Smurf Paint N' Play Workshop	Coleco	$35	$45	$75	$95
Smurf Rescue In Gargamel's Castle	Coleco	$9	$13	$25	$35
Space Fury	Coleco	$6	$9	$18	$26
Space Panic	Coleco	$7	$10	$19	$26
Spectron	Spectravision	$39	$50	$80	$95
Spy Hunter	Coleco	$25	$31	$45	$62
Squish 'Em Sam	Interphase	$10	$15	$20	$25
Star Trek	Coleco	$20	$28	$49	$65
Star Wars the Arcade Game	Parker Bros.	$35	$45	$75	$95
Strike It	Telegames	$15	$20	$25	$30
Subroc	Coleco	$8	$11	$20	$26
Super Action Baseball		$8	$13	$25	$35
Super Action Football		$10	$16	$29	$38
Super Action Soccer		$35	$42	$60	$65
Super Cobra	Parker Bros.	$35	$42	$65	$80
Super Crossforce	Spectravision	$35	$43	$70	$85
Tank Wars	Bit Corp.	$95	$120	$175	$210
Tank Wars	Telegames	$20	$25	$30	$35
Tapper	Coleco	$29	$36	$58	$70
Tarzan	Coleco	$20	$29	$50	$70
Telly Turtle	Coleco	$25	$32	$55	$70
Threshold	Sierra Online	$35	$45	$80	$100
Time Pilot	Coleco	$8	$12	$25	$35
Tomarc the Barbarian		$50	$60	$90	$108
Tournament Tennis	Imagic	$25	$30	$40	$49
Turbo	Coleco	$6	$10	see Driving Controller	
Tutankham	Parker Bros.	$35	$42	$65	$80
Up N' Down	Sega	$35	$43	$65	$85
Venture	Coleco	$5	$8	$15	$25
Victory	Coleco	$8	$11	$20	$26
War Games	Coleco	$13	$19	$35	$49
War Room	Probe 2000	$15	$21	$35	$50
Wing War	Imagic	$18	$24	$45	$62
Wizard of Id's Wiz Math	Sierra Online	$29	$37	$59	$75
Word Feud	Xonox	$49	$59	$95	$110
Zaxxon	Coleco	$4	$6	$15	$25
Zenji	Activision	$15	$20	$25	$30

Emerson Arcadia 2001

Game	Manufacturer	Cart Only	W/ Instructions & Overlays (if applicable)	Complete in Box	New
3D Bowling	Emerson	$10	$15	$20	$25
Alien Invaders	Emerson	$10	$15	$20	$25
American Football	Emerson	$10	$15	$20	$25
Baseball	Emerson	$10	$15	$20	$25
Brain Quiz	Emerson	$15	$22	$29	$35
Breakaway	Emerson	$10	$15	$20	$25
Capture	Emerson	$10	$15	$20	$25
Cat Trax	Emerson	$10	$15	$20	$25
Escape	Emerson	$10	$15	$20	$25
Grand Slam Tennis	Emerson	$10	$15	$20	$25
Jungler	Emerson	$12	$18	$25	$30
Missile War	Emerson	$10	$15	$20	$25
Ocean Battle	Emerson	$10	$15	$20	$25
Red Clash	Emerson	$65	$80	$100	$125
Soccer	Emerson	$10	$15	$20	$25
Space Attack	Emerson	$10	$15	$20	$25
Space Mission	Emerson	$10	$15	$20	$25
Space Raiders	Emerson	$10	$15	$20	$25
Space Raiders	Emerson	$10	$15	$20	$25
Space Vultures	Emerson	$15	$22	$29	$35
Spiders	Emerson	$35	$45	$65	$75
Star Chess	Emerson	$10	$15	$20	$25
Tanks A lot	Emerson	$10	$15	$20	$25

Fairchild Channel F

Game	Manufacturer	Cart Only	W/ Instructions	Complete in Box	New
Alien Invasion	Zircon	$35	$45	$75	$90
Backgammon / Acey Deucey	Fairchild	$10	$14	$25	$35
Baseball	Fairchild	$6	$9	$16	$25
Bowling	Fairchild	$12	$15	$25	$35
Casino Poker	Zircon	$30	$39	$65	$80
Cat & Mouse / Paranoia / Double Paranoia / Maze / Jailbreak	Fairchild	$10	$14	$22	$31
Checkers	Zircon	$50	$65	$100	$120
Desert Fox / Shooting Gallery	Fairchild	$6	$9	$15	$22
Dodge It	Fairchild	$10	$14	$23	$32
Drag Strip	Fairchild	$8	$12	$20	$30
Galactic Space Wars	Zircon	$15	$20	$30	$45
Hangman	Fairchild	$13	$18	$29	$40
Magic Numbers / Mindreader / Nim	Fairchild	$10	$15	$23	$32
Math Quiz - Add, Subtract	Fairchild	$10	$15	$23	$32
Math Quiz - Multiply, Divide	Fairchild	$10	$15	$23	$32
Memory Match	Fairchild	$13	$18	$29	$40
Pinball Challenge	Fairchild	$12	$16	$28	$39
Pro Football	Fairchild	$10	$14	$23	$32
Slot Machine	Fairchild	$15	$20	$30	$45
Sonar Search	Fairchild	$12	$17	$28	$39
Space War	Fairchild	$10	$14	$23	$32
Spitfire	Fairchild	$10	$14	$23	$32
Tic Tac Toe / Shooting Gallery / Doodle / Quadradoodle	Fairchild	$6	$9	$15	$21
Torpedo Alley / Robot War	Fairchild	$10	$14	$23	$32
Video Blackjack	Fairchild	$8	$12	$20	$29
Video Whizball	Fairchild	$13	$18	$29	$40

GCE Vectrex

Game	Manufacturer	Cart Only	W/ Instructions & Overlay	Complete in Box	New
3D Crazy Coaster	GCE	$65	$85	$110	$125

Game	Manufacturer	Cart Only	W/ Instructions	Complete in Box	New
3D Minestorm (must include 3D imager to be considered complete in box)	GCE	$60	$75	$500	$600
3D Narrow Escape	GCE	$65	$85	$110	$125
Animaction	GCE	$45	$53	$75	$85
Armor Attack	GCE	$12	$21	$29	$35
Armor Attack	Milton Bradley	$25	$34	$42	$48
Art Master (must include light pen to be considered complete in box)	GCE	$35	$42	$215	$295
Bedlam	GCE	$20	$35	$45	$55
Berzerk	GCE	$15	$25	$35	$45
Berzerk	Milton Bradley	$25	$35	$45	$55
Blitz	GCE	$13	$24	$31	$38
Clean Sweep	GCE	$12	$21	$28	$32
Clean Sweep	Milton Bradley	$24	$33	$40	$44
Cosmic Chasm	GCE	$14	$25	$35	$42
Cosmic Chasm	Milton Bradley	$28	$39	$49	$56
Flipper Pinball	Milton Bradley	$35	$48	$60	$75
Fortress of Narzod	GCE	$35	$55	$75	$85
Heads Up Soccer	GCE	$30	$50	$65	$78
Hyperchase	GCE	$12	$21	$29	$35
Hyperchase	Milton Bradley	$25	$34	$42	$48
Melody Master	GCE	$50	$59	$75	$85
Polar Rescue	GCE	$65	$95	$115	$125
Pole Position	GCE	$60	$85	$105	$115
Rip Off	GCE	$13	$22	$29	$34
Rip Off	Milton Bradley	$25	$34	$41	$46
Scramble	GCE	$12	$20	$26	$29
Scramble	Milton Bradley	$25	$33	$39	$42
Soccer / Football	Milton Bradley	$40	$50	$75	$85
Solar Quest	GCE	$15	$25	$34	$39
Solar Quest	Milton Bradley	$25	$35	$44	$49
Space Wars	GCE	$24	$35	$55	$65
Space Wars	Milton Bradley	$35	$46	$65	$75
Spike	GCE	$18	$29	$41	$49
Spike	Milton Bradley	$29	$40	$52	$60
Spinball	GCE	$25	$38	$50	$65
Star Castle	GCE	$45	$65	$85	$98
Starship	Milton Bradley	$45	$60	$85	$95
Star Hawk	GCE	$18	$29	$39	$45
Star Trek	GCE	$15	$25	$38	$49
Web Warp	Milton Bradley	$45	$65	$85	$95
Web Wars	GCE	$35	$52	$75	$85

Magnavox Odyssey 2

Game	Manufacturer	Cart Only	W/ Instructions	Complete in Box	New
Alien Invaders Plus	Magnavox	$4	$6	$10	$15
Alpine Skiing	Magnavox	$4	$6	$10	$15
Armored Encounter / Sub Chase	Magnavox	$4	$6	$8	$13
Attack of the Timelord	NAP	$6	$8	$13	$19
Atlantis	Imagic	$30	$38	$60	$75
Baseball	Magnavox	$4	$6	$10	$15
Blockout / Breakdown	Magnavox	$4	$6	$9	$14
Bowling / Basketball	Magnavox	$4	$6	$10	$14
Casino Slot Machine	Magnavox	$5	$8	$13	$19
Computer Golf	Magnavox	$4	$6	$10	$14
Computer Intro	Magnavox	$4	$10	$17	$25
Conquest of the World	NAP	$15	$20	$50	$68
Cosmic Conflict	Magnavox	$4	$6	$10	$15
Demon Attack	Imagic	$30	$38	$60	$75
Dynasty	Magnavox	$4	$6	$10	$15
Electronic Table Soccer	Magnavox	$6	$9	$15	$22
Football	Magnavox	$4	$6	$9	$14
Freedom Fighters	NAP	$4	$6	$9	$15
Frogger	Parker Bros.	$60	$70	$95	$105
Great Wall Street Fortune Hunt	NAP	$15	$20	$50	$68
Hockey / Soccer	Magnavox	$4	$6	$9	$14
Invaders From Hyperspace	Magnavox	$4	$6	$9	$14
I've Got Your Number	NAP	$4	$6	$10	$15
K.C. Munchkin	NAP	$4	$6	$9	$14
K.C.'s Crazy Chase	NAP	$5	$8	$12	$17
Keyboard Creations	NAP	$6	$9	$14	$18

Game	Manufacturer	Cart Only	W/ Instructions	Complete in Box	New
Killer Bees	NAP	$19	$25	$35	$45
Las Vegas Blackjack	Magnavox	$4	$6	$9	$14
Matchmaker / Buzzword / Logix	Magnavox	$4	$6	$9	$15
Math A Magic / Echo	Magnavox	$4	$6	$9	$14
Monkeyshines	NAP	$6	$10	$15	$20
Nimble Numbers Ned	NAP	$4	$6	$10	$15
Out of This World / Helicopter Rescue	Magnavox	$4	$6	$10	$15
Pachinko	Magnavox	$5	$8	$12	$17
Pick Axe Pete	NAP	$8	$12	$18	$24
Pocket Billiards	Magnavox	$8	$12	$18	$23
Power Lords	NAP	$180	$200	$300	$345
P.T. Barnum's Acrobats	NAP	$8	$12	$18	$24
Q*bert	Parker Bros.	$50	$60	$90	$100
Quest for the Rings	NAP	$15	$20	$50	$68
Showdown in 2100 AD	Magnavox	$4	$6	$9	$15
Sid the Spellbinder	NAP	$8	$12	$18	$24
Smithereens	NAP	$6	$9	$14	$18
Speedway / Spinout / Cypto Logic	Magnavox	$3	$4	$8	$13
Super Cobra	Parker Bros.	$50	$60	$90	$100
Take the Money and Run	Magnavox	$4	$6	$10	$15
Thunderball	Magnavox	$4	$6	$10	$15
Turtles	NAP	$25	$32	$50	$65
Type N Tell	NAP	$6	$10	$15	$20
UFO	Magnavox	$6	$9	$15	$19
Volleyball	Magnavox	$4	$6	$10	$15
War of Nerves	Magnavox	$4	$6	$10	$15

Mattel Intellivision

Game	Manufacturer	Cart Only	W/ Instructions & Overlays	Complete in Box	New
ABPA Backgammon	Mattel	$5	$10	$15	$25
Advanced Dungeons & Dragons	Mattel	$4	$8	$14	$20
Advanced Dungeons & Dragons - Treasure of Tarmin	Mattel	$6	$11	$19	$25
Armor Battle	Mattel	$3	$6	$10	$15
Armor Battle	Sears	$3	$9	$18	$29
Astrosmash	Mattel	$3	$6	$10	$15
Astrosmash	Sears	$3	$9	$19	$31
Atlantis	Imagic	$5	$10	$19	$27
Auto Racing	Mattel	$5	$9	$14	$22
Auto Racing	Sears	$5	$11	$27	$36
B-17 Bomber	Mattel	$4	$8	$14	$21
Backgammon	Sears	$8	$16	$31	$42
Baseball	Sears	$4	$10	$26	$35
Basketball	INTV	$5	$9	$15	$22
Basketball	Sears	$4	$10	$26	$35
Beamrider	Activision	$9	$15	$25	$29
Beauty & the Beast	Imagic	$5	$10	$17	$25
Big League Baseball	INTV	$4	$8	$25	$35
Blockade Runner	Interphase	$15	$23	$36	$47
Body Slam Super Pro Wrestling	INTV	$45	$52	$75	$85
Bomb Squad	Mattel	$6	$11	$19	$25
Bowling	Sears	$5	$12	$27	$38
Boxing	Mattel	$7	$14	$25	$29
Bump N Jump	INTV	$8	$14	$25	$35
Burgertime	Mattel	$4	$7	$12	$19
Buzz Bombers	Mattel	$10	$18	$27	$36
Carnival	Coleco	$7	$10	$19	$28
Centipede	Atarisoft	$9	$15	$25	$32
Championship Tennis	INTV	$19	$28	$46	$65
Checkers	Mattel	$5	$10	$18	$25
Checkers	Sears	$5	$13	$29	$41
Chess	INTV	$19	$25	$35	$47
Chip Shot Super Pro Golf	INTV	$19	$28	$46	$65
Commando	INTV	$16	$25	$38	$49
Congo Bongo	Sega	$90	$100	$165	$190
Defender	Atarisoft	$15	$20	$35	$40
Demon Attack	Imagic	$5	$10	$17	$25
Dig Dug	INTV	$35	$40	$65	$75
Diner	INTV	$35	$41	$65	$79
Donkey Kong	Coleco	$4	$6	$12	$19

Game	Manufacturer	Cart Only	W/ Instructions & Overlays	Complete in Box	New
Donkey Kong Jr.	Coleco	$12	$16	$29	$39
Dracula	Imagic	$9	$16	$28	$39
Dragonfire	Imagic	$6	$11	$19	$28
Draughts	Mattel	$50	$65	$110	$140
Dreadnaught Factor	Activision	$15	$25	$35	$42
Electric Company Math Fun	Mattel	$6	$11	$22	$31
Electric Company Word Fun	Mattel	$6	$11	$22	$31
Fathom	Imagic	$70	$95	$135	$155
Football	INTV	$4	$9	$15	$20
Football	Sears	$3	$10	$25	$35
Frog Bog	Mattel	$4	$8	$14	$20
Frogger	Parker Bros.	$5	$8	$15	$23
Golf	INTV	$4	$8	$15	$22
Golf	Sears	$4	$9	$22	$34
Happy Trails	Activision	$13	$21	$32	$39
Hockey	INTV	$6	$10	$17	$24
Hockey	Sears	$5	$12	$27	$39
Horse Racing	Mattel	$4	$9	$17	$26
Hore Racing	Sears	$4	$11	$28	$36
Hover Force	INTV	$25	$31	$49	$55
Ice Trek	Imagic	$12	$21	$35	$45
Jetson's Ways With Words	Mattel	$39	$57	$95	$115
Kool Aid Man	Mattel	$13	$23	$39	$52
Ladybug	Coleco	$10	$15	$25	$35
Las Vegas Poker & Blackjack	Mattel	$2	$5	$9	$15
Las Vegas Poker & Blackjack	Sears	$2	$7	$15	$23
Las Vegas Roulette	Mattel	$4	$8	$14	$18
Las Vegas Roulette	Sears	$4	$10	$22	$32
Learning Fun I	INTV	$20	$33	$50	$65
Learning Fun II	INTV	$25	$40	$55	$70
Lock N Chase	Mattel	$4	$8	$13	$19
Loco Motion	Mattel	$8	$15	$25	$35
Major League Baseball		$3	$6	$10	$16
Masters of the Universe	Mattel	$12	$21	$35	$50
Melody Blaster	Mattel	$35	$45	$70	$85
Microsurgeon	Imagic	$6	$12	$21	$33
Mind Strike	Mattel	$28	$42	$65	$75
Mission X	Mattel	$9	$16	$25	$33
Motocross	Mattel	$13	$22	$35	$45
Mountain Madness Super Pro Skiing	INTV	$30	$45	$70	$85
Mouse Trap	Coleco	$8	$12	$21	$30
Mr. Basic Meets Bits N Bytes	Mattel	$25	$38	$55	$65
NASL Soccer	Mattel	$4	$8	$14	$20
NBA Basketball	Mattel	$4	$8	$14	$20
NFL Football	Mattel	$3	$8	$13	$19
NHL Hockey	Mattel	$5	$10	$15	$22
Night Stalker	Mattel	$4	$8	$14	$19
Night Stalker	Sears	$4	$10	$23	$32
Nova Blast	Imagic	$17	$28	$43	$55
Pac-Man	Atarisoft	$19	$24	$39	$48
PBA Bowling	Mattel	$4	$8	$15	$22
PGA Golf	Mattel	$3	$7	$14	$21
Pinball	INTV	$10	$17	$31	$40
Pinball	Mattel	$12	$19	$36	$48
Pitfall	Activision	$5	$8	$15	$22
Pole Position	INTV	$45	$55	$70	$79
Popeye	Parker Bros.	$12	$17	$30	$42
Q*bert	Parker Bros.	$18	$24	$37	$49
Reversi	Mattel	$6	$11	$19	$27
River Raid	Activision	$18	$35	$49	$59
Royal Dealer	Mattel	$5	$10	$19	$29
Safecracker	Imagic	$16	$27	$45	$55
Scooby Doo Maze Chase		$45	$65	$95	$115
Sea Battle	Mattel	$3	$6	$10	$16
Sea Battle	Sears	$3	$9	$19	$27
Sewer Sam	Interphase	$15	$23	$39	$49
Shark Shark	Mattel	$10	$16	$25	$38
Sharp Shot	Mattel	$7	$13	$21	$30
Skiing	INTV	$5	$8	$16	$22
Skiing	Sears	$4	$10	$25	$38

Game	Manufacturer	Cart Only	W/ Instructions & Overlays	Complete in Box	New
Slam Dunk Super Pro Basketball	INTV	$30	$45	$70	$79
Slap Shot Super Pro Hockey	INTV	$32	$48	$75	$85
Snafu	Mattel	$5	$9	$16	$24
Snafu	Sears	$5	$12	$29	$39
Soccer	Sears	$4	$10	$24	$34
Space Armada	INTV	$4	$7	$12	$16
Space Armada	Mattel	$3	$6	$10	$15
Space Armada	Sears	$3	$8	$15	$21
Space Battle	Mattel	$3	$6	$10	$15
Space Battle	Sears	$3	$8	$15	$21
Space Hawk	INTV	$5	$8	$13	$19
Space Hawk	Mattel	$4	$8	$12	$18
Space Hawk	Sears	$4	$10	$19	$28
Space Spartans	Mattel	$5	$9	$15	$21
Spiker - Super Pro Volleyball	INTV	$45	$60	$80	$90
Stadium Mud Buggies	INTV	$50	$65	$95	$110
Stampede	Activision	$9	$17	$26	$34
Star Strike	INTV	$4	$6	$11	$15
Star Strike	Mattel	$3	$6	$10	$15
Star Strike	Sears	$3	$9	$16	$24
Star Wars - Empire Strikes Back	Parker Bros.	$20	$30	$55	$70
Sub Hunt	Mattel	$5	$10	$17	$25
Super Cobra	Parker Bros.	$75	$90	$125	$150
Super Pro Decathlon	INTV	$30	$42	$65	$75
Super Pro Football	INTV	$25	$35	$55	$66
Swords N Serpents	Imagic	$10	$19	$32	$45
Tennis	Mattel	$4	$8	$15	$22
Tennis	Sears	$4	$10	$25	$32
Thin Ice	INTV	$30	$38	$55	$70
Thunder Castle	INTV	$17	$24	$38	$45
Thunder Castle	Mattel	$18	$25	$40	$50
Tower of Doom	INTV	$25	$32	$50	$60
Triple Action	Mattel	$4	$8	$15	$24
Triple Action	Sears	$4	$10	$25	$33
Triple Challenge	INTV	$27	$40	$65	$75
Tron Deadly Discs	Mattel	$6	$11	$25	$35
Tron Maze a Tron	Mattel	$6	$11	$25	$35
Tron Solar Sailer	Mattel	$9	$16	$29	$37
Tropical Trouble	Imagic	$22	$35	$51	$62
Truckin	Imagic	$20	$39	$58	$69
Turbo	Coleco	$50	$60	$85	$95
Tutankham	Parker Bros.	$75	$90	$125	$150
US Ski Team Skiing	Mattel	$4	$8	$15	$22
USCF Chess	Mattel	$20	$30	$50	$62
Utopia	Mattel	$4	$8	$15	$23
Utopia	Sears	$4	$11	$27	$38
Vectron	Mattel	$6	$11	$19	$27
Venture	Coleco	$14	$20	$35	$45
White Water	Imagic	$25	$37	$55	$65
World Championship Baseball	INTV	$35	$45	$70	$85
World Cup Soccer	INTV	$30	$40	$65	$75
World Series Championship Baseball	Mattel	$40	$55	$79	$99
Worm Whomper	Activision	$13	$21	$35	$47
Zaxxon	Coleco	$25	$33	$55	$70

RCA Studio II

Game	Manufacturer	Cart Only	W/ Instructions	Complete in Box	New
Baseball	RCA	$12	$16	$25	$35
Biorhythm	RCA	$25	$32	$45	$60
Blackjack	RCA	$10	$14	$21	$29
Gunfighter / Moonship Battle	RCA	$20	$27	$39	$50
Space War	RCA	$18	$24	$35	$46
Speedway / Tag	RCA	$13	$17	$26	$36
Tennis / Squash	RCA	$10	$14	$20	$29
TV Schoolhouse I	RCA	$25	$35	$50	$65
TV Schoolhouse II	RCA	$25	$30	$45	$60